THE RAMBLER'S HANDBOOK

First published in Great Britain in 2023 by Greenfinch
An imprint of Quercus Editions Ltd
Carmelite House
50 Victoria Embankment
London
EC4Y 0DZ

An Hachette UK company

A CIP catalogue record for this book is available from the British Library.

TPB ISBN 978-1-52942-144-6
eBook ISBN 978-1-52942-145-3

10 9 8 7 6 5 4 3 2 1

Design by Tokiko Morishima
Map Illustrations by Barking Dog Art
Text by Susan Kelly

Printed and bound in China

Papers used by Greenfinch are from well-managed forests and other responsible sources.

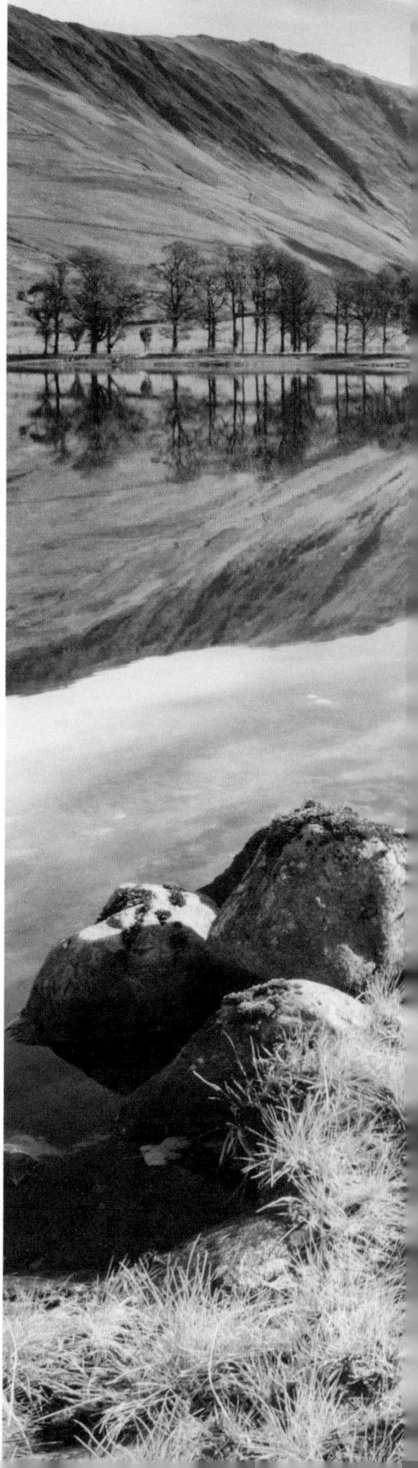

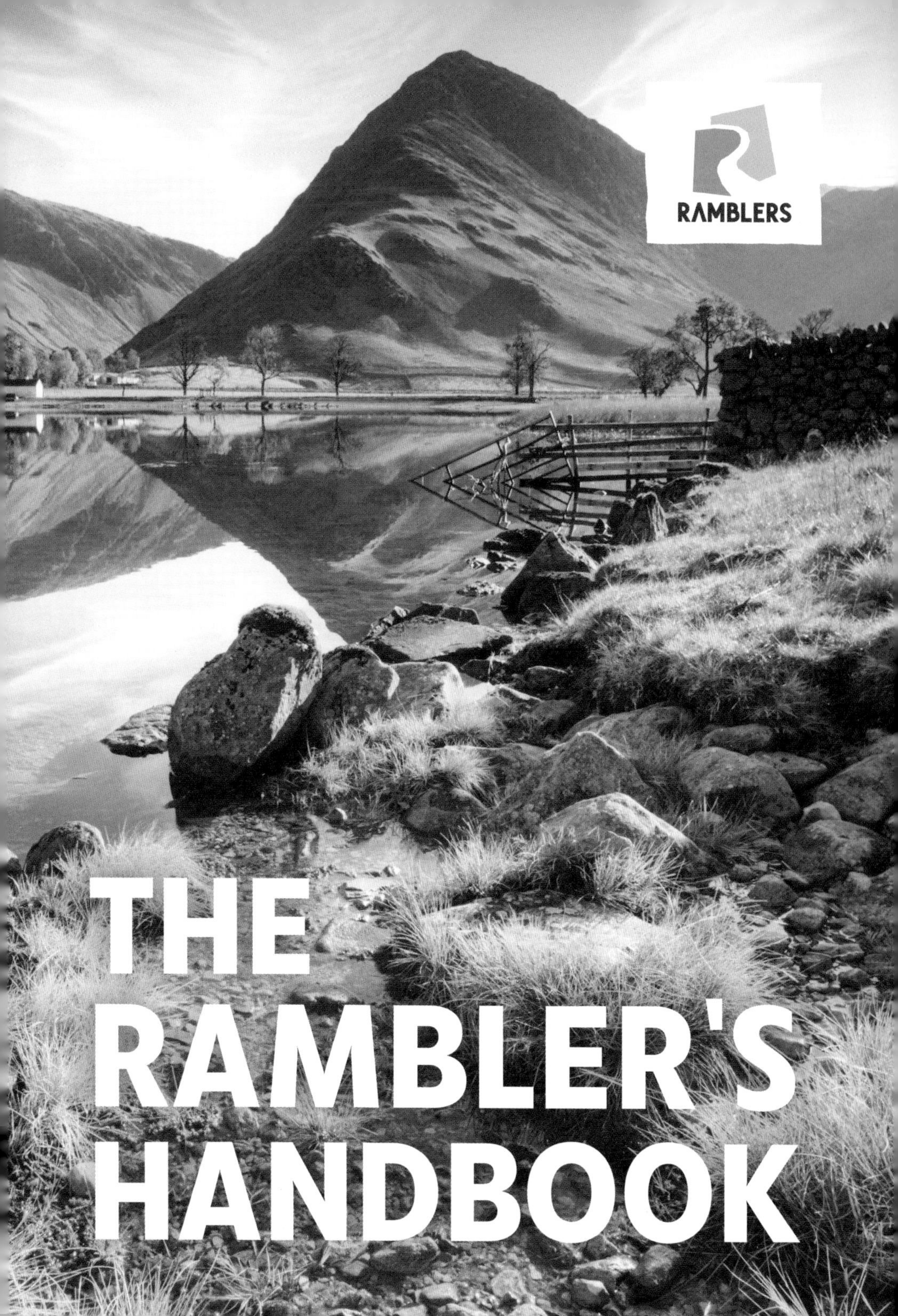
RAMBLERS
THE RAMBLER'S HANDBOOK

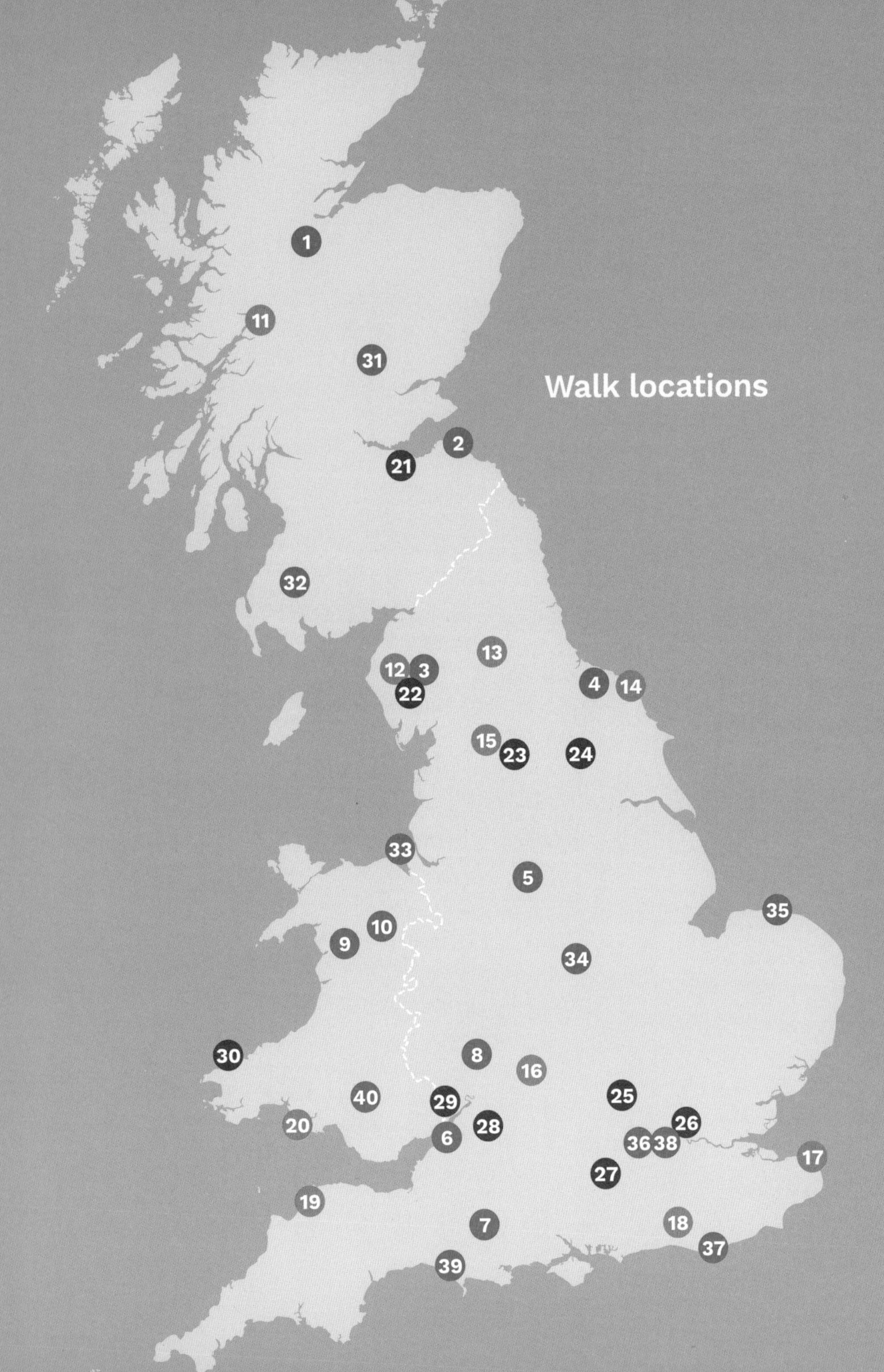
Walk locations
1
11
31
2
21
32
13
12
3
22
4
14
15
23
24
33
5
35
10
9
34
30
8
16
40
29
25
20
28
26
6
36
38
17
27
19
7
18
37
39

contents

introduction

More of us than ever before are making time to enjoy the great outdoors. Combining the promise of fun and fresh air, opportunities for self-care and wellbeing, the pure pleasure of doing something we love, and time spent away from the usual stresses of daily life, walking is the perfect way to reconnect with nature, ourselves and each other.

Research shows the numerous benefits of strengthening our relationship with nature and taking the time to notice the world around us – improved mental health, lower anxiety levels, increased happiness and heightened satisfaction with life in general. Crucially, spending time outdoors also reduces stress, and helps us to cope more effectively with any stressful situations that do come our way. During the Covid-19 pandemic, an enormous number of people in the UK reported spending time in green spaces to improve their sense of connectedness with the natural world, and to provide opportunities for rest and reflection.

We are turning back to nature...and the best way to get there is on foot!

As a nation, walking is one of our favourite pastimes; the good news is that with a comfortable pair of boots and a plan, we can be out on our next ramble in next to no time. Walking suits the way most of us live – it doesn't require enormous investment in high-tech equipment, or a large amount of space to store our gear. A pair of sturdy boots with good socks, a decent jacket and rucksack, some wet-weather gear and a little forethought are all that most of us need to head out the door. And if you take care of your kit, it will take care of you for a long time to come.

About the Ramblers

Dedicated to encouraging people to enjoy the benefits and freedoms of exploring the outdoors on foot, for over 85 years the Ramblers has been devoted to securing the footpath network in England and Wales and access rights in Scotland. Taking care of the networks and protecting the precious places where people go walking is of vital importance if we are to all continue enjoying the countryside and green urban spaces. The Ramblers organises group walks as well as providing information and high-quality routes to independent walkers. The Ramblers also provides essential support to people looking for walking to improve their health and wellbeing, working with a range of different projects and partners along the way.

Forty of Our Favourites

This book gathers 40 of our favourite walks to guide you all around Britain, travelling through picturesque locations to soak up stunning scenery as you go. Arranged by season, each featured walk includes a description, a map, detailed route instructions and notes about landmarks or wildlife to keep an eye out for. There is no better way to enjoy the landscape, seasons and incredible diversity of our wildlife than to get out there and immerse yourself in nature. And there's no time like the present to make a start. Including varied options, from short country strolls to challenging hill hikes, gentle woodland wanders to breathtaking cliff-path adventures, there are routes here for everyone to follow, no matter their level of fitness or experience. With so many beautiful walks to choose from, the biggest challenge will likely be deciding which to embark on first.

Walk gradings are provided as a general guide only. If you have any doubt about your fitness for a particular walk, don't attempt it. Bear in mind the distance of the walk, regional differences in terrain and the possibility of bad weather, which can make a walk more difficult than planned. Hiking, backpacking and other outdoor activities all have potential hazards involving risk of injury or death, and each person participating in these activities needs to understand the risks involved, obtain the necessary training and take any necessary precautions. You are responsible for your own safety when walking. If you're unsure of your fitness level, try a short walk first – it's much better to find a walk a little too easy than to exhaust yourself. Whether you have several leisurely days to devote to rambling or just a few hours to stretch your legs, a walk is always worth it.

Routes Grading Guide

EASY ✪ walks for everyone using easy access paths, though some further research on suitability for wheelchairs or pushchairs may be needed. Comfortable shoes or trainers can be worn.

LEISURELY ✪✪ walks for reasonably fit people with at least a little walking experience. May include unsurfaced rural paths. Walking boots and warm, waterproof clothing are recommended.

MODERATE ✪✪✪ walks for people with walking experience and a good level of fitness. May include some steep paths and open country. Walking boots and warm, waterproof clothing are essential.

STRENUOUS ✪✪✪✪ walks for experienced walkers with an above average fitness level. May include hills and rough country. Walking boots and warm, waterproof clothing are essential.

TECHNICAL ✪✪✪✪✪ walks for experienced and very fit walkers with additional technical skills. May require scrambling and use specialist equipment such as ice axes or crampons.

walking for health

Walking is excellent exercise. Importantly, it is also free, accessible and you already know how to do it. We may not always consider walking as 'exercise', because we often take it for granted and most of us do it every day almost without thinking. But walking is a wonderful way to keep moving and stay well. Heart-healthy, as well as great for bone and muscle strength, walking also supports the joints, oxygenates the blood, improves circulation and sleep quality, alleviates fatigue and depression, lowers stress, improves posture and endurance, and releases those all-important endorphins to increase our sense of wellbeing.

Walking makes us feel good. It keeps our brains engaged and active, strengthens our bodies, rewards our efforts with glorious views and helps us collect some beautiful memories along the way.

Staying physically active through walking may help prevent various illnesses. It has been shown to reduce the risk of several major health conditions such as heart disease, stroke, Alzheimer's disease, type 2 diabetes and some kinds of cancer by significant amounts, in some cases up to as much as 60 per cent. It can also lower the chances of developing osteoporosis. Regular physical exercise also helps with balance, assists in muscle and bone health, and lowers blood pressure as well as playing a part (along with diet of course) in maintaining a healthy weight.

Nothing Beats a Brisk Walk

A decent pace is important for accumulating health benefits, and regular brisk walking is the best of all – it has been shown to lower the risk of strokes and heart disease, reduce high blood pressure and improve circulation as well as strengthening the heart and lungs. But even beginners can start to feel the benefits of walking relatively quickly. Commencing with easy-paced walks will soon start to bring improvements in flexibility and strength, and as your endurance and your confidence build so your walks can both lengthen and increase in pace. The most important thing is to start at whatever pace and distance feel most comfortable to you – walking must, after all, be first and foremost a pleasure.

As with all forms of exercise, frequency and regularity are key. There are much greater health benefits to be gained from hour-long walks taken several times a week than from just one or two enormously challenging hill hikes embarked on twice yearly. Walking 'little and often' is particularly important when you are first starting out, to increase your fitness to the point where you can begin to enjoy a few more satisfying walks (and feel proud of your efforts too).

Being active also brings a number of benefits relating to mental wellbeing and keeping the mind healthy. Physical activity has been shown to significantly reduce the risk of depression, as well as providing a key part of the path to recovery for those who already suffer from this debilitating illness. Physical activity improves sleep quality, attention and memory, and enhances self-esteem and confidence. Staying active also reduces fatigue, stress and anxiety. Regular walking is a long-term investment in your health, mental as well as physical.

Mindful Walking

While our mental wellbeing will naturally improve as we start to walk more, we can accelerate these benefits simply by learning to pay attention and position ourselves 'in the now'. Mindfulness – deliberately and carefully noticing our surroundings and the way we feel as we move, breathe and sit or stand – is a wonderful way to enjoy walking, and a great practice for supporting our mental health. It helps us to separate from our racing thoughts, decreases stress, heart rate and blood pressure, and increases our sense of wellbeing while heightening our feelings of gratitude and contentment. Mindfulness helps us to take a pause and check in with ourselves, and reminds us to pay attention to our breath and listen to our bodies. Opening our awareness to the natural world is an inevitable consequence of quietening the mind-chatter that so many of us live with day in and day out – suddenly, as we ease the ropes of stress and tension we rely on to yank us through the day, we find ourselves free to see, hear and experience so much more. Walking is the perfect activity to encourage and enhance this mindful approach, thanks especially to the easy, instinctive, repetitive rhythm we fall into taking step after step. Walking can be a meditation.

As we adopt a more mindful awareness while walking, we engage more meaningfully with the world around us and with ourselves. Our sense of connectedness with nature deepens, and so too the weight of the load we seem to carry through life lightens. Perhaps we realise that we can put troubles and worries aside for a while, maybe even abandon them altogether. We might choose to offload some of that emotional weight we carry, and leave it behind us on the path as we carry on with our journey. Our ability to show ourselves and others kindness and compassion increases. We take the time to notice our steps and experience the sensation of walking, feeling our feet planting firmly on the ground and then lifting away. We realise how the air we breathe in different locations smells, tastes and feels as we inhale and exhale, the sensations in our bodies as we walk and then also as we stop walking to drink in yet another stunning view. We feel grateful for the act of walking, for the beauty of nature

surrounding us and for our own ability to place one foot in front of another in this way. We notice how our breath speeds and slows, and we notice our steady, purposeful steps. We allow ourselves to experience the simple joy of meeting nature on its own terms, in its own wild places and surrounded by its own wild elements.

Year-round Walking

One of the purest joys of regular walking is the opportunity to experience the seasons as they flow, shift and change throughout the year. As we travel around the sun, the natural world seems to expand from early spring through to late summer, exploding in a froth of blossom and the eager unfurling of shoots and leaves. Flowers, fragrance and fruits follow, until all of the natural world is resplendent, flourishing, vibrantly alive. Then the leaves change colour, some in a swansong blaze of reds and golds. Nature begins to turn inwards again, directing energy back towards the earth, into the secret chambers of seeds and roots, shedding all that no longer serves it in autumn, then pulling all the nourishment of warmth and light captured during the spring and summer months deep inside during winter.

Plenty of people in Britain, and indeed in many places around the world, find the winter difficult to endure – as nights close in, mornings grow darker and days are more often low and grey, the wind, rain and cold can at times seem unrelenting. Seasonal Affective Disorder (SAD) – sometimes referred to as 'winter depression' – usually manifests more during the colder months, the main theory attributing this to lack of sunlight. But there is no surer way to find some peace (and perhaps even joy!) within this complicated season than to confront it head on. If you, like so many others, find yourself dreading the winter, it is time to do something about it – after all, winter does keep coming around.

Once again, walking is the answer. Rather than hiding indoors and wishing time away, pull on your boots, hat and a good jacket and start exploring. Remember the wonderful Norwegian saying, 'There is no bad weather, only inappropriate clothing.' Continuing your walking in nature throughout the winter will get you out in the daylight, improve circulation, increase serotonin (that all-important feel-good hormone) and help to regulate sleep and appetite. There are plenty of new locations to discover or old favourites to revisit, winter wildlife to spot and all the fierce weather to enjoy as well as a fresh appreciation of this dramatic season to be gained. Be bold about spending time walking outdoors during winter; you may very well be surprised at the difference it makes to how you feel.

Staying Active

For many people, especially those with existing health conditions, trying to stay active can be a challenge. But with so many proven health benefits, walking can be an incredibly positive way to commit to your own health and stay well. It might even help you improve any health problems you are living with and start feeling better. Trained walk leaders organise the Ramblers walking groups up and down the country, and these can support you in building confidence and increasing your activity levels. Joining a group is a great way to meet new people, stay motivated and enjoy yourself. Information about walking with specific health conditions is available on the Ramblers website, as are contact details for making further enquiries.

forest bathing

Shinrin-yoku, translated into English as 'forest bathing', is a decades-old therapy first developed in Japan, focusing on the health and wellbeing benefits of immersion in a forest environment. We instinctively understand that spending time among trees has a calming and mood-brightening effect.

Studies show that positive effects of forest bathing range from reduced cortisol (the stress hormone) to notable reductions in depression, anxiety and sleep problems. These significant mental, emotional and physical benefits result from unplugging, de-stressing and developing a conscious awareness of our surroundings. Research even suggests that the fragrance of the forest, plant compounds called phytoncides, may act as natural aromatherapy and strengthen our immune systems to fight infections and inflammation.

So, how do we do it?

Forest bathing is essentially a mindfulness practice, and one you can enjoy in any wooded green space away from the sounds of traffic and other man-made noise. If possible, plan to spend a couple of hours soaking up the atmosphere, quiet and undisturbed. If time is tight, even as little as 15 minutes will be of benefit. If forest bathing with others, make sure you each have enough space to wander about on your own, and agree to remain silent and disconnected. Leave phones and other electronic devices behind, or at least switch them off. The purpose of this is to firmly locate yourself 'in the now', rather than diverting your attention with all the usual distractions.

Ensure you are wearing comfortable clothing, warm enough to keep you cosy (or light enough to keep you cool). A few layers are ideal, so you can maintain a comfortable temperature. Weather allowing, you might even consider removing your shoes to go barefoot.

Once you have found your space, simply move about without thinking, analysing or recording. Relax your body. Your goal is just to be where you are, wandering aimlessly, led by your senses. Release your thoughts, worries and anxieties, allowing them to float away. Bring your attention instead to your body, to your senses. What can you see, hear, touch, taste and smell? Notice the feeling of the forest air on your skin. What does it smell like?

Close your eyes, or soften your gaze, and notice your breath. Draw the cool scent of the forest deeply inwards. Feel your ribcage expand, the space across your back widening as you inhale. Drop further into the present moment with each exhale. Visualise each in-breath delivering nourishment to even the smallest cells in your body. Notice your feet, firmly grounded as you stand, the earth beneath supporting you, holding you, welcoming you.

Turn your attention outwards, to your surroundings. Notice the myriad shades of green, or examine the intricacies of tree bark. Notice the broad canopy stretching above you, the constant small movements of leaves and branches. Place your hands upon a tree trunk, feeling the structure of the bark. Bring your awareness to the interplay of light and dark, watching the movement of sunshine through the leaves, the richness of the darker places that lie beneath. Feel the warmth of sunshine upon your skin, the coolness of the shade.

Stay as long as you wish. Enjoy your time in nature. All is well.

how to get started

Making the choice to start walking is a decision that can change your life – the whole wide world is out there waiting for you to discover it. While a gentle stroll around a few country lanes might not be too taxing, before long you will likely develop an appetite for something a little more challenging. So first, there are a few practicalities to attend to.

Health and Fitness

How much exercise do you take at the moment? If only a little, or none at all, it would be wise to begin with some easy outings and build up to bigger walks gradually, setting yourself small, enjoyable targets (say, three short, easy walks each week) to begin with. As your fitness and confidence improve, so too can the length and duration of your walks. But it is important to start off slow and easy, to work out what you can do – then take it from there.

If you have any existing health conditions, or any potential issues (such as heart disease) that run in your family, it might be wise to consult your doctor for a check-up before embarking on a new type of exercise.

Perhaps you already feel strong and confident in your fitness levels. Still, take it easy as you get used to walking and maybe join an experienced group or friends for your first few walks. It pays to get a sense of how capable you are before setting yourself any major challenges in terms of terrain or distance. Err on the side of caution; be careful not to overstretch yourself, don't choose overly ambitious routes to start with, and cut your walk short if you start to tire, feel unwell or the weather worsens and you feel at all uncertain about continuing.

Allow Enough Time

Just as you should make a habit of familiarising yourself with your route before making a start, you should also learn to work out how long it will take you. About 3km (2 miles) an hour is most people's average walking speed, which still allows enough time for short breaks along the way. Experienced walkers will likely move more quickly. If your fitness levels have room for improvement, allow yourself more time so that you can enjoy the walk at your own pace.

More challenging walks – on difficult terrain, climbing hills, across tricky surfaces like mud or sand, or in poor weather conditions – may well prove slower going and require more time. Hill-climbing time is usually estimated by adding an extra 30–60 minutes for each 300m you plan to ascend.

Let someone know where you are going and when you plan to return. And don't forget to let them know later on that you have returned safe and well!

What to Wear

Most importantly, you will need a strong pair of shoes or boots that fit well and will not cause blisters. They should be lightweight, with sturdy soles and decent arch support. For tougher terrain, proper walking boots will be essential. Always wear good walking socks.

One of the most important rules of walking is to always be prepared for changeable weather. Cloud, rain and mist pose challenges with staying warm and dry. Heat may be equally problematic, raising the risks of dehydration, sunburn and possibly heatstroke. Check the weather forecast, and tide times if relevant, so you have some idea of what to expect, and dress in comfortable clothing appropriate for the expected weather conditions. See pages 16–17 for more on what to wear.

What to Carry With You

A small **rucksack or backpack** is the best solution for carrying your supplies, as it leaves your hands free and is the most efficient way of distributing any weight. Your bag should have comfortable straps and a volume of about 25–40 litres.

Be sure to carry **enough water** to drink along the way; you may find yourself more thirsty than usual due to exertion. Some walkers like to carry a hot drink in a Thermos flask, especially when walking in the colder months. On longer or more difficult walks a few **high-energy snacks** are good idea as well. See page 16 for some snack suggestions.

Other important things to remember include a **paper map** of your route in a **waterproof plastic wallet**, a **whistle** (if walking alone) and perhaps a **torch** and **compass**, and a **mobile phone**. In cold weather, be sure you also have enough **warm clothing**, including a hat and gloves, and extra food. In warm weather, a **sun hat** and extra **sunscreen** are advisable. You should always carry a **waterproof jacket** in case of rain.

A small **first-aid kit**, including blister plasters and a bandage, insect bite/sting cream, tweezers and insect repellent is also a useful addition to your pack. A basic first-aid kit for walkers may be purchased online or from outdoor stores.

walking with the seasons

With a well-deserved international reputation for changeability, the British climate is nothing if not interesting – it certainly keeps us all on our toes. When it comes to walking, we can be assured of plenty of varied weather while we are out and about, and we must always be sure we have what we need to make the most of our walks.

Britain generally enjoys a temperate climate, with temperatures seldom dropping below −10°C (14°F) and only occasionally rising above 35°C (95°F). However, conditions can shift markedly and surprisingly rapidly, especially at higher altitudes. Extremes of temperature and weather are less common, when compared to the rest of the world, but with frequent changes in air pressure and a high level of rainfall year-round, a single day can often see a surprising range of weather in a single location.

Spending time in nature and enjoying walking in our wild spaces is a great way to recalibrate, relax and recharge, providing those all-important opportunities to step away from the stresses and strains of day-to-day routine. Our need for this chance to refresh our bodies and minds is not restricted to fair weather, so we must make it as easy as possible for ourselves to say 'yes' to a walk whatever the outlook. Preparedness and having appropriate clothing and other equipment to hand play a significant part in making it easy to get ready and go.

Remember to wear sunscreen to protect your skin year-round; even in the winter or on overcast days, UV rays can cause skin damage. A waterproof rucksack and jacket, good strong shoes or boots (see page 17), good-quality walking socks and comfortable, weather-appropriate clothing are all essential. And pack a snack: chocolate, bananas, trail mix, nuts and seeds, bliss balls and cereal bars are all good choices to combat hunger or tiredness, as well as providing a cheerful little interlude.

Cold Weather Walking

During winter months, wear plenty of light layers to keep you as comfortable as possible and wrap up warm with a hat and gloves. Mittens worn with liner gloves underneath are an excellent idea, as the warmth from all your fingers nestles together inside the mitten-bundle. Merino-wool base layers are a good investment as they are sweat-wicking and breathable, so will keep you from overheating. Sweating too much will make you cold.

Remember to check what time the sun will set, and take a torch. Plan to either finish your walk or be sure you will be on decent paths by the time darkness descends. Pack a warm drink in a flask along with your water bottle, and add some snacks from the list opposite to your rucksack as well, to keep your energy levels up.

Remember that our bodies require more fuel than usual to keep warm when the weather is cold. Avoid sitting or standing still when exposed to wind, rain or the cold; choose sheltered spots for any rest breaks along the way and add an extra layer (such as a lightweight insulated jacket) as soon as you stop moving. Remember, it is much easier for your body to simply stay warm than it is for it to cool down and then warm back up. Winter walks are a brilliant way to make the most of this season – just ensure you are well prepared.

On Warmer Days

When spring rolls around, the days start to lengthen and the sunshine delivers a bit more warmth. Temperatures may continue cool though, even when the sun is out, so remember to wear layers, and carry a waterproof jacket with you even if the day looks fine, just in case.

Summertime walking requires loose and lightweight clothing, with a focus on staying cool so you don't overheat. Take a sunhat to protect your face and head, plenty of water to drink, and sunscreen to reapply at regular intervals. Take a waterproof jacket for those summer showers, and remember that temperatures will be cooler if you are walking in the hills, so pack an extra layer or two.

In autumn, temperatures start to drop again, so it is wise to follow a similar checklist to that for your winter walks. Remember that the long, light evenings of summer quickly slip away during the autumn – don't be caught out by the shortening days; carry a torch and plan your walks carefully.

Check the Weather

Understanding and responding to weather conditions is essential to your own comfort and safety. Check main sources of weather information when planning your walk, especially the UK Met Office, and check on the day you plan to walk for any updates. Weather changeability is most marked in hill and mountain areas, so it is important to have a good idea of the weather you might expect.

Wherever you are, you can walk in all weathers, as long as you are well prepared.

Check the forecast

If you are hill or mountain walking, the UK Met Office supplies a specialist Mountain Weather Forecast covering the Lake District, the Peak District, the Yorkshire Dales, the Northwest and Southwest Highlands, North Grampian, South Grampian and Southeast Highlands, the Mourne Mountains, the Brecon Beacons and Snowdonia. Forecasts are issued in the afternoon before 6pm, then updated in the early hours before 6am, to cover a full 24 hours as well as a brief outlook over the next three days.

rambler profiles

Louise Trewern

Louise Trewern discovered a love of walking when looking for ways to manage chronic pain. Walking for health benefits turned into walking for enjoyment – so much so, that Louise and her wife, Karen, set up their own Ramblers Wellbeing Walks group in Newton Abbot, Devon.

1. How did you first get into walking?

I started walking for health reasons about 3 years ago. I have arthritis and fibromyalgia and for many years I was on strong painkillers. I eventually had to give up work and was becoming less and less engaged with daily life. I went into hospital to come off high-dose prescription opioids (strong pain medications) and while I was in there the consultant said, 'In order to manage the effects of withdrawal, you should pace the ward, it will trigger endorphins – the body's natural pain killers!'

I was amazed that it worked, so when I got home, my wife Karen and I would drive out to somewhere flat like Teignmouth sea front to walk. At first I had a wheelie walker but gradually progressed to walking sticks, then walking poles and now I don't use any aids. I left hospital weighing 159kg (25 stone) and not very active, however we walked every day and gradually I built up my fitness and I lost weight.

I wanted to set up a walking group for people who live with pain and/or disability and long-term health conditions and Karen suggested we use the Ramblers framework! That's when we met Tom from Active Devon and completed our walk leader training, then set up our walk at Decoy Country Park with the help of Chrissy from Teignbridge District Council and we meet every Thursday morning rain or shine. On a good week we will have as many as 14 walkers and they come for the friendship and social interaction as much as the wildlife and nature connection.

2. What is your favourite walk?

It's difficult to choose because I have so many favourites. I love coast path walks with the stunning scenery, especially on a sunny day, but I also love woodland walks with the abundance of nature and wildlife all around. I discovered how beautiful it is to hug the trees and I don't care if people laugh. If I had to choose a favourite it would have to be the circular walk known as Bolt Head walk near Salcombe, which takes in the breathtaking views of the sea framed by rugged cliffs!

3. What is your top rambling tip?

Always have two things in your rucksack: a waterproof coat and hat because the weather is unpredictable, and a sit mat which gives just enough cushioning on hard stone or metal seats and is toasty warm in winter!

Lahari Parchuri

Lahari moved to Sheffield from Hyderabad, India, to study an MBA at Sheffield Hallam University, where she joined the Sheffield 20s & 30s Ramblers' Association walking group.

1. How did you first get into walking?

I didn't really get a chance to go out walking in the village where I grew up, and especially not in Hyderabad – a big, polluted city. Now, I take the Peak District for granted because it's on our doorstep, but we all realise how lucky we are to have it.

I came here knowing no one and the university circles were not where I wanted to be, mainly because everyone had different interests. Staying in Sheffield after studying was certainly not part of the plan, but now I've lived here for over 6 years! I even considered going back halfway through my course because it was very isolating, but then one of my Indian friends, who is now back in India, suggested joining a walking group.

In a university, it's a bit of a bubble and I wanted to learn about the local community and people, and the things that they would do here. Being part of the Ramblers has been a massive help in establishing my personal network in the UK. I literally went from thinking, 'Oh my god I can't live here, I want to go back', to not wanting to go back at all because all my friends are here.

I definitely wanted to meet new people and to build new friendships. In hindsight, I don't think I realised how much of a motivation this was for joining the Sheffield 20s & 30s walking group. And now, all my best friends are from the group, we socialise a lot outside of the walks, and it's fantastic to be a part of it.

2. What is your favourite thing about walking?

It is underrated how much walking and being in touch with green spaces keeps you well mentally. If I am having a busy and stressful day, I just take 15 minutes to get out into the park across the road. That 15 minutes' walk changes my mood and relaxes me. I don't think I'd be able to do that if it wasn't for the green space.

3. What is your top rambling tip?

Make sure to have the right gear for all weathers and the right mindset for any obstacles. But the top tip has to be: enjoy walking and the nature, it's not about how many mountains you climb or how much distance you walk or what fancy gear you buy, it's about enjoying the outdoors and the peace and calm that walking brings to one's mind through just putting one step in front of another.

the
walks

spring

A wonderfully optimistic season, the British spring is a time of awakening and new growth in the most beautiful range of fresh, vibrant greens. The first buds and shoots appear after winter, daffodils blossom and creatures hatch, emerge from hibernation or migrate back to our shores. Though there may be some mixed weather in store, temperatures rise and days lengthen; it is a magical season to get out into the countryside and witness the miracle of Mother Nature's annual regeneration.

Falls of Foyers, Loch Ness

Time: 4 hrs | Distance: 11.1 km (6.9 miles) | Difficulty: ✪✪

A must-see on any Loch Ness visit, the impressive Falls of Foyers can be safely viewed from well-made wooden steps and railings. This lovely loop walk includes short sections of the South Loch Ness Trail, leading through the trees to stunning view points over the Loch and from there on to the Falls.

Start location

The Forestry Commission Scotland car park, Inverfarigaig, Inverness-shire, nearest postcode IV2 6XS (grid ref: NH522238).

Getting there

By car: Using satnav, the nearest postcode is IV2 6XR. Follow the B852 towards Inverfarigaig. From Inverfarigaig, take the turning to Errogie, also marked with Forestry Commission signs to Farigaig. The car park is about 100m up this road on the right.
By public transport: D&E Coaches' bus 302 from Inverness to Inverfarigaig runs every day except Sunday Inverness is well served by trains UK-wide.

Before you start

* Should you be in need of either, both accommodation and refreshments can be found at Foyers.

1 From the car park at Inverfarigaig, follow the blue South Loch Ness Trail (SLNT) waymarker steeply up for a short distance, before leaving it by taking a sharp right at a signpost for the Loch Ness View Point. After taking in the view, continue along the path up through woods before descending sharply down to the main trail. Turn left, as if returning to the car park, for a short distance before turning right and following the yellow waymarkers.

2 Follow this wide track up through trees for approximately 1km (½ mile). You will come to another great view point overlooking Loch Ness and the massive rock buttress of Dun Deardail. From here, continue on for a short distance and you will come to the small, picturesque Lochan Torr an Tuill. Past the lochan, the track meanders slowly downhill for 1km (½ mile) before emerging at the side of the road through Gleann Liath. At this point, stay on the track-side of the road and head back into the woods on a much narrower and steeper path.

3 This path makes its way up through trees before emerging into a more open area. Shortly afterwards the path splits: at this point you should take a left and follow the red waymarkers. The path rises steeply through dense woods before emerging into heather and small trees. This is the highest point on this walk, with wonderful views of Loch Ness and the Monadhliath Mountains.

Having climbed through the trees from Inverfarigaig Forestry car park, this is your first peek at stunning Lock Ness; what a way to begin your walk.

The River Foyers creates a sensational display as the Falls of Foyers feed into Loch Ness. This is a popular natural beauty spot.

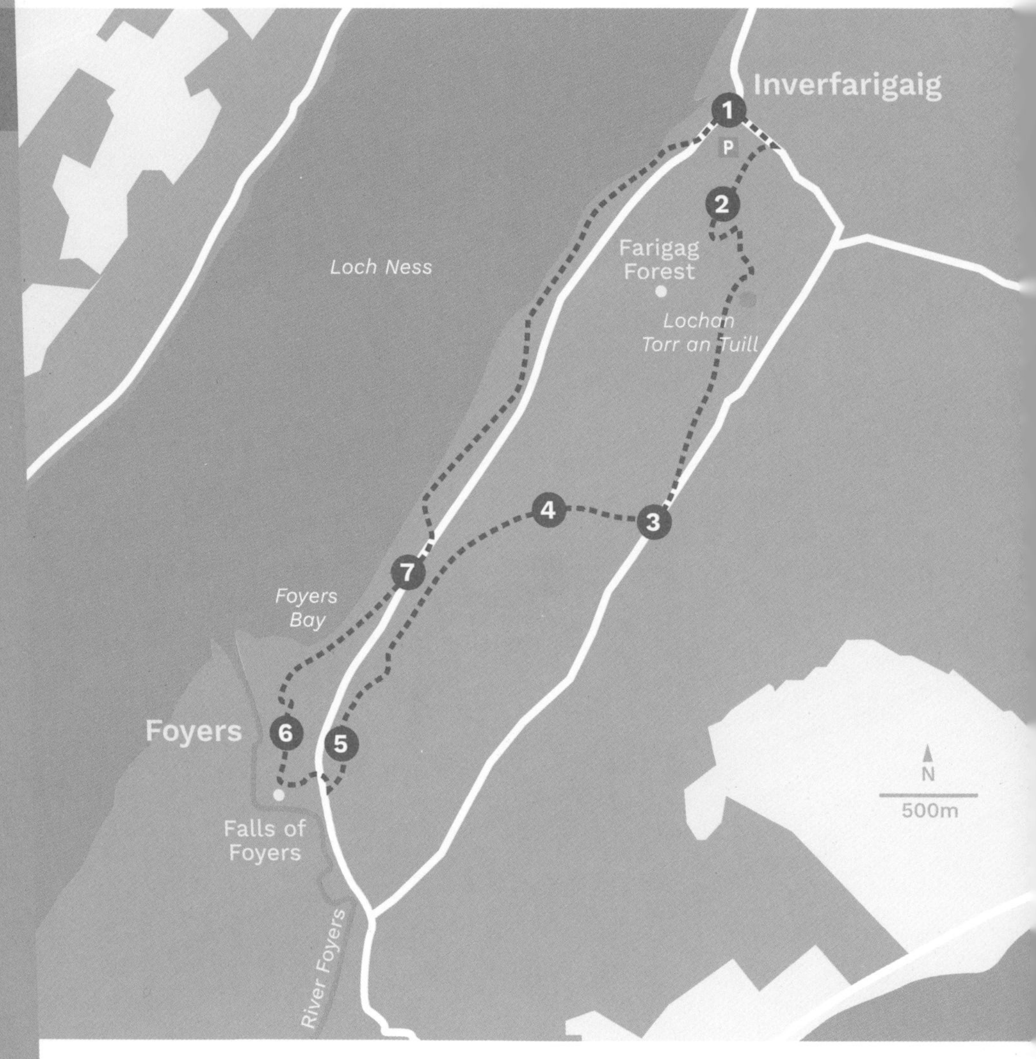

4 From here, the path descends steeply until you reach a forestry track. Here you should turn right and follow it down, past a hydro service tunnel, until you pass the back of a primary school on your right and come out onto the road. Turn left here, at the South Loch Ness Trail (SLNT) waymarker, and walk a short distance uphill to the Waterfall Café and Foyers Gift Shop. The wooded area opposite the shop is another good spot for a red squirrel sighting (see Notes of Interest on page 27).

5 Directly opposite is the gated path down to the Falls of Foyers. There are two view points. After your visit, climb back up to a path junction, signposted for Lower Foyers. Follow this direction – it meanders along the edge of the gorge before emerging at Foyers House guesthouse. There are some blue markers (not SLNT ones) for guidance.

Native to the UK, red squirrel numbers have declined across much of England and Wales. They still thrive in wilder, more remote locations such as this forest.

6 From the entrance to the guesthouse, turn left and descend to the road. Here, turn left again, past the medical centre and down to where the road splits again. At this point you will see a large stone building; this is the old aluminium works. Follow the road past this and, immediately after the fish hatchery, look out for a blue waymarker (again, not an SLNT one). Turn right here and then, at the first bend, turn left and follow the track uphill to the road.

7 At the road, turn left for a short distance past the Foyers Lodge. Immediately after the Lodge, take the path to the left, marked 'Inverfarigaig', and descend through mixed woodland to a single-track road. Turn right here, then walk up past the electrical substation. Just past here, turn left onto a path that descends gradually, almost to Loch level, before emerging beyond a house on the right. A short distance past the house there is a small track down to the shore of the loch, where you will find a seat. Back on the path – now a rough track – you will pass a few more houses before coming out at Inverfarigaig Pier. From the pier, head up the tarred track to join the B852. At the road, turn left and then take the first right, marked 'Errogie', to return to your start point at the car park.

Notes of interest

★ While walking through the conifer plantations, there is a good chance of spotting red squirrels – they prefer to stick to the canopy, so remember to look up! Most of the year red squirrels tend to live alone, but in the springtime they perform courtship displays in the trees, chasing each other through the branches.

walk
2

Ravensheugh Sands and Seacliff, East Lothian

Time: 3 hrs 15 mins | Distance: 13.2 km (8.2 miles) | Difficulty: ✪✪✪

A stunning circular route along Ravensheugh Sands to Seacliff on the breathtaking East Lothian coast, with views of Bass Rock and incredible scenery and wildlife to be seen along the way. One short section at Scoughall Rocks may be impassable at high tide so check tide tables before starting.

Start location

Tyninghame Links car park, East Lothian, nearest postcode EH42 1XW (grid ref: NT627809).

Getting there

By car: Tyninghame Links car park is pay and display, and is located on Limetree Walk, Tyninghame. Use postcode EH42 1XW to make your way there using satnav.
By public transport: There is no public transport to Tyninghame Links car park. Bus service 120 leaves from North Berwick and Dunbar to Limetree Walk, on the A198. This leaves a 2km (1¼ mile) walk to the start of this route.

Bass Rock, or The Bass, is a tiny steep-sided island about 2km (1¼ miles) offshore, formed by volcanic rock. It is home to the world's biggest colony of northern gannets.

Before you start

* It is important to consult tide tables as you plan your day, as the rocks may be impassable at high tide.

* Even when the tide is out, the route along Scoughall Rocks can be dangerous, as the rocks are covered with slime and seaweed.

* Don't forget to pack your binoculars if you want to take a closer look at the hustle and bustle of seabird life on Bass Rock.

Along with the gannets, Atlantic puffins also nest on Bass Rock; they arrive, ready to breed, in March and April, then depart in August.

1 Begin from Tyninghame Links car park, which sits 2km (1¼ miles) east of the A198. Walk through the car park passing a 'Path to beach' signpost. Once through the gate, you should follow the woodland track southeast towards the coast. After 1km (½ mile) the track splits; keep left and continue through a line of large concrete blocks, remnants of Second World War sea defences. When you reach an old wall, continue to the gate and turn right where a broader track soon leaves the woodland behind and proceeds over scrubby grassland, culminating at the rocky headland of St Baldred's Cradle.

2 Bear left and walk northwest along a grassy path which becomes a sandy path. When you reach the information board, descend onto the golden expanse of Ravensheugh Sands. This stretches north, providing a superb view of Bass Rock, an island 1.5km (1 mile) off-shore.

During spring and summer, Bass Rock is home to around 150,000 northern gannets, making it the largest colony in the world – you will see their nests densely packed together. During April, puffins also return to Bass Rock to lay their eggs, along with gulls, shags and guillemots. Walk along Ravensheugh Sands, crossing a couple of burns as you go – these should pose no problems at low tide, but higher tides may mean wet feet. Beyond Peffer Sands, the route reaches Scoughall Rocks.

3 At particular points, this section can be a little awkward underfoot as stones and larger rocks need to be crossed. It may also be blocked at high tide. However, these difficulties are short-lived, and this part of the route is particularly diverse, passing a series of coves containing interesting geological features. Once you have passed through an obvious gap between two crags, round the headland to pass St Baldred's Cross to reach Seacliff.

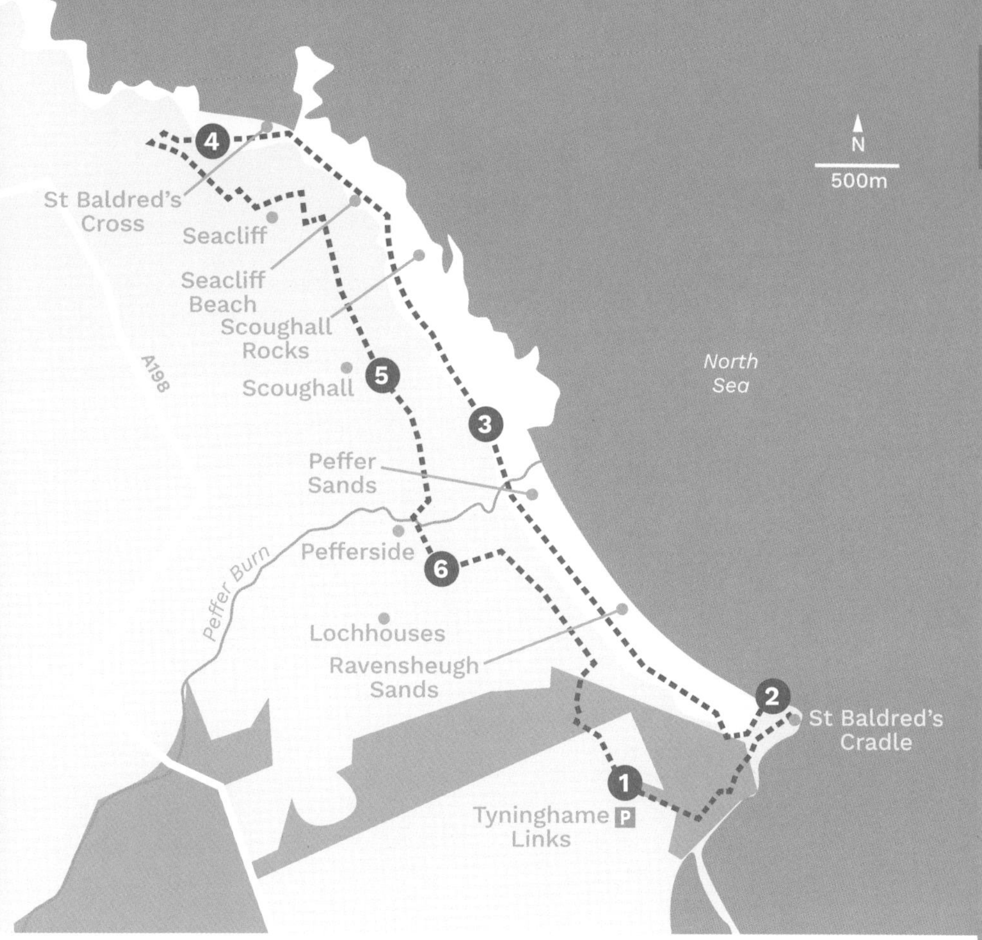

4 Retrace your steps about halfway along the top of the beach, then climb wooden steps to a small car park. Turn right, follow a single-track road, and then beyond a barrier turn left onto a minor road. Just before a cottage you should fork left, follow the road past an archway, and then head left at the next fork. The road proceeds through open countryside. At the crossroads go right, where a track skirts woodland to meet another track on the left. Follow this along next to a wall, turn right through a gap and continue south to Scoughall.

5 Just before you reach some buildings, turn right onto a road and at the next junction keep left around a gate. Follow another road that heads through Pefferside, crossing a footbridge over the Peffer Burn. From here, follow a rougher track to the crossroads that lies a little east of Lochhouses. Here take a left turn.

6 Go round a gate and follow a track towards dunes, until this swings right at a signpost for Tyninghame Links. The track now heads southeast alongside the dunes into woodland. When it splits turn left, pass through a gate, and walk back to Tyninghame Links. Make your way through one final gate, and you have reached the car park where this route began.

Skelwith and Colwith, Lake District

Time: **3 hrs** | Distance: **8.9 km (5.5 miles)** | Difficulty: ✪✪

The wonderful waterfall views at Skelwith Force and Colwith Force are spectacular on this leisurely circular walk. Although of course the falls are most striking after heavy rains, this route is well worth a wander whatever the weather.

Start location

North end of the bridge on the A593 in Skelwith Bridge, Cumbria LA22 9NN (grid ref: NY344033) just south of the junction of the A593 Ambleside to Coniston Road and the B5343 Langdale Road.

Getting there

By car: Skelwith Bridge is at the junction of the A593 Ambleside to Coniston Road and the B5343 Langdale Road. There is free unrestricted road parking on the left at the start of the B5343. If those spaces are full, there is a pay and display car park 1km (½ mile) further along the road on the right. A path opposite the entrance leads down to the main path down the valley, which the route follows, where you turn left down to Skelwith Bridge. Summer weekend parking may prove difficult if you do not arrive early, so it is worth considering the bus, especially if you are staying in Ambleside. **By public transport:** The 516 Langdale Rambler bus service stops at Skelwith Bridge, and travels through Elterwater which is an alternative start point. The infrequent X33 Ambleside to Coniston and Ravenglass service also passes through Skelwith Bridge. There is a pub, a café, a shop and pleasant riverbank to enjoy while you wait for a return bus once you have completed your walk.

Before you start

- Colwith Force is a considerable distance from any tourist car park, and is only accessible by walking. It is in a beautiful setting deep in the woods.

- 'Force' is a word from the local dialect word meaning 'waterfall', and it is used frequently in the area.

- Skelwith Force, with a popular visitor attraction centre and lots of parking nearby, is likely to be busier than Colwith Force. It is much smaller, but easier to get close to by clambering over the rocks. Take care, as a lot of water rushes through a very small gap extremely quickly. At times of flood, the iron bridge may be awash to the height of the handrail.

- Springtime is a particularly lovely season to enjoy this walk (although of course it is worth a visit any time of year) because the route will be bright with wildflowers, and many different types of waterfowl can be seen in the river.

Nestled within thick woodland, Colwith Force falls like a curtain of water as it drops along the River Brathay. In full spate it is particularly impressive.

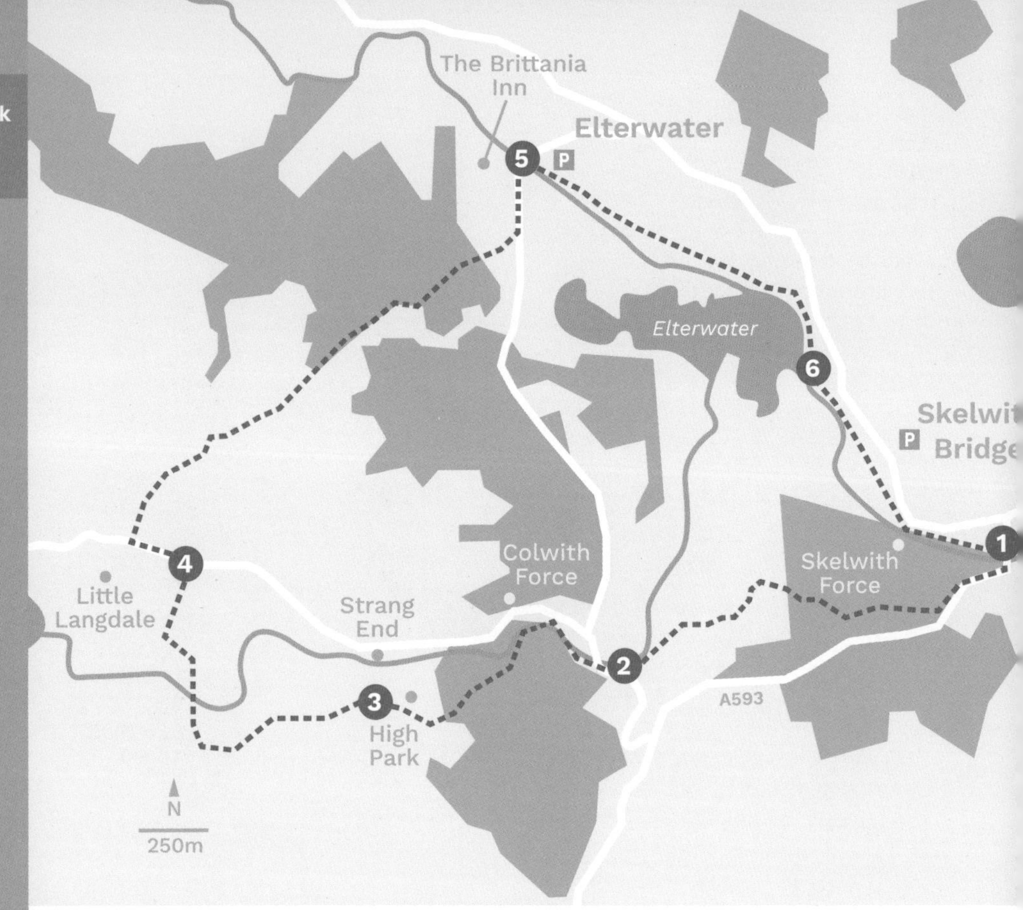

1 From your start location, cross the bridge on the A593 over the river into Lancashire, heading towards Coniston. Take a sharp right bend, ignoring a waymarked path pointing to a waterfall view point (you will see this waterfall a little later). Continue on to a second path on the right, waymarked as 'Cycle route 37 towards Colwith Bridge, Elterwater & Coniston'. A couple of steps down the drive, turn left through the gate and follow the path until you reach a T-junction with a signpost. Turn left, towards Colwith Bridge. You are now following the Cumbria Way long-distance path. The waymarks will be a little intermittent, but useful over the next section of your walk.

The path proceeds through woods and departs the woods through a gate. Keep straight on along a clear path. A track soon joins from the left, and you should keep in the same direction along the track. Go through a gate, pass cottages on the right and go through two metal kissing gates. The clear path crosses a field then enters a farmyard, go through and directly across a tarmac drive, then follow the path beyond straight on. Reach the end of a drive with a house to the right. Take the metal gate opposite and go down the field ahead until you reach a stile on the edge of the woods. Cross it and drop steeply down through the trees to meet the River Brathay and the road into Little Langdale at Colwith Bottom.

2 Turn right along the road and very soon climb left up some steps to a gate leading into National Trust land. Now turn right and

follow the path which soon reaches the river and goes upstream alongside it. You will pass a flight of stone steps up to the left, and soon reach a marvellous spot for viewing Colwith Force. After pausing to drink in the view, return to climb the stone steps you just passed. A short path turns right at the top to allow you to explore the top of the falls. The main path continues on, swinging left uphill through trees to eventually reach a cross path travelling along the top of the wood. Turn right after a short distance and pass through a gate into a field. Keep ahead on the stony path towards the white buildings at High Park – here you will find refreshments for sale and a beautiful garden you may wish to enjoy (especially if the weather is fine).

3 Now leaving the Cumbria Way, which goes left, you should proceed through the gate in High Park farmyard out onto a narrow tarmac lane beyond. Follow this as it goes right, down to the cottages at Strang End. Zig-zag to the right then left through the buildings and continue descending gradually. The lane becomes unsurfaced as it passes round a wooded hill and down to a ford. Cross by the footbridge back into Old Westmorland and follow the lane to the main Little Langdale Road. There is a pub just down the road to your right.

4 Turn left uphill along the road. After leaving the village of Little Langdale, take the road on the right signed as 'Unsuitable for motor vehicles' and marked as 'Cycle route 37 to Ambleside, Challenging Option'. There is no cause for alarm – the route is challenging only for cyclists, not walkers! The tarmac ends after a house, then the rough road leads pleasantly over to the wooded land above Elterwater. Moving under the trees, ignore a bridleway up to the left and proceed straight on, making your way down a steep hill. At the bottom turn left along the road and cross the bridge into Elterwater village. The Britannia Inn, set on the village green, is an excellent choice if you are looking for a lunch stop.

Notes of interest

✳ The whole of this walk lies within the present-day county of Cumbria, which was created in 1974 when the historic counties of Cumberland and Westmorland merged with the Furness region of Lancashire. The old boundary between Lancashire and Westmorland ran along the River Brathay here, then went on up to the Three Shires Stone at the top of the Wrynose Pass, where the three old counties met. Although the old boundary no longer has any administrative significance, the old counties still live on in the hearts and minds of many local people.

5 Immediately after the bridge, a path signed to 'Skelwith Bridge & Ambleside' goes right, passing between the river and the car park. This is a clear, well-surfaced and obvious path that is suitable for wheelchairs and is deservedly popular. It runs alongside the river, then soon alongside Elterwater, although the view is restricted in summer by the leaves on the trees. On leaving the trees you reach a short stretch of lakeshore where you will be rewarded with a glorious view of the lake and the Langdale Pikes directly beyond. This is a lovely spot for children to paddle.

6 Continuing on your way, the path carries on ahead through grassland, with the river running slow and lazy over to the right. As you enter woods, the river starts its rush to Skelwith. Ignore a bridge on the right and keep ahead between the road and the river. Soon, a metal bridge on the right goes down to Skelwith Force. After viewing the Force continue downstream to return to your start location at Skelwith Bridge.

walk
4

Farndale, North Yorkshire

Time: 5 hrs 30 mins | Distance: 17.1 km (10.7 miles) | Difficulty: ✪✪

The lovely Dove Valley is renowned for the countless wild daffodils that drape its flanks in a blanket of golden yellow each spring. Beginning and ending at Low Mill in Farndale, this tranquil route climbs over paved paths, moorland tracks and farm lanes, including a steady climb and numerous stiles. Walkers are rewarded with immense panoramas across the endless heather seas of the North York Moors National Park.

Start location

Low Mill, Farndale, North York Moors National Park YO62 7UY (grid ref: SE672952).

Getting there

By car: Low Mill car park is 10km (6 miles) north of Kirkbymoorside.

By public transport: The seasonal Moorsbus service M3 passes within a mile of Low Mill. Daily regular buses service Kirkbymoorside from Scarborough and other centres.

In the heart of the North York Moors, Farndale Nature Reserve was established in 1955 to protect the famous flowers growing here.

Before you start

- The start of this walk is Low Mill in Farndale. As it is at the heart of the golden sea of wild daffodils which this area is famous for, bear in mind that this area can be very crowded around Easter when the flowers begin to bloom.

- If you are searching for somewhere to stay, accommodation may be found at both Church Houses and Hutton le Hole.

- Famously picturesque, this route has much to offer in the way of inspiration to the painter, photographer or sketchbook enthusiast. Enveloped by a lattice of grey stone walls that sneak towards the bold ridge-tops, the landscape is a patchwork of pastures and pocket woodlands. The red-pantiled cottages, farms and barns give a hint of Tuscany on the hottest days; age-old hamlets, mills and villages are linked by sinuous lanes and tracks shimmer in a purple haze.

Springtime sees the Dove Valley carpeted with vibrant wild daffodils, which grow naturally here thanks to the ideal conditions created by the meadows, woodlands and river banks.

1 Join the well-marked footpath from the gateway at the mouth of the Low Mill car park. Once you have crossed the nearby footbridge, follow the secluded, tree-lined path upstream beside the River Dove. This presently reaches the hamlet of High Mill. Walk the lane ahead for 150m, then take the gateway on the left, signed for Cow Bank, cross a boggy field and then a footbridge to commence the steady climb out of Farndale. The path rises via stiles to reach Daleside Road.

2 Turn right, then at the nearby junction bear left for Dale End. Just past Monket House, take the gated track left for Bransdale, continuing the climb out of the dale along this old pit road. The lane rises from the hamlet of Church Houses (where you will find a pub, if you are in need of rest and refreshment) and winds up to the crest. Just north of this point are the red roofs of the famous Lion Inn on Blakey Ridge. The track now climbs steadily past old coal delvings and grouse butts, with engaging views up the great, green hollow dale. Eventually the climbing eases and a long straight brings you to a major junction of ways.

The old drovers' route along Rudland Rigg runs 16km (10 miles) along the North York Moors, one of the largest heather moorland areas in the UK.

Notes of interest

★ Thanks to the campaigning efforts of West Riding Ramblers, this beautiful part of Upper Farndale isn't submerged beneath the waters of a vast reservoir as was proposed by the regional Water Board in the late 1960s. The plans were successfully seen off by the Ramblers alongside other outdoors groups after three years of parliamentary lobbying.

3 Turn left along this old Westside Road, an undulating sandy track along Rudland Rigg, a long, flat-topped hill.

This section of the route offers an extraordinary panorama across waves of ridges, deep dales and hills. For company, expect the whirring, chuckling flight of red grouse and the mournful voices of curlew and whimbrel. Passing by the trig pillar, an eerie landscape of old diggings is the foreground to a view stretching south across the Howardian Hills and the Vale of Malton to the distant Wolds.

This airy trail merges with a tarred lane; keep ahead as you cross over a cattlegrid and pass a cottage on your left.

4 When you reach the bend 150m past the cottage, turn back-left through a waymarked hand gate, onto a path that leads through boggy fir and birch woods. This eases left to pass through a gate, then carries on

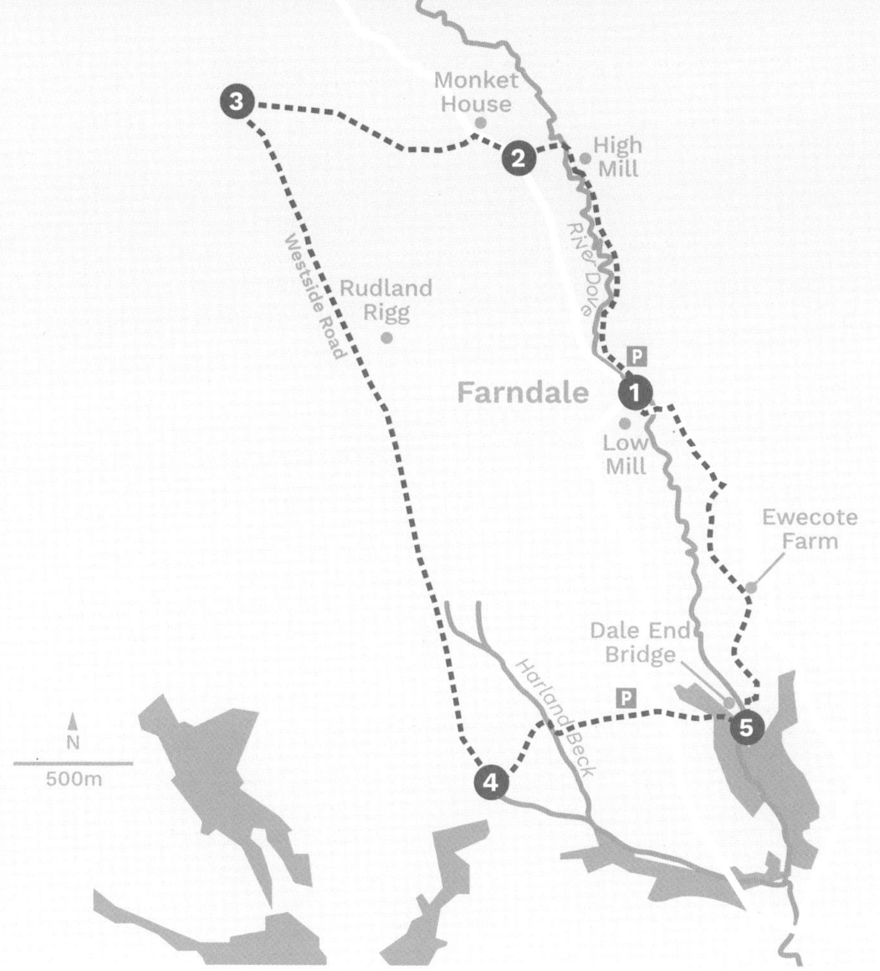

ahead to a broken wall; turn right past this to descend to a footbridge over Harland Beck. Turn right through the gate beyond onto a grassy path that curls left, widening to a track across moorland with sublime views down Douthwaite Dale. Cross straight over the lane and take the thin, waymarked path ahead, passing a walled corner and heading down to find a rough track above fir woods. Turn right for a few paces and look left across a heathery bump for a waymarked stile into the woods. From here, the path – occasionally indistinct – drops to another track at the foot of the slope. Take the signed path opposite to cross the Dale End footbridge over the River Dove.

5 Bear left up the old walled lane, which winds easily up the dale side. Cross directly over a farm access track and remain on the pleasant way now contouring Farndale's eastern flank. At Ewecote Farm, take the marked path ahead from the corner beyond the buildings, passing further buildings and emerging onto a tarred lane. Turn left and then left again to bring you back to Low Mill.

walk 5

Parwich and Tissington, Derbyshire

Time: **3 hrs 15 mins** | Distance: **10.5 km (6.6 miles)** | Difficulty: ✪✪

A circular route through picturesque limestone country, this walk begins at the village of Parwich then visits the famous village of Tissington, taking in a few stretches of the popular Tissington Trail along the way.

Start location

Parwich car park, Derbyshire, nearest postcode DE6 1QL (grid ref: SK189542).

Getting there

By car: Parwich lies on a minor road a couple of miles east of the main A515 from Ashbourne to Buxton Road. The Sycamore Pub in the village can be located using postcode DE6 1QL. Pass the pub on your left to follow the road out of the village and you will find the free car park along on the right. There is plenty of on-street parking if you find that the car park is full. More parking is available at Tissington Station (with toilet facilities) and Alsop-en-le-Dale Station (which is convenient for the A515) although you should bear in mind that both of these are pay and display car parks.

By public transport: The 442 bus between Ashbourne, Hartington and Buxton stops on the A515 outside Alsop-en-le-Dale Station. There is a reasonable Monday to Saturday service (check online for times), but no service runs on Sundays. Only school buses go to Parwich.

Before you start

- There is a code of conduct for trail users displayed at the car parks. Cyclists should cycle at reasonable speeds and sound their bells when approaching pedestrians, but do be aware that some do not. Walkers should keep well to the left, leaving plenty of room for cyclists to pass to their right. Large groups of pedestrians or cyclists should not spread out across the width of the path. As always, consideration and being mindful of other path users are key.

- The Limestone Way is a popular long-distance path that covers 74km (46 miles) across the limestone country of the White Peak, running from Castleton down to Rocester, where it connects with the Staffordshire Way. The waymarks will help you navigate from Parwich until you reach the Tissington Trail.

- The Tissington Trail follows the trackbed of the old Ashbourne to Buxton railway, which opened in 1899. Regular passenger trains stopped running in 1954 and this stretch of the line closed completely in 1963. During the 1970s, the trackbed was converted to an accessible footpath and cycleway. It has proved to be extremely popular. This is also a valuable resource for wheelchair users, providing access to some beautiful countryside.

The Tissington Trail winds its way from Ashbourne to Parsley Hay. There is plenty to see, as it passes through picturesque Tissington village and crosses the beautiful Derbyshire Dales.

1 Starting from the Parwich car park, turn left along the road, soon passing the Sycamore Inn. Just beyond, after a pond on your left, turn left on a track that follows the stream that runs into the pond. You will find a four-way fingerpost. Go straight on, signed Limestone Way, up an enclosed path that carries on alongside the stream. Just before you reach a road, and immediately after the white gates on the left, cross an un-waymarked stile on the left. Follow the left edge of the field up to and through a squeeze stile about 10m right of a gateway. Continue diagonally right up the next field and through a stile in the top hedge. Follow the right edge of the next two fields, then proceed steeply down to a footbridge over a stream – this is the Bletch Brook.

Hands Well in Tissington, dressed with flowers and natural materials to celebrate the biblical miracle of water changed into wine, for the annual well-dressing ceremony.

2 Cross the bridge and walk up to a squeeze stile you will find in the far left corner of the field. Once through this, keep straight on and climb steeply up the next field. You should keep parallel to the left-hand boundary about 20m to your left. Cross a step stile in the top wall, then continue straight on up the next field until you reach a cross track. Turn left along this track. Immediately after you cross a railway bridge, go through a small wooden gate on the left and follow the path down to the old railway trackbed, now the Tissington Trail. Turn right and carry on along this. At first there are fantastic views to the left. Later, the track runs through a cutting then goes under a bridge to reach the car park on the site of the old Tissington Station. You will find information boards as well as toilet facilities here.

3 Continue walking through the car park and turn left along the road. Soon you should fork left down into Tissington village.

One of the most popular tourist villages in the Peak District, expect to find Tissington busy on a summer weekend and at times of the well dressings. Since the time of the Civil War the village has been owned by the FitzHerbert family, who live in the impressive Tissington Hall. The beautiful little parish church contains numerous striking monuments to departed FitzHerberts. If you venture in, look out for the remarkable stained-glass window by the pulpit – it includes a notable Noah's Ark.

Just after the pond, turn right up The Street, passing a church on your right and a grand hall on your left. Continue straight on up the road, ignoring a possible right turn. When the road bends left, go straight ahead through a squeeze stile just left of a large field gate. Aim slightly left as you carry on, gradually diverging from the wall to your right, to reach and cross a step stile in the far wall. Keep on in the same direction to pass through a gate in the next wall. Now go straight on out into a large field. After a couple of hundred metres you should start walking parallel to some power lines. If

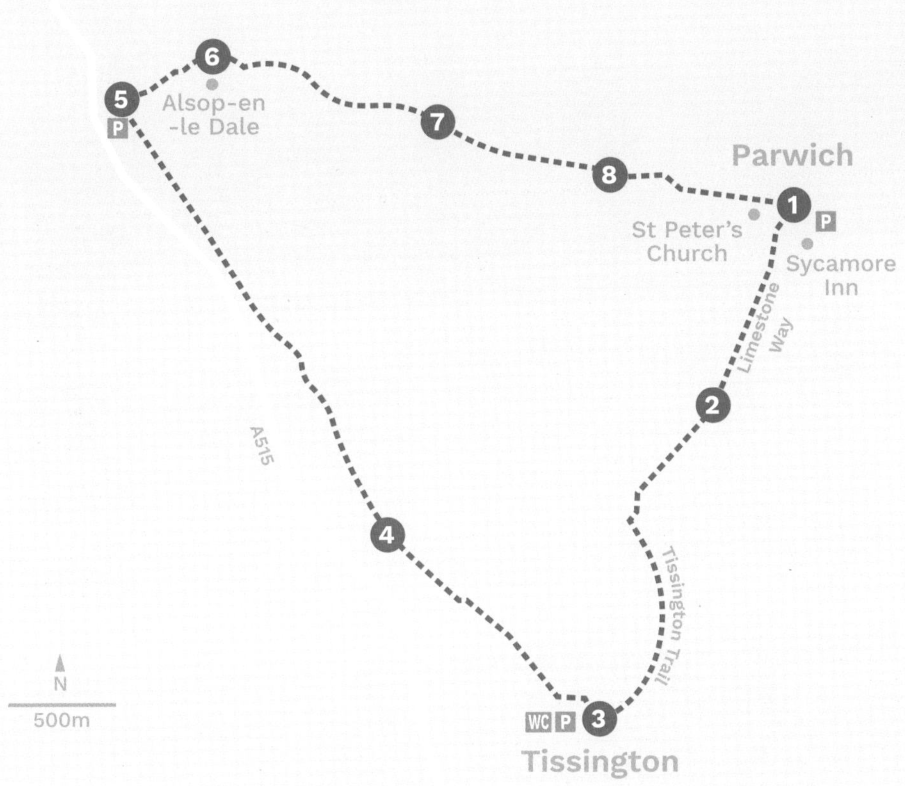

you keep these about 50m to your left you will eventually come to a squeeze stile and wooden gate in the far wall.

4 Pass through the gate, then keep straight on and pass through another gate in the next wall. Bear slightly left across this large field. Go through the two wooden gates in the wire fences either side of the cross track, and then bear slightly left to pass through a squeeze stile. Walk downhill, then cross the track you come to using two wooden stiles. Head slightly right to pass through another squeeze stile. Head up to the far top left corner of the next field, to find a gap that leads onto a track. Go right, ignoring the left turn you see soon. Just before the railway bridge, climb the steps on the right – here you are joining the Tissington Trail again. Turn left over the bridge and follow the trail until you reach the car park and picnic area on the site of the old Alsop-en-le-Dale Station.

5 Keep on the trail to the far end of the car park, then take the path that forks right down past a bench and leads you over a stile into a field. Walk down the steep hill, keeping the wall on your right. About halfway down, turn right through a gate in the wall and then left to continue downhill with the wall on your left. (If you think this path is a bit steep, spare a thought for the poor villagers who used to have

Parwich, the start and end point of this walk, is a remote village in the White Peak area. Pretty houses, built of local limestone, cluster around the green.

to drag themselves up it to catch a train!) At the bottom, cross the stile that will lead onto a road. Turn right along this road, and follow it through the little village of Alsop-en-le-Dale.

Alsop-en-le-Dale is a peaceful little hamlet only reachable through small lanes. It sits in a beautiful location at the head of a pastoral valley, and includes a handful of houses and a late 16th-century (Elizabethan) hall, which was home to the Alsop family. The little Norman church was restored by the Victorians and includes an interesting millennium window in the chancel – this is a lovely place to pause and rest awhile.

6 About 20m before the last house in the village, named The Bungalow, climb up steps on your left and cross the wooden stile into a field. Make your way diagonally right, aiming just to the right of the power-line pole, and cross a step stile about two-thirds of the way along the right-hand wall. Go slightly left and cross another stile in the wall to the left. After this, turn right walk along close to the meandering wall to your right. Now go through a wooden gate – this leads you into the end of a wood. Keep straight ahead, just inside the right edge of the wood, then cross a stile into a field. Follow the wall on your right until you reach the next stile, then go over and straight across the next field, and down to the low point of the opposite wall where you should pass through a metal gate that leads you into trees. Keep straight on down the steep path through the trees, from which you will reach a stile which you should cross into a field.

7 Carry straight on until you come to a stile a little to the right of the mid-point in the far wall. Then angle slightly left as you walk across the next field to reach a stile slightly left of centre in the far wall. Just beyond, cross a tarmac driveway via two gates. Go slightly right to the far-right corner of the next field. Here you will find a small plank bridge and squeeze stile, which will lead you into the next field. Go half right to cross a track and then through two small wooden gates. Follow the right edge of the next field to a track and turn right to follow it through a gate and onto a road.

8 Turn left to walk along the road. Immediately after you pass metal barns on the right, having reached the bottom of the descent, fork left off the road to follow a track. Go through a wooden gate at the left end of the wooden fence, then follow the wire fence on your left to a footbridge and gate leading into the next field. Keep straight on across three more fields and you will reach a road on the edge of Parwich village. This is just up from a school down on the left. Walk left down the bank, passing the parish church to your left. Although it is a Victorian rebuild, the church does contain one ancient treasure: a tympanum, sited above the west door (see Notes of Interest, right). Follow the road around to a T-junction with the main road through the village. Turn right and follow this road back to your start point.

Notes of interest

★ Tissington is famous for its Well Dressings ceremony, which takes place around Ascension Day (40 days after Easter). It is estimated that about 50,000 visitors flock to the village at this time of year. In this unique Derbyshire custom, the wells are 'dressed' with pictures made of natural materials. Large, wooden, rectangular frames are coated in mud and decorated with petals to create images. The pictures are often religious, but may also commemorate other special anniversaries or even people. These are then placed in front of each of the six wells around the village. This ancient custom has been revived in most of the villages in the area. It is thought that these ceremonies likely date back to pagan thanksgivings for full wells even during times of drought.

★ Visit the parish church at Parwich to see its tympanum – a semi-circular carved stone placed above the doorway. This one is dated by experts as being carved between 700 AD and 1200 AD – the huge 500-year possible range is testament to its uniqueness – and is decorated with animals symbolizing the Redemption. Inside the church you will find an exact replica at eye level at the back, which is easier to inspect than the original above the doorway. There is also an information board which does a superb job of explaining all the images and symbols incised in the stone.

nature in spring

As nature awakens, shaking off the memory of winter's frosty cloak, the great outdoors beckons with its increasingly irresistible invitation. Springtime in Britain spans March, April and May, and is a wonderful season to get out for a walk.

Some say it is more likely to snow at Easter than Christmas...but of course this depends where you are (and when the moveable feast of Easter falls). One thing is for sure though – the spring heralds the beginning of lengthening light hours and shrinking dark. Vernal equinox, the first day of spring, brings with it a pleasingly balanced 12 hours of darkness and 12 hours of sunlight. All across the UK, the average spring temperature is about 7–8°C (44–46°F), but again, how warm or cool it is will depend very much on where you are.

Early spring often brings wind and showers, and a traditional saying promises these will 'bring forth May flowers'. The transition into spring certainly appears to herald a period of unsettled weather, especially in April, as increasing warmth and low pressure systems seem to arrive on our shores at the same time. Spring air seems fresher, more fragrant, and it turns out science backs this up by pointing to increased moisture levels in the air around this time of year. Then when May sweeps in, resplendent in those glorious fresh greens and blushing blossoms once again, we know that summer is just around the corner.

Spring is the time of nature's great reawakening, and there is so much to see, hear and smell when you are out and about. British birds appear early in March and burst into song designed to both defend their territories and attract mates. Blackbirds, robins, skylarks and song thrushes all compete to be heard, along with sand martins and chiffchaffs who arrive to spend the spring and summer before heading off to spend our winter somewhere warmer. These birds are easiest to spot in early spring, with tree branches still relatively bare and as they search hungrily for food.

Hares, although increasingly rare, make a fascinating spectacle if you can find them boxing in the early spring, while vegetation is still not yet tall or thick enough to hide them from view. The brown hare is the most common of three hare species to be found in the UK, and, if you are lucky, may be spotted on flat farmland and grasslands, where they consume wildflowers, herbs and grasses. March walks in locations including Norfolk, Suffolk, Cheshire, the Marlborough Downs in Wiltshire, Anglesey, the Peak District and Cambridgeshire are recommended if you are particularly keen to spot the hares, and you are most likely to see them in the early morning and evening.

Woods carpeted with nodding, fragrant little bluebells are one of Britain's iconic signs of spring, with walkers and day trippers alike making their annual pilgrimages in April and May to drink in the exquisite colour and scent. Both British and Spanish bluebells can be found growing wild across much of Britain during these months, although only the British bluebells release that heady fragrance so evocative of springtime in the woods. Remember to tread carefully to avoid damaging the blooms; the native bluebell is a protected species and extremely delicate.

Some of the best places to spot bluebells include Loughrigg Fell in Cumbria, Grizedale

Forest in the Lake District, Sissinghurst Castle Garden in Kent and Urquhart Bay, Great Glen. There are of course plenty more places you can find seas of these sweet-smelling beauties in season; a quick search online will provide more detailed information about when and where to spot them in your preferred area, to help you plan your walks.

Leaves of wild garlic may be foraged during April and May, and the flowers too later in the season, where the plants grow on damp ground in woodlands and forests. Be sure you have correctly identified the plant before consuming it – wild garlic's distinctive aroma, small white flowers and pointed green leaves make it an easy one for beginner foragers to spot. Usual foraging rules apply – be careful not to damage the plants, take only a little and be sure to harvest only in areas where plants are healthy and plentiful. Wild garlic's relatively gentle flavour may be enjoyed in soups or sauces, pesto or salads...really, it can be added to pretty much anything you might enjoy the flavour in. The leaves can also be washed, dried and frozen to preserve them for use later in the year. An online search should yield a number of recipes and easy serving suggestions.

There are plenty more examples of spring plants and wildlife to look out for all over Britain, including: breathtaking Adonis blue butterflies, an iconic species living on the South Downs in Sussex, which start flying in early May; wild daffodils, which can be spotted in various locations such as West Dean in Sussex; bell heather in Scotland, a super-attractor for bees and butterflies; and early spring greens such as chickweed, dandelion and pale hawthorn leaves (followed closely by pale pink blossoms). Wherever your walks take you in springtime, Britain in bloom promises to reveal the very best that nature has to offer.

A Somerset apple orchard in blossom, with a sheep and her lambs enjoying the springtime.

walk 6

Portbury, North Somerset

Time: 1 hrs 30 mins | Distance: 6 km (3.7 miles) | Difficulty: ✪✪

A short, undulating ramble passing through mixed woodland which you will find carpeted in bluebells in springtime. Bluebells aside, this gentle loop on the outskirts of Bristol makes a lovely outing at any time of year.

Start location

Portbury, North Somerset BS20 7TJ (grid ref: ST498752).

Getting there

By car: Portbury is reached from Junction 19 on the M5, or the A369 from Bristol.

By public transport: There are various bus services available from Bristol city centre; the closest bus stop to the start of this walk is Sheepway, Station Road. Check online for schedule details.

During the spring, Prior's Wood is carpeted with a sea of delicate bluebells. The views are particularly striking in the southern and west parts of the wood.

Before you start

❊ You will find a pub in Portbury, where this walk begins and ends, if you require refreshments.

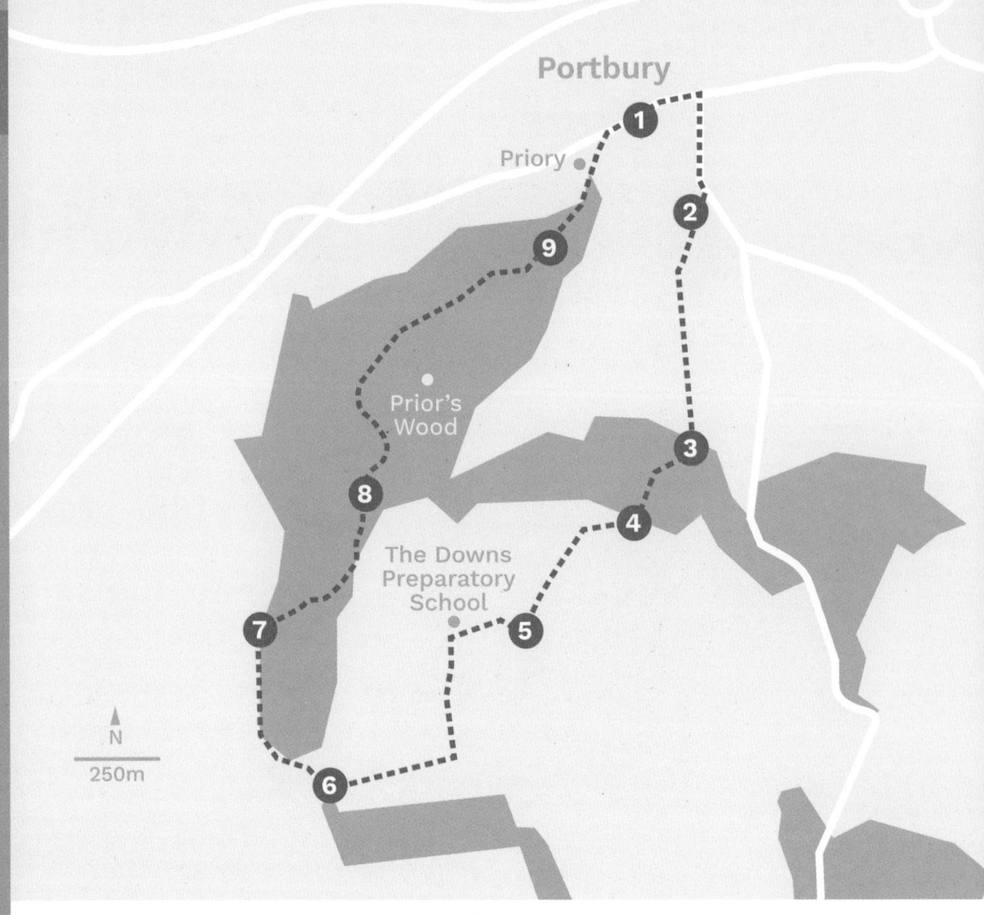

1 Park near the war memorial on the corner of Station Road and Caswell Lane, or take a short walk there from the bus stop at Sheepway, Station Road. Then walk back to Mill Lane on the right. Follow Mill Lane, turning right into Mill Close where, in a few metres, you should pass through a kissing gate on the left.

2 Cross the field diagonally right towards the boundary hedge. Climb two stiles either side of a stream, then turn left and walk on with the hedge on your left. At the top of the field, go through a gate, then another gate (or stile) on the right. Continue up this next field, keeping the boundary on your left, to a gate and stile with track beyond. Cross the track, climb the stile ahead and continue a few yards to a path junction. Here, take the signed path to the right.

3 Climb through the woodland to the path junction, where you should turn left then immediately right. Now climb again until you emerge at a stile with farmland beyond.

4 Head in a gentle right direction across the field corner to a gate, beyond which you should veer slightly left. You will pass a pond on your right and should aim for the further stile in the field boundary. Cross over, and head for the stile in a new fence by a ruined barn.

5 Cross the stile and turn right, walking with the fence now on your right, until you reach a driveway. Turn right along this driveway with the main building of the Downs School (formerly Charlton House) now visible on the left. Turn left at the next driveway and walk for 300m to a stile in the fence on the right. Waymark signs offer two routes across this field. Take the one going slightly left, skirting to the left of an old hedge boundary (now a row of trees) and continuing down the field until you reach a stile at the bottom.

6 Once you have crossed the stile, you are confronted with a broken stile (take care as you cross this) and then a 2m-high fence. Turn right and, keeping the fence to your left, you will soon reach woodland on your right. Continue down, ignoring a gate into Prior's Wood, at first climbing steeply then more gently, and passing two fields to your left as you go. You will reach a path junction. Here, turn right and descend into ancient woodland, rich with wildlife, where you will also find streams and plantations. In winter, a golden carpet of beech leaves covers the ground, only to be replaced in spring and early summer by the sea of bluebells for which Prior's Wood is so famous. Move quietly and you may even spot deer beneath the trees.

7 Take the steepish path down through the trees to a crossing track. Go left here and in a short distance you will reach a fork. Take the lower, right-hand path to cross a wooden bridge over the stream. (To see the best bluebells, you will need to make a diversion: do not cross the bridge, but instead take the path down to the left, with the stream on your right.) Returning to the broad path over the bridge, this now climbs and passes a track that has been opened up on the left. Ignore this and continue to the obvious cross track at the top of the rise.

8 Turning left, you now have some easy walking, ignoring a number of minor, indistinct turns. Carry on straight ahead at a crossing path, and you will reach an obvious fork in the track. Here, take the higher, right-hand route and walk with woodland to your left. You will find a high, wire fence to your right after a few metres.

9 Once you have walked 500m, go through the gate next to a former gamekeeper's cottage. From here the vista opens out on your left and you have just a short distance to walk before a gate provides you access to the road. Turn right and walk to the road junction, and you have once again reached your starting point.

Notes of interest

★ Prior's Wood was once part of the Tyntesfield Estate, but was bought by Avon Wildlife Trust when the National Trust purchased Tyntesfield.

★ Just before the road junction that marks the end of this walk, the tall building on your left was a priory, dating from the 12th century. Now much altered, the existing structure is 15th century and served as a school from the 19th century until 1972.

walk 7

Child Okeford, Dorset

Time: 2 hrs 50 mins | Distance: 11.9 km (7.4 miles) | Difficulty: ✪✪✪

Featuring stunning vistas across Blackthorn Vale, this circular walk links two Iron Age forts and several delightful Dorset villages. From the summit of Hambledon Hill one can see across three counties – Somerset, Wiltshire and Dorset – a reminder of why this was such an excellent choice of location for a hillfort. Plan your visit for late spring for a good chance of seeing one of the five species of wild orchids that thrive in this chalky grassland. Bird watchers and butterfly spotters will also find plenty to interest them here, including skylarks, kestrels and willow warblers, as well as the green hairstreak butterfly and the rare Adonis blue.

Start location

The Baker Arms, Child Okeford, Dorset DT11 8ED (grid ref: ST 83502 12729).

Before you start

- This is an area with a long history – do read the Notes of Interest on page 55 before you set out if you are interested in learning more.

- Note that this route includes moderate hill climbing, and also that it can be marshy at particular points (noted in the route description).

Getting there

By car: there are various parking spots in the village, either at one of the pubs or alternatively at the Hambleton Hill car park on the edge of the village.

By public transport: The X10 bus runs through the village from Yeovil to Blandford Forum. Find details of this service online.

1 Begin outside the Baker Arms, a pub in the centre of Child Okeford. From the pub's entrance turn left then, past the war memorial where the road forks, take the right lane up Upper Street. Follow the road as it gently climbs for about 400m, then take the right path once you have passed Hambledon Cottage. This path runs along a line of trees east and then climbs up the imposing ramparts of Hambledon Hill (see Notes of Interest on page 55). Once you've crossed the hill, take in the view then wander along the ridge (the hill is open access land, so you are free to wander as you wish) to the southeast corner of the hill.

The earliest occupation of Hambledon Hill was during the Neolithic period, when a pair of causewayed enclosures were dug out at its top, linked by a bank and a ditch. Two long barrows were erected within the complex and a third enclosure was also built. The total earthworks covered more than a square kilometre. The hill was further developed during the Iron and Bronze Ages and is now a classic example of an Iron Age hillfort. Rows of embankments and earthworks can be found around the hill's edges. The fort had three entrances, with the southwestern entrance protected by a 100m-long horn work. This seems to form the first in a series of connected earthworks which end at the Iron Age port of Hengistbury Head. The site seems to have been abandoned around 300 BCE and residents decamped to Hod Hill.

The breathtaking view down towards Child Okeford village, from Hambledon Hill. This is one of the best preserved Iron Age hillforts in Britain.

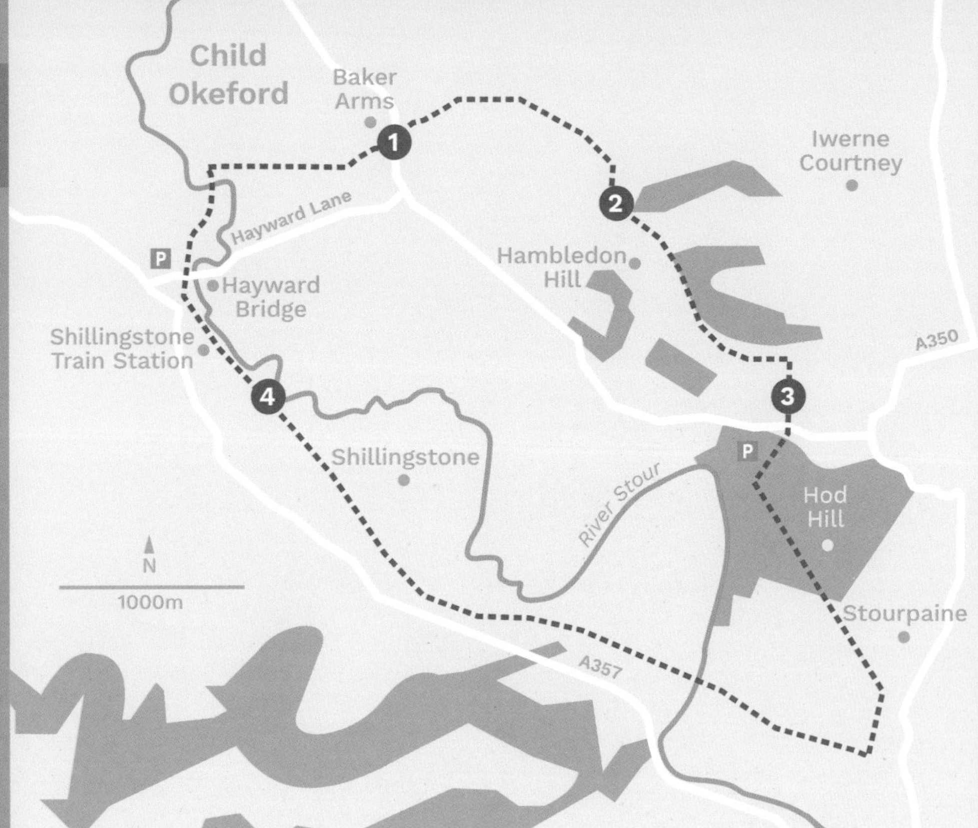

2 Pass through the gate and follow the path as it climbs southeast up to the trig point. Follow along the trackway (which may become very muddy in parts) and keep to the Stour Valley Way path, which will run left when the two paths fork. This path slowly curves around along the north edge of the hill, before dropping gently down. When you reach the barn, turn hard right to follow the track down to the road.

3 At the road, cross and climb straight up again to reach our second hillfort of the day, Hod Hill. Hod Hill sits at 143m high and is topped by a hillfort of the same name. The fort is roughly rectangular and encloses an area of 22 hectares – considerably less than the Hambledon Hill fort. On one side, this fort is protected by a steep natural slope down to the River Stour while the other sides are protected by an artificial rampart, ditch and counterscarp.

The hillfort was built about 500 BCE, around the time Hambledon Hill was abandoned. During the late Iron Age Hod Hill was inhabited by a local tribe, the Durotiges. It is notable as having been captured by the Roman Second Legion (Augustia), commanded by the future emperor Vespasian, during the Roman invasion of Britannia. Following the Roman invasion, the fort was used as a camp by the Romans before passing out of use around 40 ad, when it seems it was likely abandoned. The site was excavated in the 1950s and is now noted as an important calcareous grassland habitat.

Follow the path as it climbs sharply to the northwest corner of the fort, taking the right path when it forks. When you've gone through the gate, pass through the ramparts into the fort and walk across it to the southeast corner. Now follow the path down into the village of Stourpaine. Once in the village, you should head down Manor Road and then turn right and carry on past the village hall and football pitch onto the North Dorset Trailway.

The North Dorset Trailway extends from Sturminster Newton to Spetisbury, linking many of the Blackmore Vale's villages and providing an off-road trail for walkers, cyclists and horse-riders. The Trailway runs along the abandoned line of the Somerset & Dorset Joint Railway, which was closed in 1963.

Follow the trailway 3km (1¾ miles) or so to the village of Shillingstone, another village featured in the Domesday Book. Shillingstone was once noted as the site of the tallest maypole (26m) in Dorset. It was also nicknamed 'the bravest village in Britain' during the First World War due to the high proportion of residents who signed up to fight. These days, the village is noted for its parish church, originating from the 12th century, and its railway station, which is undergoing extensive restoration.

4 Follow the trailway onwards through Shillingstone and pass by the train station. You'll come to a bridge over Hayward Lane. Take the path to the right before you cross the bridge across the road. Take the right path over the field towards Child Okeford. Follow the path along, cross the bridge and then turn right to take the gate through the eastern wall. Beware that the ground can be very marshy at this point. Follow the path east as it passes through the fields until it comes to the road. Follow the road up towards the Baker Arms where this walk began. Take care when crossing the road here as the traffic moves quickly and again be aware that this section of the walk can also be very marshy.

Notes of interest

★ The picturesque village of Child Okeford is first recorded in the Doomsday Book as 'Acford', with a total taxable value of 10 geld units. By 1227, it was known as Childacford. The name derives from the Old English 'cild' (noble-born son) added to 'ac' (oak tree) and 'ford'.

★ In the Civil War era the Clubmen – a group of locals keen to protect their lands rather than to fight for either the Royalist or Parliamentarian causes – used Hambledon Hill as their base in August 1645. Led by a local rector, 2,000 Clubmen assembled on the hill. They baited local Parliamentarian patrols and made an unsuccessful attempt to take Shaftesbury. Eventually, they were dispersed by a troop of dragoons sent by Cromwell. Several were killed, around 300 arrested and the rest of their force dispersed. The prisoners were later released, Cromwell calling them 'poor, silly creatures'.

★ During the Norman conquest Stourpaine was of some importance – it was mentioned in the Domesday book and taken from its Saxon owners to be given to William I's chamberlain. By the 1800s however the parish was relatively isolated and noted for its poverty; its vicar testified to the Poor Law commissioners about the impoverished conditions suffered by his parishioners.

South Malvern

Time: 3 hrs | Distance: 8.9 km (5.5 miles) | Difficulty: ✪✪✪

This circular ramble through the southern end of the Malvern Hills leads you through the hamlet of Whiteleaved Oak, where the counties of Herefordshire, Worcestershire and Gloucestershire meet. In spring the woods will be adorned with bluebells and the air filled with birdsong, including the calls of the song thrush, nuthatch and pied flycatcher. This area is also home to a number of different species of bat – 13 at last count – although of course these will remain sensibly hidden during the day.

Start location

Off the left of the A438 between Eastnor and the B4208 east of Hollybush, Worcestershire.

Getting there

By car: There is an unsigned free car park on common 200m before church car access and car park (grid ref: SO 7665 3680)

A sunny May morning in the South Malvern Hills. The serenity of the lush green woods is enhanced by birdsong and bluebells.

1 This walk begins from the car park, with your back to the main A438 road. Set off past the house low on your left, and the half-timbered cottage on the right, heading along a grassy track. Continue downhill for 500m to the left bank of the Golden Valley millpond you will see ahead. Go round the north (far) edge of the pond and carefully across the dam on the stepping blocks. Bear left, keeping both the hedge and the thatched cottage on your left. When you reach the track, go right then immediately turn left to make your way up a stony track. Proceed on Coombe Green Common for 300m and then bear slightly right past willow trees and a cottage on the right, crossing over a concrete bridge. After another 200m you will reach the phone box on the B4208 road.

2 Cross the road and turn right along the road verge. Carry on along here for 400m, until you reach a farm gate and stile low on your left. Cross over, and in the field bear diagonally right to go through the gap/gate you will find in the cross field fence. Then continue to the farm gate which lies under the trees in the far corner. Through the gateway, follow the hedge on your left for 200m, and then keep on in the same direction but now with the hedge on your right. At the end of the field, climb over the stile. Continue forward with the hedge and stream on your right, then head over another stile into the road at Rye Street.

3 Turn right along this road, walking for 100m until you come to a road junction. Here, cross the A438 to the Duke of York pub. Go down the hedged track through the gate on the right of the pub. At the end of this track, cross over a stile and into the field. Follow the hedge on your right around to reach the double stile in the far hedge. Cross these stiles and walk up the field with a hedge on the right. At the top of this field cross the stile onto the road and turn left, noting the pond on your left. Proceed along the road, passing Berrow House on your right as you go, for 250m.

4 When you reach the road junction (an offset crossroads), turn sharply right and follow the minor road for 800m to a T-junction. Turn right here (signposted 'Hollybush 1.5 miles'). Just past a large house on the left, go through the gate on the left to walk along a farm track next to a collapsing wooden barn. Now in the field, follow the perimeter around to

Chase End Hill is the southernmost of the Malvern Hills and is 191m above sea level. It offers stunning views at all times of year.

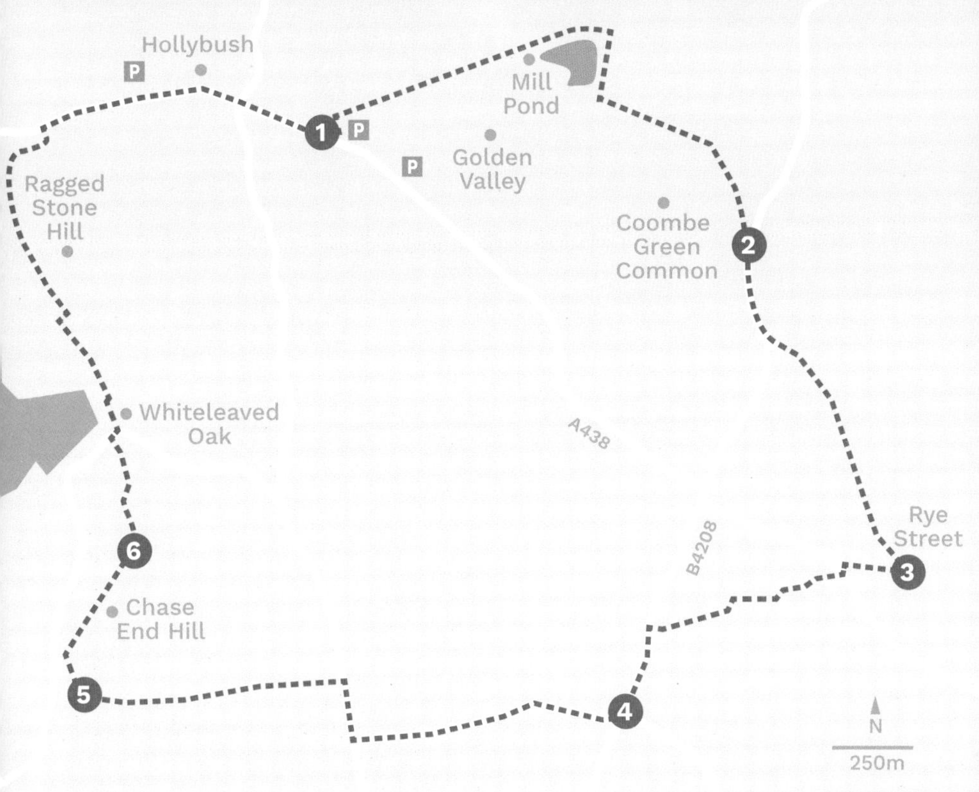

the left and then right to proceed uphill towards the wood, with a hedge on your left. At the top left corner, proceed through the gate, cross the forestry road, and continue forward uphill through the trees for another 200m. At the junction bear right heading uphill; after 100m go through the hunting gate onto the track. Turn right on the track, follow it through the farm gate and immediately turn left uphill through the coppice to reach the open access land of Chase End Hill.

5 Now cross over to the wooded area on the far side of the open access land, then turn right to follow a good path for 600m along the western slope of the hill (on your right) to the path T-junction – where it meets an incoming path from the top of Chase End Hill.

6 At the T-junction, bear left and carry on downhill for 300m. Soon you should pass through a pedestrian gate into a hedged track/gully, passing a cottage on your right, and then join a metalled lane. Turn right along the lane for 50m, and you will reach the hamlet of Whiteleaved Oak. Ignore the road leading to the right, and instead turn left and walk along that track for 50m. Just before the waymarked farm gate across the track, turn right uphill taking the obvious path to reach another gate. This wooded path uses access land for 1.1km (3/4 mile) along the western slopes of Ragged Stone Hill. Towards its end, the path curves right and you will eventually need to bear left on another obvious path. This will lead you downhill to a gate onto the A438. Turn right, then walk along the A438 road for 1km (1/2 mile) to return to your start point in the car park.

Near Dolgellau, Snowdonia

Time: 1 hr 37 mins | Distance: 5.3 km (3.3 miles) | Difficulty: ✪✪✪

Paths, tracks and lanes make up this short, scenic loop near Dolgellau, as it winds through woods and farmland, and alongside rivers. Scattered with stunning glimpses of the surrounding hills and the wonderful sights of rocky streams, rapids and waterfalls, this is a lovely ramble at any time of year. You will be rewarded with the best views of the rapids while the trees are still bare or just beginning to leaf in early spring.

Start location

The entrance to the driveway of the Dolserau Hall Hotel, Dolgellau, Snowdonia National Park LL40 2AG (grid ref: SH 755192).

Getting there

By car: Dolserau Hall Hotel is situated on a minor road running between the A470 and the A494 near Dolgellau, signed for the Torrent Walk and Dolserau Hall Hotel. There is very limited roadside parking near the footpath sign at Waypoint 1. Take care when you park your car that you are not blocking a passing bay or obstructing other traffic.

By public transport: The layby at Waypoint 4 is an alternative start point for this walk, and a good option if you are using public transport. Take the X27 bus from Dolgellau, and ask for the 'Tabor, Torrent Walk' stop – it is just a 5-minute ride. The bus will drop you on the main A470 road at the junction with the B4416. Walk 200–300m along the B road to find the permissive path sign at Waypoint 4, on the left.

View through Torrent Woods along the Clywedog river on the edge of Dolgellau. The gorge is home to many unique plants and fascinating wildlife.

Before you start

* Take extra care on this route in wet weather, as paths and stiles in the early parts of the walk may be slippery and paths may be boggy in some sections. Certain streams you will cross along the way may be quite full following heavy rain, and you should be mindful to stick to the path, as there are some steep drops along the way.

* The popular Torrent Walk follows paths on either side of the River Clywedog as it tumbles 100m down through a wooded gorge. The gorge is designated a Site of Special Scientific Interest because of the wildlife and plants to be found here, such as otters and dormice, and includes areas listed in the Ancient Woodland Inventory.

The tiny and seriously endangered hazel dormouse spends a lot of time high up in the trees, and depends on a diet of berries, nuts, seeds, insects and flowers.

1 With the Dolserau Hall Hotel behind you, turn left along the lane and walk towards the river. Look out for a footpath sign on your right before crossing the river. Taking this path, which turns back to walk alongside the river, you should cross a stile almost immediately. Follow the waymarked path over stiles and through fields and woodland. You will emerge from a short section of woodland to bear slightly right (again, this direction is waymarked) and continue below the mossy, tumbledown wall, towards a gate ahead. Head through the gate, with a cottage on your right, bearing right beyond the cottage where another gate leads you onto a track. Turn left along the track, fording a stream to pass immediately through a second gate. Continue a short distance along the track, walking through forest.

2 Look out for a stile on the right – cross this and enter the wood. Follow the clear path up the hill guided by yellow marker posts. After a stile, the path splits at a waymarked post. Take the option pointing right. The path crosses further stiles and crosses a stream, approaching a wall which is crossed by a ladder stile. Beyond the ladder stile the path becomes indistinct but if you continue in the same direction through the woods a further stile will soon become clear. Cross the stile. Now look out ahead, and slightly to the left, for a waymarked gate.

3 Head through this gate into a neat and well-kept cottage garden, crossing through this to another gate on the far side. Exiting from the garden, turn right on to a track and immediately through a further gate. Follow the track, soon bearing left, and walk along the tarmac lane to the B4416. Turn right, and walk about 1km (½ mile) along the road, passing St Mark's Church (see Notes of Interest on page 63) on your left. Take extra care here; the traffic, although unlikely to be heavy, can be fast-moving on this B road. However, there are decent verges that you can safely walk on.

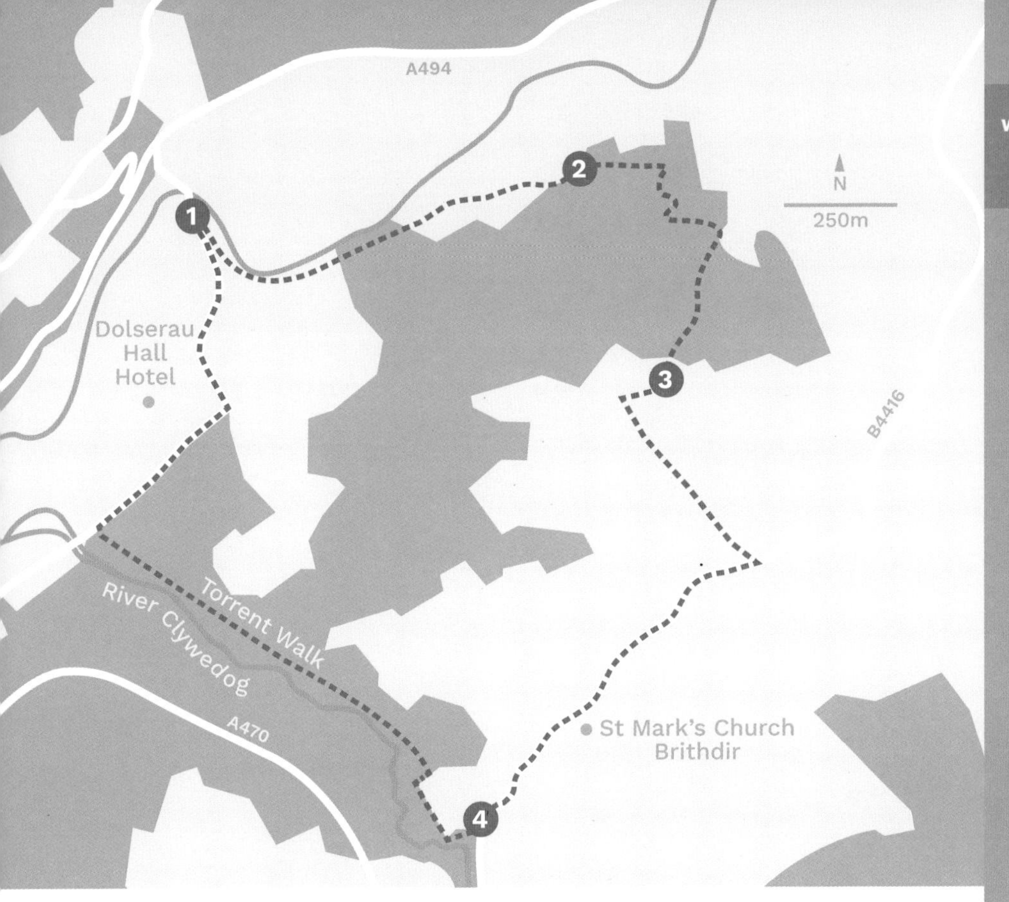

4 Once you have passed the church and a school, at the end of a layby on the right you will see a permissive path signed through a gate. Follow this to descend on a clear path, initially signed with marker posts, through woodland and alongside the stream. You will soon have excellent views of the spectacular rapids and waterfalls below you. Be careful to stick to the path, staying well away from the steep drop down to the river below. Our route descends on one of the Torrent Walk paths. At the bottom, the path joins a lane. Walk ahead onto the lane and then almost immediately straight down a short stretch of track. You will now join the minor road which takes you back to the start point.

Notes of interest

★ St Mark's at Brithdir is a fine example of an Arts and Crafts church. Built between 1895 and 1898, it was designed 'to appear as if it had sprung out of the soil'. It is designated a Grade 1-listed building, particularly notable for the boldness of its architecture and its intricately detailed, naturalistic fittings. The church is no longer in use but is cared for by the wonderfully named 'Friends of Friendless Churches'.

walk
10

Cadair Berwyn, North Wales

Time: 5 hrs | Distance: 10.5 km (6.3 miles) | Difficulty: ✪✪✪

The Berwyn Mountains, high ground to the east of Snowdonia, offer this incredible circular ramble through wild scenery and across a high undulating ridge – ramblers are rewarded for their efforts with truly exceptional views across much of North Wales. Not to be missed!

Start location

The car park is by a lane near Pistyll Rhaeadr SY10 0BX (grid ref: SJ076294).

Getting there

By car: Head for the start point – the car park by a lane near Pistyll Rhaeadr waterfall.
By public transport: The nearest station is 6.5km (4 miles) from the start – at Gobowen, near Oswestry – from where bus 79A stops at Llanrhaeadr-ym-Mochnant; check online for specific details. Walking to the start point will take you about 1 hour 20 minutes, so remember to factor this in.

The view down to Llyn Lluncaws from the summit of Cadair Berwyn. At 832m, this is the highest point in the Berwyn Mountains.

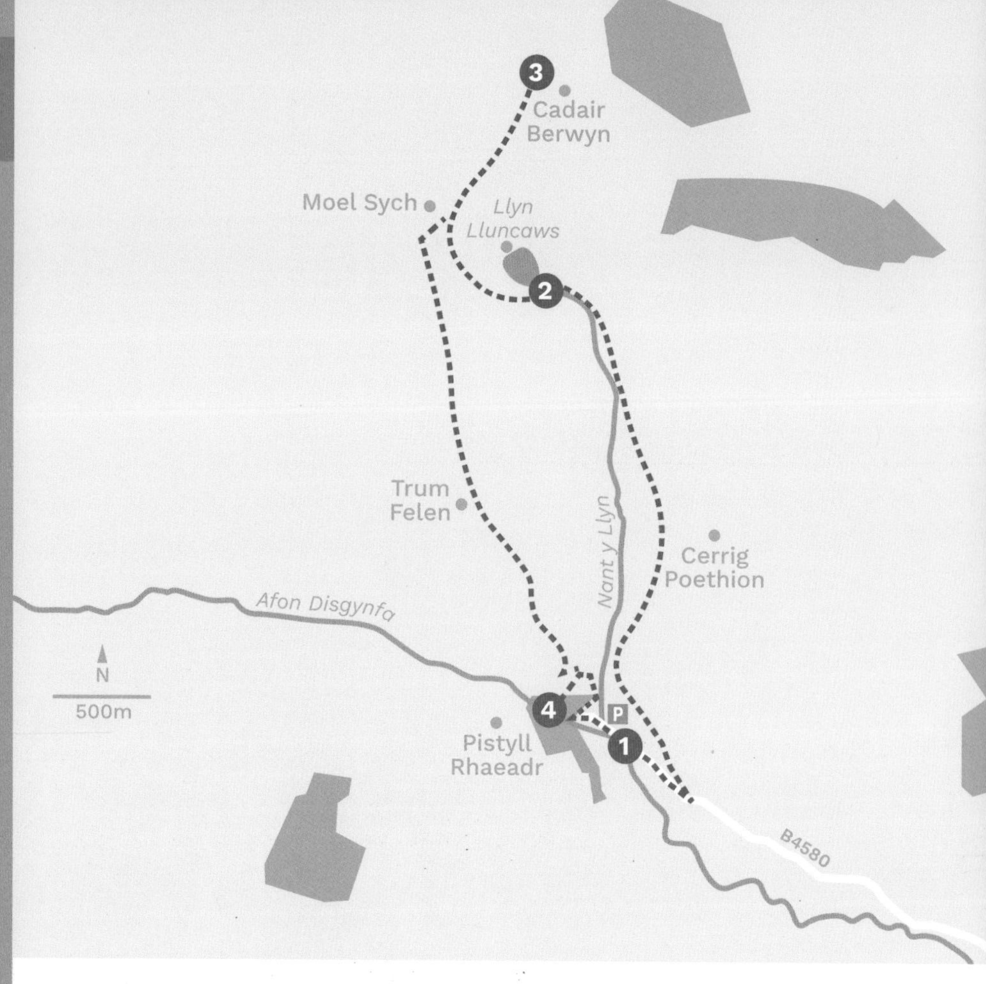

1 Starting at the car park, set off 200m east of Pistyll Rhaeadr, turn right and walk down the lane for 350m. Take the gate on the left that leads to a grass track. This track gradually climbs northwest, then swings north, proceeding through two gates, to contour along the east side of the long, empty valley of Nant y Llyn. You will see the crags of Cerrig Poethion rising on the right. Continue ahead as the valley narrows – the track becomes a path through heather which crosses the headwaters of Nant y Llyn. Eventually the track turns northwest to reach the shores of Llyn Lluncaws.

2 This perfectly formed mountain lake is a fine place to pause for a scenic refreshment break. When you are ready, continue along the path that now climbs a steep spur, with some outcrops, above the south side of the lake. It veers northwest, then north, above the crags to meet the main ridge between Moel Sych and Cadair Berwyn. Head north, along the crest of the ridge, for 700m to the southern summit of Cadair Berwyn (the highest point on the ridge at 832m) and continue for another 500m. Here there used to be a ladder stile, which has now been replaced with barbed wire cut down to above thigh-high. Cross (carefully!) here and carry on until you reach the trig point. This is slightly lower than the ridge, at 827m, although it was thought to be the true summit until a re-survey was carried out in the 1980s.

3 Enjoy the wide panoramic views – you are atop the highest mountain in Wales outside the National Parks – before retracing the route back to the cairn on Moel Sych. Now follow the path that leads southwards down the hill, keeping the fence on your left. You will descend to a small dip before rising again to the lower top of Trum Felen. After 15m, head through a gap in the fence at the bottom, and continue southeast for 400m, now keeping the fence on your right, (after entering the bracken there is a clear fork – you need to take the left path). The path descends towards the steeper ground above Pistyll Rhaeadr and the woodland that surrounds the waterfall will soon become visible. The path meets a rough track and at this point it is possible to go right, via a gate, on a path into trees which leads to the top of the high cascade, where Afon Disgynfa suddenly crashes over the precipice.

4 Now return to the track and descend east for 150m, crossing open slopes above the trees, to rejoin the track. This will lead you down to a stile by a small walled enclosure, with the waterfall tumbling between the tall trees beyond the café and associated buildings. A footbridge crosses the river and pools below the cascade. This is the perfect place from which to both appreciate and photograph the stunning view. From here, walk back up to the café and continue along the lane for 250m to return to your start point.

Notes of interest

★ Flowing with water from the Berwyn Mountains, Pistyll Rhaeadr is 74m tall and the highest single-drop waterfall in both England and Wales.

★ 'Llyn Lluncaws' is Welsh for 'the lake of cheese', and according to Arthurian legend is home to a wise fish. Local legend says a winged serpent has been known to fly down the valley and seize children, women and animals to feast on.

Often referred to as one of the Seven Wonders of Wales, Pistyll Rhaeadr is formed by the Afon Disgynfa dropping 73m into the Afon Rhaeadr below.

summer

The most sublime season of all, summer is full of sound, scent and promise. The sun shines more often, and birdsong carries on a soft breeze. Daylight hours lengthen languidly towards summer solstice. June is typically the sunniest month and July the warmest. The daylight lasts longer the further north one travels, although temperatures might not average much more than 15°C (59°F) in the Northern Isles. In the south of England, temperatures in the mid 30s (around 95°F) are these days more likely than they used to be.

walk 11

The Ring of Steall, the Highlands

Time: 9 hrs | Distance: 15.3 km (9.5 miles) | Difficulty: ✪✪✪✪✪

There are astounding views throughout this diverse circular walk, which travels through the spectacular woodland and waterfalls of Steall Gorge to arrive in Steall Meadows – home to the fantastic An Steall waterfall. A wire bridge here provides a novel way of crossing the Water of Nevis to reach the base of An Gearanach. The Ring of Steall, above Glen Nevis, is one of the classic mountain day-treks, taking in seven mountains – four of them Munros (An Gearanach, Stob Coire a' Chàirn, Am Bodach and Sgurr a' Mhàim). Fantastic narrow ridges link many of the mountains, the most spectacular being the Devil's Ridge linking Sgurr an Iubhair and Stob Choire a' Mhail. It is a long, tough walk, but enormously rewarding and entirely unforgettable.

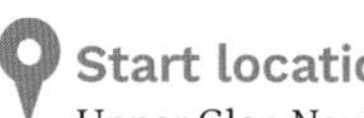

Start location

Upper Glen Nevis car park, Glen Nevis, Highland PH33 6SY (grid ref: NN168691).

Getting there

By car: Driving is the best way to reach the start point.
By public transport: There's no public transport direct to the start. Regular Scotrail services or Citylink bus 916 from Glasgow go to Fort William. From there, Stagecoach bus 41 takes you as far as Glen Nevis Youth Hostel, but that still leaves a 5km (3 mile) walk to the start (for more information, check online).

The 120m waterfall viewed here from the meadow. Steall Falls is also known as 'An Steall Bàn' meaning 'White Spout' in Gaelic.

Before you start

* Munros are Scottish mountains over 914m high.

* There are excellent paths and tracks through Steall Gorge and over the mountains. There are several steep ascents and descents throughout, making this walk a long, tough one. There's also an exposed ridge and a wire bridge en route. The ridge can be negotiated using narrow paths but as it is exposed, it could be problematic during the winter months. We recommend tackling this route during the summer.

1 From the car park at the end of the Glen Nevis single-track road walk east along an excellent path, climbing through the beautiful woodland of Steall Gorge high above the Water of Nevis. The path can be uneven at points and care should be taken. After approximately a kilometre (half a mile) the path emerges from the woodland into the beautiful Steall Meadows, which provides incredible views of the Mamores and An Steall. Continue through the meadows along the main path, then bear right onto a narrower path leading down to the wire bridge, comprising of two cables for hands and one for feet. Carefully cross the bridge (or if this doesn't appeal, remove your boots and wade across the river) then turn left to pass Steall Hut. Continue through wooded slopes and across a burn, passing beneath Steall Falls. After crossing one more burn, you reach the base of An Gearanach.

2 Turn right and climb the initially steep path, which then begins to zig-zag its way up the rocky slopes. Superb views open out along the length of Glen Nevis and up to Ben Nevis. The path continues to reach the 982m summit An Gearanach, the first Munro of the day. Its central position within the Mamores

This walk offers many richly varied views and landscapes. Here, the glen broadens out into a grassy meadow, guarded by steep mountainsides.

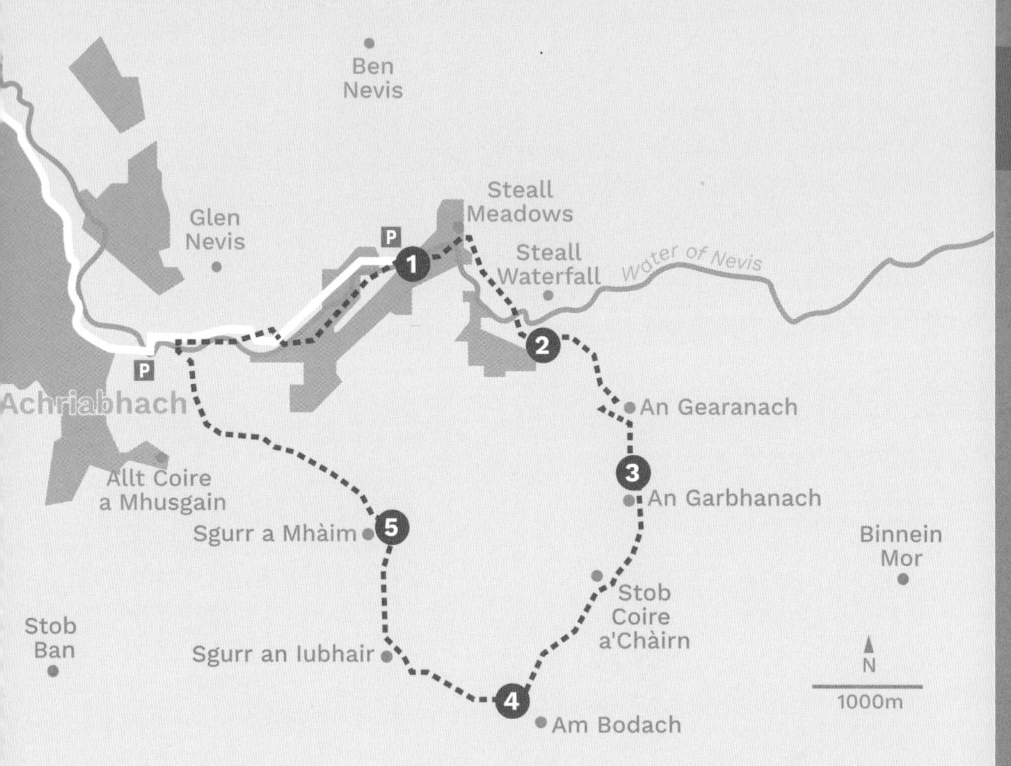

range allows for wonderful views of Binnein Mòr and Binnein Beag.

3 From the summit, continue south along the narrow ridge over An Garbhanach . A steep descent and re-ascent climbs to the cairn on the second Munro of Stob Coire a' Chàirn, which has a commanding view of Am Bodach. The gradient eases slightly as it descends southwest to reach the base of Am Bodach. However, a thigh-punishing climb southwest up a rocky path is required to reach the lofty summit. When you get there, you will be rewarded with superb views as far afield as the Paps of Jura.

4 A path now descends west to a narrow bealach (Gaelic for 'pass'), which then climbs onto the summit of Sgurr an lubhair. This is where the trickiest part of the route begins. Ominously named 'the Devil's Ridge', the path descends northwest to another bealach, then heads north over the short, but very narrow and exposed, Devil's Ridge. Depending on your head for heights, you may want to opt for a slightly less exposed path descending left from the ridge. But take care and pay attention – whichever route you choose requires extreme caution. Once across the ridge, the wide, quartzite slopes climb easily to reach Sgurr a' Mhàim. This is the highest Munro of the day, presenting great views of Stob Ban and Mullach nan Coirean.

5 From Sgurr a' Mhàim, a path zig-zags northwest down an obvious ridge into Glen Nevis to reach a path beside the Allt Coire a' Mhusgain. From here, bear right and follow the path down to the Glen Nevis road at the Achriabhach car park. Cross over a bridge, turn right and follow the road for approximately 3km (1¾ miles) to take you back to your start point.

walk 12

Buttermere, Lake District

Time: **2 hrs** | Distance: **6.9 km (4.3 miles)** | Difficulty: ✪✪

One of the loveliest lakeside walks in Britain. This route loops gently around Buttermere, with spectacular scenery everywhere you look. Walking is popular here, particularly in the summer, but it doesn't suffer from the same weight of numbers as more easily accessible areas such as Derwent Water or Windermere.

Start location

The Bridge Hotel, Buttermere, Cumbria CA13 9UZ (grid ref: NY174169)

Getting there

By car: Driving is the easiest way to get to Buttermere as local public transport options can be few and far between depending on when you visit. Do be aware that the roads in the Lakes are very narrow and steep with the pass between Borrowdale and Buttermere hitting a 25 per cent gradient at some points. There is a central car park in Buttermere next to The Fish hotel, although this fills up quickly during the summer high season.

By public transport: The village is served by the 77/77A bus service, a seasonal service that runs up to ten times a day during the summer.

Before you start

- Buttermere is a famously attractive spot for wild swimming, and if you are a confident swimmer you may well be tempted to take a dip. It is worth bearing in mind though that the steep underwater edges mean this is not a suitable paddling location for beginners or children.

- Nesting sandpipers lay their eggs on the lakeside shingle along the north edge of Buttermere from April through to late June. A small section of permissive footpath may be closed during this time to keep the eggs and new chicks safe from walkers and dogs.

Nestled in among the northern fells, Buttermere makes the ideal focal point for a relatively short and easy ramble through beautiful scenery.

The Fish features in local legend The Maid of Buttermere. It tells the tale of Mary Robinson, the beautiful daughter of the 18th-century landlord.

1 This route begins in the centre of Buttermere hamlet, a small hamlet with a population of 121, where the Bridge Hotel sits on the B5289. Take the lane to the left-hand side of the hotel and walk towards The Fish hotel. From there, take the fenced track to the left-hand side and follow this along. Turn left, pass through a gate, and then bear right through a further gate before following the track down towards the lake. Turn right here and follow the path along until it meets the lakeshore, passing through a gate and two bridges en route.

Buttermere is home to a small church, named for St James, which contains a stone tablet set into the south window as a memorial to British fell walker and guidebook writer Alfred Wainwright. The window looks out over Haystacks, his favourite place to walk and the place where his ashes were eventually scattered.

2 Follow the path as it runs down the southwestern flank of the lake, keeping left. At the end of the lake, continue a little further and take the first left turn through a gate and over Peggy's Bridge. The path runs into a lane leading to Gatesgarth Farm. Walk through the yard and up to the road.

3 Turn left when you reach the road and walk up the hill. The road will swing right where it meets the lakeshore, then left. Where it bears right, moving away from the shoreline, a path runs down the left to the shoreline; this path is signposted 'Buttermere via Lakeshore Path'. Follow this along the northwest side of the lake.

Notes of interest

★ Buttermere lake sits at the head of the River Cocker and is surrounded by fells. There are two theories about the origins of Buttermere's name. One holds that it comes from 'the Lake by the Dairy Pastures', or the 'Butter Lake', while the other suggests that the name is a corruption of the old Norse 'Buthar', the lake's original name being 'Buthar's Lake' or 'Butharmere'.

★ Despite its small size, Buttermere has a long and significant history which draws in the Norse conquest, the beginnings of Romanticism and the start of Lake District tourism. Famous local figures include Mary Robinson, the famous 'Maid of Buttermere', a shepherdess and the daughter of the landlord of The Fish hotel, which this walk passes, and a noted local beauty. Her story inspired Melvin Bragg's 1987 novel *The Maid of Buttermere* and a play of the same name in 2009.

A notable feature here is the small, tunnelled section of the path. This tunnel was forged in the 19th century, on the instruction of George Benson who then owned the Hassness Estate and wished to walk around the lake without straying far from the shore. The tunnel was created so he needn't leave the lake's edge to pass a ridge.

Note that this section of the walk contains some road walking; be careful of traffic, make sure you are visible and keep to the right-hand side of the road.

4 Where the lake bank turns left, continue straight on and follow the path as it runs uphill towards Buttermere village. The path will lead towards Wilkinsyke Farm and, from here, it's an easy walk out to the road just short of the Bridge Hotel. Turn left to walk along the road, returning to your starting point.

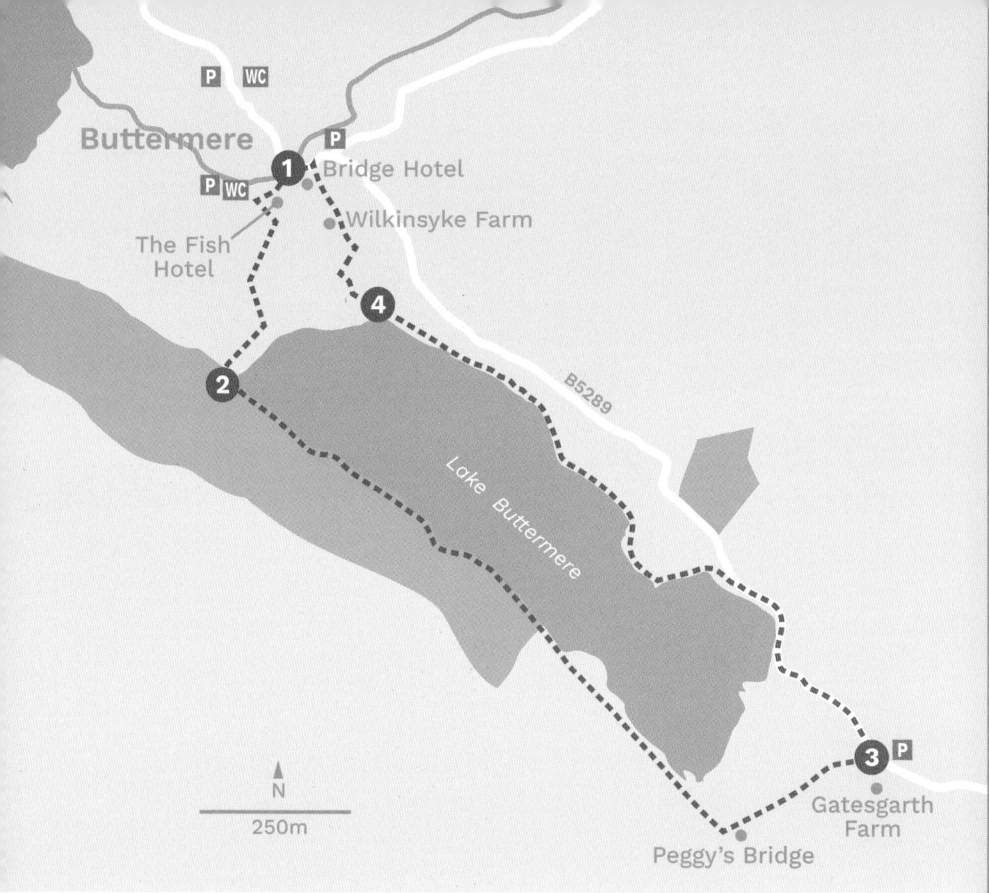

Buttermere
P WC
P
P WC
1 Bridge Hotel
Wilkinsyke Farm
The Fish Hotel
4
2
B5289
Lake Buttermere
3 P
Gatesgarth Farm
Peggy's Bridge
N
250m

The Church of St James was originally built on a rock outcrop overlooking Buttermere village in 1507. The present building dates from 1840 and was restored in 1930.

walk 13

High and Low Force, Upper Teesdale

Time: **4 hrs** | Distance: **13.1 km (8.1 miles)** | Difficulty: ✪✪✪

A spectacular circular walk in Upper Teesdale, passing Low and High Force waterfalls. High Force is one of the most impressive waterfalls in England, where the River Tees drops 21m from Whin Sill rock into the plunge pool below. Low Force is especially dramatic after rain.

Start location

Bowlees car park, Upper Teesdale, County Durham DL12 0XF (grid ref: NY 908283).

Getting there

By car: Bowlees is on the B6277 5km (3 miles) west of Middleton in Teesdale. The car park is signed up a side road off the main road. There is a visitor centre nearby where you can get refreshments and toilet facilities available. A donate and display scheme runs at the car park, with a minimum recommended payment – income from parking helps to maintain the attractive surroundings and support the visitor centre.

By public transport: There is a very limited 73 bus service which runs once on Wednesdays only, from Barnard Castle.

High Force is one of the most impressive waterfalls in England. The rocks it plunges over are more than 300 million years old.

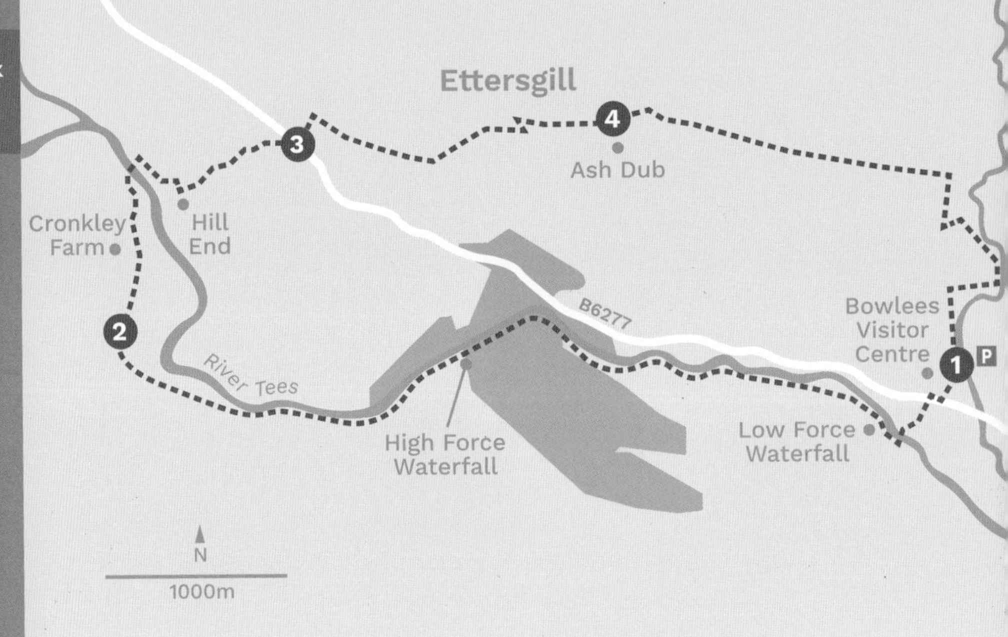

1 From your start point at the Bowlees car park, cross the footbridge and go past the visitor centre, which is an old chapel. Go straight on down the access road to the main road, turn right for 30m, then take a signposted path on the left. Follow this across the fields, through a squeeze stile and down a rocky path to the River Tees. Cross over the Wych suspension bridge and turn right to follow the river past the Low Force waterfall. Continue alongside the river, passing a footbridge and then climbing a hill. You should now follow the river deep down into a gorge to your right. When approaching High Force, look out for a small path going right through a black metal fence. Make a quick diversion along this path to come out on a rocky outcrop with an outstanding view of the waterfall. Return to the main path and continue past the top of High Force. Continue alongside the river passing a quarry on the opposite bank and then climbing a hill, gradually diverging from the river. At the top of the hill, fork right at stone marker posts and go down to a stile in a wire fence close to a wall corner. The section of this walk along the river bank follows the Pennine Way, one of Britain's premier long-distance footpaths, running for 434km (270 miles) from Edale to Kirk Yetholm.

2 Cross the stile, turn right and follow the flagged footpath with a wall on the right. Go through a gate, then cross a stile in the wall and go down a steep hill to Cronkley Farm. Go ahead to the near right corner of a large wooden barn. The path has been diverted at this point; you should use the new route which goes left through a gate and clockwise around the barn to a wooden gate leading onto the farm access road. Follow the access road to a bridge over the river. Cross this and bear right on the track, then follow it uphill passing Hill End on your right. Continue on the track around to the left, go right at a T-junction and carry on to the main road. Turn right, walking along the road for 50m until you reach a chapel.

3 Turn left up a side road, follow the road uphill and round to the right at the top.

Stay on the road – passing a former chapel on your left – to its end. Fork left through a gate at the end and continue ahead with a wall on your right. Go up a hill and through a gate in a corner. Immediately after the gate, bear slightly left down the field to its opposite corner. Cross a small stile in a fence and immediately go right through a farm gate. Go slightly left downhill to another gate just beyond, follow a track across a stream and up into another field. Go to the far end and, just left of black barns near a house, go through a gate and through the house's parking area to a road. Turn left and carry on for nearly 100m. Just after a farm, turn right on a signed footpath and follow the track steeply downhill. Cross a footbridge and climb up the track beyond the bridge. Where the track bears left, carry on straight ahead and then bear left up a field and cross a ladder stile in the facing wall. Go straight ahead, passing the right side of the nearest barn, and then through a gate at the far end of the barn that leads into the farmyard at Ash Dub. The waymarking is poor in this section. Pay extra attention to your navigation.

4 Turn left up out of the farmyard and then right along a track with a wall on your right. Pass through a gate, keep straight on to cross a stile in the far right corner. Then cross a stream ahead and climb to another farm gate in the top right corner. Go straight ahead across the next field (there is no visible path), and cross a stone stile in a wall. (Most of the wall climbs steeply from right to left, but you will find the stile in a short, level section – it may be waymarked.) Bear very slightly left across the next rough field to a gate in the far left corner. Continue through the next rough field, bearing very slightly right, aiming just right of the left end of the line of conifers ahead. Soon, you will spot a lone tree down in a valley ahead, with a small young plantation just beyond it. Pass this tree and climb a hill with a wall on your right. At the top, turn right across a stile and go through the next field with the conifers on your left. Soon cross a stile into the wood, and then turn right to follow a track to the bottom of the wood. Turn left back into the Bowlees car park, and you have returned to the start.

One of the most beautiful waterfalls in the north of England, Low Force is a series of small cascades on the River Tees as it makes its way down the dolerite gorge.

walk 14

Robin Hood's Bay, North Yorkshire

Time: 1 hrs 15 mins | Distance: 4.2 km (2.6 miles) | Difficulty: ✪✪✪

A beautiful short walk following the old Scarborough & Whitby Railway to the famous fishing village of Robin Hood's Bay. This route then follows the steep, winding main street down to the sea before returning along the coast path on the Cleveland Way. During the summer months, you can expect to see plenty of sea birds around this area, congregating for breeding season, including guillemots, gannets, kittiwakes, oystercatchers and perhaps even puffins. There are land birds too of course, including skylarks, linnets and goldfinches, as well as wagtails and pipits. Keep an eye on the sea as you walk; harbour porpoise and grey seals are often spotted along the coast here during the summer.

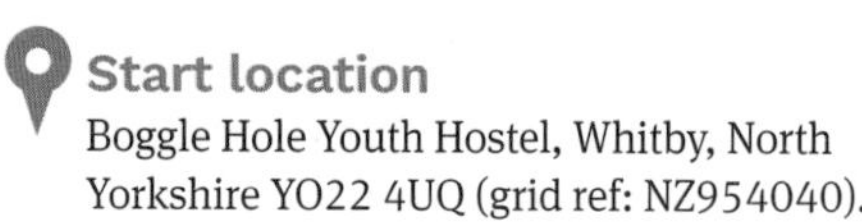

Start location

Boggle Hole Youth Hostel, Whitby, North Yorkshire YO22 4UQ (grid ref: NZ954040).

Robin Hood's Bay, seen from the cliffs. At low tide, a small sandy beach can be reached from the clifftop path.

Getting there

By car: Boggle Hole is on minor roads east of the A171, a mile or so south of Fylingthorpe village. At the top of the driveway to the hostel, which you are not allowed to drive down, there is a large marked-out parking area on the side of the road, available for the use of both hostellers and non-hostellers. A large pay and display car park is also available in Robin Hood's Bay.

By public transport: Boggle Hole cannot be reached by bus, but the X93 Scarborough to Whitby and Middlesborough bus service stops in Robin Hood's Bay, by the crossroads at Waypoint 4.

Before you start

* Although this is quite a short walk, note that there are three quite significant ascents and descents along the way.

* If you are looking for accommodation, try the youth hostel at Boggle Hole (where this walk begins); for more information see the YHA website.

* Robin Hood's Bay is a popular local tourist attraction, so it gets extremely busy on a summer weekend. Its popularity means there are plenty of public toilets available, and several places to buy refreshments. There is a tiny fish and chip shop on Albion Street at the bottom of the village, should you fancy fish and chips on the beach.

1 From the start point at the youth hostel, cross the footbridge over the stream and climb up to the road. Turn right and go steeply up to the road junction at the parking area. Turn right and follow the road between houses and farm buildings. At the far end of the buildings, go through a gate (which may well be propped open), cross the road and follow the road steeply down to a ford.

2 Cross the footbridge over Mill Beck, which is the stream that runs into the sea further downstream at Boggle Hole. Go ahead a few steps and turn left to follow a narrow path with a wire fence to your right. Soon, cross an old stone stile and reach the road again. Turn right and head steeply uphill. At the top, go through a gate across the road, next to a green bench (which may be handy if you need a rest!). The lane now goes gently downhill. Ignore a right turn along the dead-end Mark Lane and continue for another 30m to reach the old railway path.

3 Turn right along the old railway, which is signed 'Railway Path to RH Bay'. Keep on the main track, ignoring all side paths, aiming for the odd-looking church tower with the red-tiled sloping roof that lies ahead of you. This track eventually becomes tarmac and continues on to reach a road. Turn right and follow this road to St Stephen's Church. As the church has been in view for most of the last mile, you might like to look inside – it is normally open from 8am to 4pm. Built in 1870, it has high lofty vaults and is a nice example of Victorian architecture. Keep straight on past the church on your left and continue past the bus stops to reach a T-junction. This section of the route follows the trackbed of the old Scarborough & Whitby Railway (see Notes of Interest, right).

4 Turn right and follow the road downhill, to reach a turning circle by the Victoria Hotel. Keep straight on across a small green furnished with lots of benches, then start going steeply downhill on a paved path, keeping a green

Notes of interest

★ Robin Hood's Bay is a beautiful little fishing village that plunges down steep streets to the sea, with a maze of narrow alleyways going between the buildings, which are fun to explore. The bottom of the village, known as Baytown, is now famous as the eastern terminus of Wainwright's 'Coast to Coast' walk. There is a map of the route on the wall by the slipway, and you may well see tired but happy walkers going for a paddle after completing a tough, but beautiful, trek across the width of England.

★ The route along the coast follows part of the Cleveland Way, with its distinctive white acorn logo that signifies it is a National Trail. This popular route runs for 175km (109 miles) around the North York Moors National Park from Helmsley to Filey, including a long coastal stretch.

★ The old Scarborough & Whitby Railway was a 32km (20 mile) line opened in 1885 and closed as part of the Beeching Cuts in 1965. It was a slow route, with a number of sharp bends and steep inclines making it difficult to run steam trains along it, especially when sea mists made the tracks damp and slippery. After closure, the route was purchased by the local council who have converted it into a popular walking and cycling route. It is branded 'The Cinder Track', as the ballast on the route was made from cinders rather than stone. With cinders being a cheap waste product from steam engines, they were often used on low-grade lines to save costs.

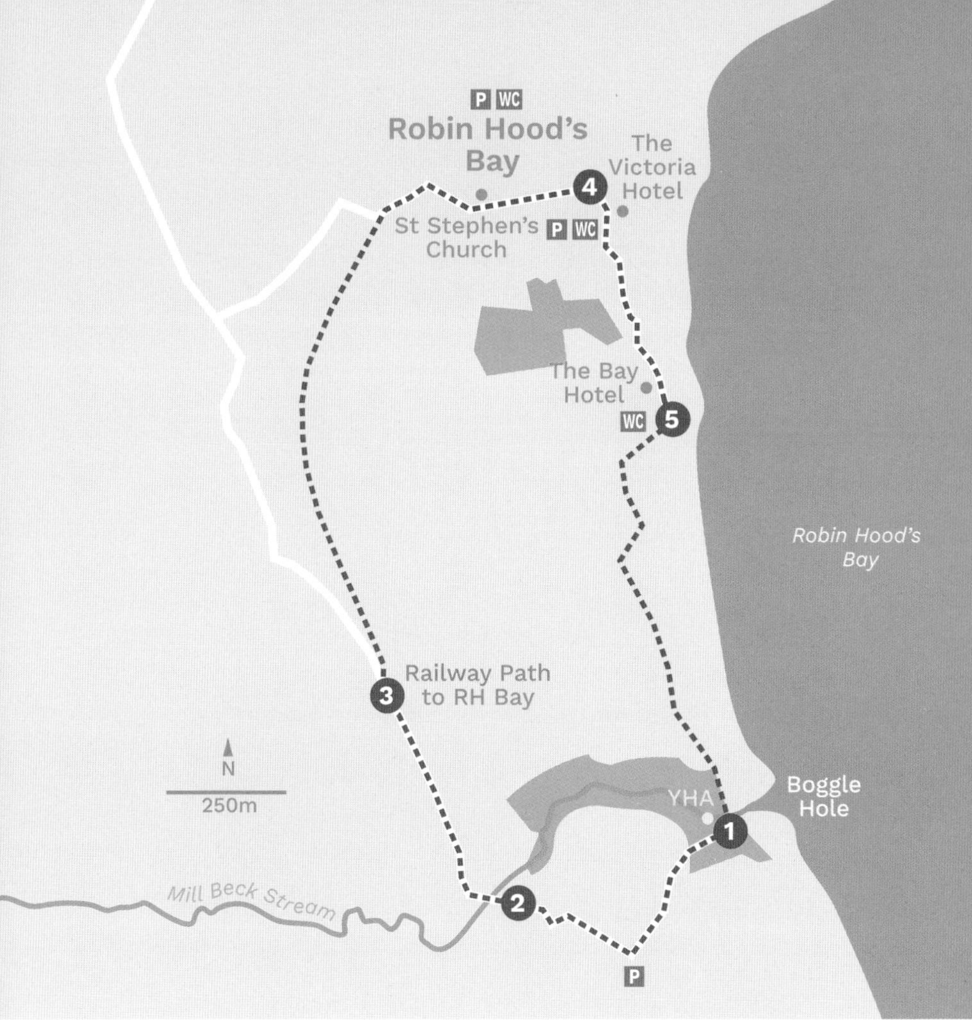

metal fence between you and the road. When the fence ends, continue down the main street to reach the Bay Hotel and slipway at the bottom of the village.

5 With your back to the slipway, go up the road ahead past the public toilets, then turn left along Albion Street, which lies between Dollies ice cream shop and the Smugglers Restaurant. At the last cottage on the left, Flagstaffe Cottage, go left up a flight of stone steps. You will come to some wooden steps with a handrail, turn right up these. At the top, continue along the coast path with the sea on your left. Just after a sharp right bend, turn left on a path with a 'Cleveland Way' sign pointing to Boggle Hole. Soon, you should pass a National Trust sign marking the entrance to Boggle Hole, and, just beyond, descend a steep flight of steps to return to your start point at the youth hostel.

Malham Cove, North Yorkshire

Time: **3 hrs 30 mins** | Distance: **11.3 km (7 miles)** | Difficulty: ✪✪✪✪

This incredible walk is packed with an extraordinary share of Britain's natural wonders, and is worth scheduling for early summer, when the limestone slopes are ablaze with wildflowers. Full of glorious and wildly contrasting vistas, the route covers the dramatic landscapes of Malham Cove, Gordale Scar, Janet's Foss waterfall and Malham Tarn (Britain's highest lake), and will bring you alongside gigantic white cliffs, rushing waterfalls and some outlandish rock formations as well.

Start location

Malham National Park Visitor Centre, Malham, North Yorkshire BD23 4DA (grid ref: SD900626).

Getting there

By car: Malham National Park Visitor Centre has a car park and an electric car charger point in the car park.

By public transport: Regular buses and Royal Mail post buses run during the week from Skipton, the nearest railhead. On weekends, you can also get there from Skipton and Ilkley on the Malham Tarn Shuttle bus. Timetables for these services are posted online.

Before you start

- Due to the environmental sensitivities of this iconic natural landmark, an alternative route may be suggested in accordance with conditions at the time of walking.
- There are well-made paths throughout, however some cross steep, rocky ground that can become slippery in wet weather.
- Summer is a great season to take this walk, but be aware that Malham village draws large crowds on bank holidays and weekends.
- The view from the top of Malham Cove stands as a grand finale to a circuit that's been a popular excursion since Victorian times, when its landforms inspired J. M. W. Turner, John Ruskin and Charles Kingsley. More visitors than ever are now coming to Malham to experience these great sights but, thanks to sensitive management by the National Trust, walking remains the only way to reach the most impressive view points, which has ensured these limestone treasures remain undiminished by the attention lavished on them.

Just over half a mile north of Malham lies Malham Cove, a huge curved cliff carved out of limestone by millions of years of water and ice movement.

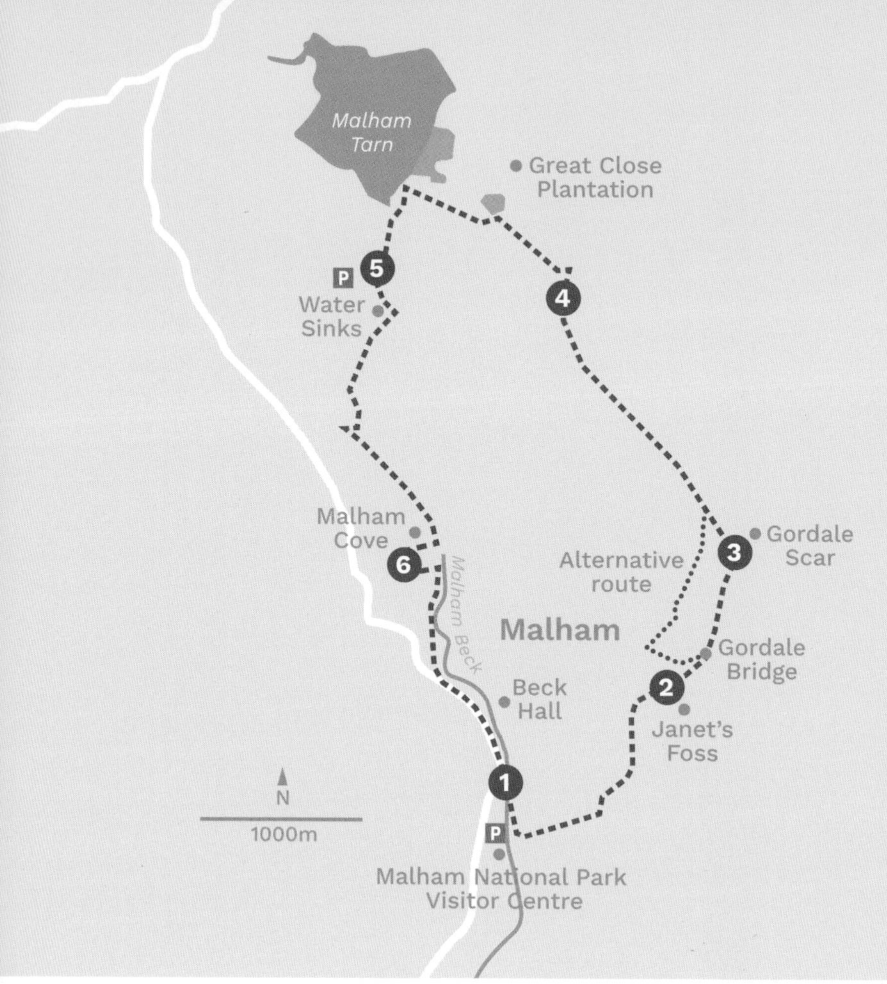

1 Turn left out of the National Park Visitor Centre onto the main road through the village, past the methodist chapel on your left. Opposite the River House hotel you'll see an old smithy, behind which a stone clapper bridge crosses to the far bank of Malham Beck. Once you have crossed over this, turn right and follow the Pennine Way downstream. After passing through two swing gates, you reach a kissing gate where you should turn left off the Pennine Way in the direction of Janet's Foss, as indicated. The path winds along the side of a wall and Gordale Beck for about 15 minutes, passing three handsome old stone barns and a concrete bridge to the right which you should ignore. Another gate leads into the National Trust-owned Janet's Foss woodland, past a succession of mossy crags and fallen tree trunks on its approach to the famous waterfalls and pool.

Janet's Foss plunges over an outcrop into a deep pool ringed by mossy boulders and trees. 'Foss' derives, like its namesake 'force', from the Norse word for 'waterfall'; 'Janet' is a fairy queen of local folklore, suggesting this magical glade has been popular with the area's inhabitants for many centuries. As you approach the falls through the wooded gorge below them, look out for fallen tree trunks into which people have

The impressive natural gorge at Gordale Scar is a fascinating 100m limestone ravine; it attracts thousands of visitors every year.

hammered lucky pennies as offerings to the fairies who inhabited these glades.

2 The path climbs left of the falls and on across a field to meet Gordale Lane. Turn right on to the tarmac and follow it for a few minutes, past Gordale Bridge until you reach a right bend. Go through a gate on the left and along a footpath, signposted to Gordale Scar, past the campsite. Continue along a well-made path running to the right of the stream to reach the ravine itself. Hidden until the last second by a bend in the surrounding cliffs, Gordale Scar comes as a complete revelation – a vertical trench bounded by 100m cliffs that seem almost to meet at their tops. Through this narrow defile the stream froths down two superb waterfalls, the higher of the pair cascading over a rock arch above the first.

3 While walkers can do a brief scramble at this point, the Yorkshire Dales National Park Authority now recommends this 'walk-round' suggestion because climbing the footpath up the waterfall may damage the soft

Notes of interest

★ The geological explanation for Gordale Scar is that the gorge was formed by the collapse of a massive underground cavern, but this fails to convey the gloomy magnificence of the scene, which has long fascinated visiting artists. The Romantic poet Thomas Gray (1716–71) claimed he could only bear to stay in the scar for a quarter of an hour at a time, and then, 'not without shuddering'. And after being invited here by the local landowner, Lord Ribblesdale, in 1811, James Ward declared the vista 'unpaintable', before proving himself wrong with a rendition as awe-inspiring as it was huge. His enormous canvas, measuring 3.7m x 4.3m, now hangs in Tate Britain.

tufa rock. The alternative route should be used to avoid further environmental damage, as well as for safety, especially when the falls are frozen or the river is in spate.

Alternative route: Once you've admired the falls, return back down the path to the tarmac road. Turn right and follow the road for 40m until you reach a gateway on your right at Gordale Bridge, signposted 'Malham Cove 1 mile'. Go through this gate and keep to the clear path ahead, which runs up the side of a drystone wall to a second gate. Turn sharp right (northeast) after the gate, making for a third gate visible on the far side of the field, just beyond a wall junction. From the other side of this gate, a clear path strikes steeply right up the hillside to the crags above. Running in parallel with the drystone wall lining the cliff edge, it then goes along the top of the ravine before making a slight descent to rejoin the main Gordale Scar path at a ladder stile over a wall.

Once atop the gorge, keep to the obvious path, which gradually drifts to the left of a dry valley in the direction of the Malham Tarn road. After crossing the ladder stile where the alternate route rejoins, continue along the wide path. The last stretch shadows a drystone wall, funnelling you into a corner where a stile carries you over to Street Gate.

4 Continue straight ahead from here along the broken-surfaced track, heading due north, with a wall to your right. Bending away left from this wall, the path eventually drops downhill to arrive at a gate next to Great Close Plantation. Ignore the trail leading ahead beyond the gate and instead turn left along the side of the wall bounding the trees. Ignore the small wood on the hillside to the left and when a second coppice appears ahead of you make for the left of it. Skirt the south edge of this second clump of trees until you arrive at a gravel track, where you should turn right and then left almost immediately onto the Pennine Way, as indicated by a fingerpost sign. From here you can either keep to the Pennine Way, which glances the southern tip of nearby Malham Tarn, or follow a broader track southwest to crest a rise; this will give you the best views of the lake and house.

Originally formed by glacial meltwater, the lake Malham Tarn – the highest in Britain – presents a serene spectacle against its backdrop of moorland ridges. The eastern shore is dominated

by the stately façade of Malham House, an elegant aristocratic bolthole that formerly belonged to Lord Ribblesdale (see Notes of Interest on page 89). The mansion nowadays serves as a field centre run by the National Trust.

5 Both trails eventually converge on a small car park. Turn right on to the road, cross the stream and pick up the Pennine Way, which turns left through the gate just beyond stream. After approximately 100m, turn left again as indicated by a fingerpost sign to pass the famous Water Sinks. The next leg down Watlowes follows an obvious path but is rocky, muddy and hard going in wet weather. After 5 minutes or so you reach a small clearing; stay with the clear path going left, which then circles right to a stile on the left. Cross the stile and descend a steep, rocky path. This eventually takes you to the lower level of the valley, where it splits below some dramatic crags. Once on level ground the rest of the route to the head of Malham Cove is relatively plain sailing.

6 Turn right along the Pennine Way when you reach the rim of the cove – our featured view point – picking your way across the limestone pavement, or over the crags to its right. At the point where the rocks peter out, the path plunges left through a gate in a drystone wall to start its stepped descent back to Malham. After passing through a gate at the bottom of the steps it is worth making a short detour on a path to the left to admire the cliffs from below. The remaining stretch into the village runs above the stream via a good path, scaling a rise to rejoin a lane on the northern fringes of Malham. Turn left onto this tarmac lane and follow it for 5 minutes past the entrance to Beck Hall into the centre of the village. The National Park Visitor Centre lies a few minutes' walk further down the same road, past the Buck Inn and methodist chapel on your right.

Malham Tarn is one of only eight upland alkaline lakes in Europe. At 377m above sea level, it is also the highest lake in England.

Notes of interest

★ Arguably the most majestic sight on this route extends from the rim of Malham Cove itself, a spectacular amphitheatre of escarpments from whose foot a dark river mysteriously emerges. Back in the last Ice Age, this same river used to plunge over the top of the precipice, but when the ground thawed the water began to flow underground, leaving in its wake an elaborately ribbed 'pavement' of blue-grey limestone that today forms a surreal foreground to the panorama of lush hills and dales enfolding from below it.

★ The defining feature of the landscape lining the south and west perimeters of the Yorkshire Dales National Park is the Craven Fault – a geological fault line dividing the park's limestone uplands from the gentler pastures below. Formed 330 million years ago, when the area lay beneath a tropical ocean sprinkled with coral islets, its bedrock of carboniferous limestone was lifted by earth movements and gradually eroded by millennia of rainfall and glacial action. Limestone is unique among the hard rocks of Britain for being soluble, and the stepped plateau to the north of Malham is also honeycombed by invisible channels that allow water to drain rapidly away. Walk on a wet day up Gordale Beck, the stream followed by the early stages of our route, and you'll gain a vivid sense of the volume of water pouring from the high ground.

nature in summer

Summer in Britain bridges the beautiful months of June, July and August, with the summer solstice in late June, the longest day of the year, when the sun reaches its highest point in the sky. These long, often sultry, days of summer are the perfect time to ramble, when nature is in full bloom.

All through the summer rainfall can be variable – this is Britain, after all! Scotland and northern England tend to see the coolest temperatures during summer, and the southeast and London the highest with warm days generally hovering around the mid-20s (about 77°F). The hottest temperature so far recorded in the UK was 40.3°C (104.5°F). Long periods of warm, bright weather are not uncommon, but the warmth and moisture in the summer air also create perfect conditions for thunderstorms. As ever, higher altitudes or coastal locations may experience stronger winds and cooler temperatures, and conditions can change quickly so walkers should always be prepared.

If you are looking for inspiration and adventure, summer is a wonderful time to see the gentler side of the long, sandy beaches of South Wales, and to explore the coastlines of Devon and Cornwall.

Plan a walk to include the stunning Bempton Cliffs on the North Yorkshire coast, where half a million seabirds, including gannets and guillemots, gather for their breeding seasons over the summer months. Colonies of puffins also spend the summer here, leaving around mid-August – they make a truly memorable sight. You may also spot puffins on Skomer Island in Wales, on Northumberland's Farne Islands and Coquet Island, and on the Shetland and Orkney Islands.

Further inland there is plenty more birdlife to see; birds of prey, such as the common buzzard, can be spied hovering watchfully during their hunt for small mammals and rodents. Red-faced goldfinches feast on the seeds of thistles and teasels in parks, woodland and farmland. Birds provide the soundtrack to the summer and, if you tune in your ears, they may be even more help than your eyes in identifying birdlife during your walks. Blackbirds, woodpeckers, blackcaps and starlings, as well as summer visitors such as swifts and barn swallows can be spotted all over the country.

Naturally, summer is buzzing with a surge of insects as they have emerged from their resting phase as winged adults. Dragonflies and butterflies will be out in force on balmy, clear days – common darter dragonflies shimmer and flit around in wetlands, near rivers and ponds. Crickets may be heard chirping on warm summer evenings – the frequency of chirping rising with the temperature.
Summer is also a good time to see marine life, particularly from the coastal path walks around the northeast. Bottlenose dolphins and porpoise can often be spotted in the waves, and it's sometimes possible to see grey seals a whole lot closer than that if you are lucky! Don't forget to pack binoculars to make the most of any spotting opportunities.

Many British plants are in their element during midsummer, and the countryside provides walkers with a visual feast of every different shade of green one can imagine. Plenty of plants are in bloom, including the fragrant and frothy meadowsweet, a native plant which you will find along riverbanks or in fresh, damp meadows. You can recognise it by its sweet, strong scent, and the delicate creamy white of its small, clustered flowers. Chaucer refers to it as 'meadwort', and it is sometimes known as 'Queen of the Meadow'.

Edible plants, flowers, herbs and fruits all flourish in the lazy warmth. While walking during the summer, it pays to pack a container of some sort; if you have any interest in foraging wild foods, you can take your pick. Plump, juicy blackberries can be eaten now or frozen for later use. Honeysuckle flowers make a fragrant tea or a delicious cordial or may be infused into refreshing summer drinks. Ground elder, with luxuriant leaves particularly tender in June, grows low in shaded places and can be used cooked or raw, like parsley or spinach. Synonymous with the British summertime, elderflowers explode in sweetly scented clouds of blossom early in the season; gather the flower heads to make into cordial or champagne, but be sure to leave enough that the elderberries will still appear in early autumn.

One of the most evocative summer scents of Sussex – blackberry bushes loaded with ripening fruit, fragrant in the warm afternoon sunshine.

walk 16

Stow-on-the-Wold, Cotswolds

Time: 3 hrs 30 mins | Distance: 12.7 km (7.9 miles) | Difficulty: ✪✪✪

A beautiful circular walk over the high Cotswold Hills to two beautiful, contrasting villages. This route includes a mixture of quiet road walking, unsurfaced lanes and field paths, with one fairly long ascent on a track after about a mile.

Start location

The Stag at Stow, Cheltenham, Gloucestershire GL54 1AF (grid ref: SP191257).

Getting there

By car: Stow is at the Junction of the A429 Fosse Way, the A436 and the A424. Parking in the Market Square is restricted to two hours before 6pm. There is a pay and display car park by the Bell hotel close to the start of the walk, which can be found off the A436 leading east out of the town. If you prefer to park for free, at the expense of a few hundred metres' extra walking, go to Tesco, just north on the A429. At the far right side, separated from Tesco's car park by a wall, is the town car park, which is a free long-stay car park. From there, turn left along the Fosse Way, left at the fork and past the stocks to The Stag at Stow on the left.

By public transport: The 801 bus service runs hourly between Cheltenham and Moreton-In-Marsh, and stops in Stow Market Square.

1 From the front of The Stag at Stow turn left along the street, pass the Market Cross in Market Square on the right and fork left at the bank. Turn left down the main road and cross over to the far side as soon as you can. Fork right at a postbox and walk ahead down the minor road. Pass the Bell hotel on your left and continue ahead for a kilometre (half a mile), on a clear tarmac footpath on the right side of the road, to reach Maugersbury.

The large market square of Stow-on-the-Wold. It's size, as well as the narrow, winding alleys leading off, is a reminder of the square's history as a major sheep market.

2 Go straight on over a staggered crossroads past The Lower House on your left and continue down a small lane. Follow the lane as it swings right, then after 20m go left, steeply down a dead-end road. At the bottom, pass through the brick abutments of the old railway bridge (this was once the Great Western branch line between Banbury and Cheltenham) and start going uphill. Head to the right of some concrete barns and continue uphill, ignoring a track going right from the barns. The climb eventually eases and great views open up back to Stow and over the Evenlode Valley to the left. Go straight on when you reach a road, then left downhill at a T-junction. Turn right at a triangular T-junction with a house in the centre. Go through the village of Icomb to a T-junction at the war memorial.

The beautiful church at Icomb you pass on your left is worth visiting. It contains the interesting tomb of Sir John Blaket, who died in 1431 after fighting with Henry V at the Battle of Agincourt.

3 Turn right, and when the road swings right go left, then immediately right onto a footpath. Go through a gate 50m ahead and turn right along the fence up to a rusty kissing gate. Follow the next hedge on the left uphill until it ends, then go slightly left up towards

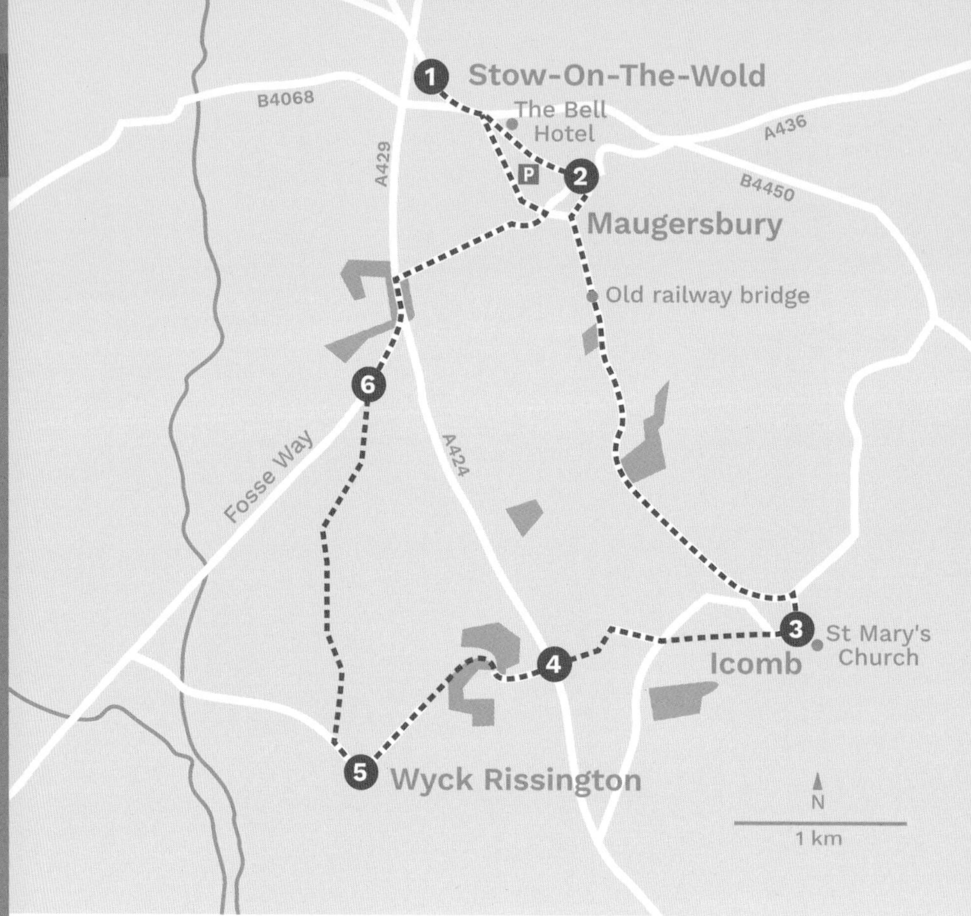

trees at the top of the field. Pass through a gap in the top corner and continue slightly left across the next field to a footpath sign on a prominent high post. Cross straight over the road then up the drive to the curiously named Icomb Proper farmhouse. Just before the house, follow the waymarks right along a short road that soon loops back onto the drive you have been walking up, just beyond the house. Go ahead on a short track that goes through trees and into a field. (If you have an OS map, it may show the path angling through the trees, but the path has now been diverted around the edge.) Turn left along the field edge to the corner, then turn right and make your way downhill, with the hedge on your left, to a main road.

4 Now cross straight over to a bridleway that goes down through the trees and soon reaches a tarmac drive. Turn left, heading downhill. Keep right at a fork, then at the gate marking the entrance to Orchard House you should fork right down an enclosed path. Go through a rusty gate and swing left, keeping close to the trees on the left as views open up to the right. When a house at the bottom of the field comes into view, aim for the metal gate just to the right of it. Go through and ahead along the drive to the road at Wyck Rissington. If you decide to explore the village, return to where you joined the road afterwards.

5 Turn right and follow the road to a gate and path on the right, 10m beyond a zig-zag sign. Head across a field to double gates. Follow the right edge of a long field to a gate at the far end. Head up to just right of a cottage at the top of the next field and find a gate in the field corner by an old barn. Go right on the lane for 10m then left over a stile. Turn right along the edge of the field to pass through a wooden kissing gate, then left down to another gate in the left hedge 25m on from the near corner. Go slightly right across a narrow field to a gate on the opposite side. Do not go through this gate, but turn right and follow the hedge on the left to a stile just before the far corner. Go through, over the old railway, to a gate. Turn right to a kissing gate in the next corner, then go diagonally left across the next field to a gate in the far corner that leads onto the busy Fosse Way. The kissing gate may be in disrepair, so take care when passing through.

6 Cross straight over and turn right, uphill, along the grassy verge. 20m beyond the traffic lights, cross back over at an island with bollards in the middle of the road. Turn left uphill on a clear tarmac path. Just after you pass two redundant signpost poles, turn right on a lane that is blocked to motor traffic (with a locked gate). Continue ahead as the lane soon becomes a normal tarmac lane, which contours the side of a valley and has lovely views down to the right. Follow this lane all the way to Maugersbury. At a crossroads approximately 200m from the village sign, turn left uphill between gateposts, and carry on past some wonderful buildings. When the tarmac ends, carry straight on along an unsurfaced track that ends back at the Bell at Stow. Retrace your steps back uphill to the left, then right at the small green back to the Market Square where you will see your start point again – The Stag at Stow.

Notes of interest

★ Icomb is a Cotswold gem you will only find if you leave the beaten track. Strangely, the village used to belong to Worcestershire, despite being well into Gloucestershire. Such areas, which are called exclaves, were all abolished by an Act of Parliament in 1844. Before then, in the days when early police forces only had power in their own counties, exclaves were often hotbeds of crime, as criminals only had to get into them to escape, and the host county could rarely be bothered with policing such small, remote areas. In Icomb, a notorious band of three brothers from the Dunsden family made their name as highwaymen. Their names are still known today: they were the original Tom, Dick and Harry.

★ Wyck Rissington is another beautiful Cotswold village, and worth a diversion if you have time. In contrast to Icomb, where many houses were built crammed together, the cottages here are all well spaced out along a wide village green. There is a ramp down into the pond, built in the days of carts with wooden wheels. Drivers often soaked the wheels so the wood expanded and gripped the iron rim better. The church contains a remarkable mosaic maze on the north wall. It was created by the local rector in 1950 after he saw it in a dream. A life-size version of it existed in the vicarage for a few years. A board next to it explains all the symbolism. The English composer Gustav Holst, who is most famous for his Planets suite, was the choirmaster and organist at this church for a while.

walk 17

Margate to Broadstairs, Kent

Time: 3 hrs 20 mins | Distance: 10.8 km (6.7 miles) | Difficulty: ✪

A beautiful, relaxing walk along the white cliffs of Kent, with far-reaching views especially on fine summer days, plenty of places of interest and opportunities for beach stops on the way. There are steps and gradients in a few places, but the route is largely flat and paved.

Start location

Margate Station, Kent CT9 5AD (grid ref: TR348705).

Getting there

By car: Parking is available in Margate.
By public transport: Both stations are served by Southeastern trains from London Victoria or by the high-speed service from London St Pancras. Coach services are available from London Victoria.

Before you start

- This route is mainly paved and flat if you choose the right alternatives, but you cannot avoid gradients so it cannot claim to be wheelchair friendly. The most favourable section is that running between Margate and Kingsgate.
- There are plenty of opportunities to stop for refreshment along the way.

The beautiful wide sweep of Stone Bay. The promenade leads on to Broadstairs, and the main beach at Viking Bay.

1 Leave Margate Station and go down the approach road, bearing right through the standing stones then crossing All Saints' Avenue to reach the seafront. Continue past Dreamland (see Notes of Interest, right) then cross at the pedestrian lights and continue on the promenade towards the clock tower. Carry on past the clock to reach the stone pier known as the Harbour Arm with its lighthouse, the Tourist Information Centre and the Turner Contemporary gallery in its stark, grey shed (see Notes of Interest, right). As you come to the seafront, on your left is a statue of a lifeboatman, commemorating the wreck of the Margate surfboat *Friend to all Nations* in 1897, when nine of the 13 crew were lost.

2 Continue to the left of the Turner building then along the promenade. You pass the big white building which is the Margate Winter Gardens theatre (see Notes of Interest, right). Shortly afterwards, bear right up the ramp which is signed 'Viking Coastal Trail'. Go through the gateway at the top, then turn left down the steps to reach the Lido (see Notes of

Turner Contemporary Modern Art Gallery designed by architect David Chipperfield. Its name was inspired by the town's association with the English painter J. M. W. Turner.

Notes of interest

★ Dreamland started as 'The Hall by the Sea', an unwanted railway station converted into an entertainment centre and developed by 'Lord' George Sanger in 1874. The station was replaced in 1894 and in 1919 the conversion into the American-style 'Dreamland' began, including the installation of the wooden rollercoaster. The existing building opened as a cinema in 1933. This site became derelict as recently as 2005, but in 2015 its restoration as a 'heritage theme park' began.

★ The Turner Contemporary art gallery opened in 2011 after a gestation period of nearly 20 years. The gallery is on the site of Mrs Booth's guesthouse, where the artist J. M. W. Turner stayed during his trips to Margate.

★ The Winter Gardens theatre was opened in 1911 by Margate council to provide a superior form of entertainment, a mission which it continues to this day. The building received troops returning from Dunkirk, and was later bombed.

★ Completed in the 1920s, the Lido was built to cater for an increase in sea bathers as the pastime became ever-more popular. The Lido was built on the existing Clifton Baths Estate, beneath which ran many passageways that had been used by smugglers in previous centuries. The underground complex consisted of bars, cafés and a warm sea-water pool with nearby changing facilities. The Lido was hugely popular from its construction right through to the 1960s.

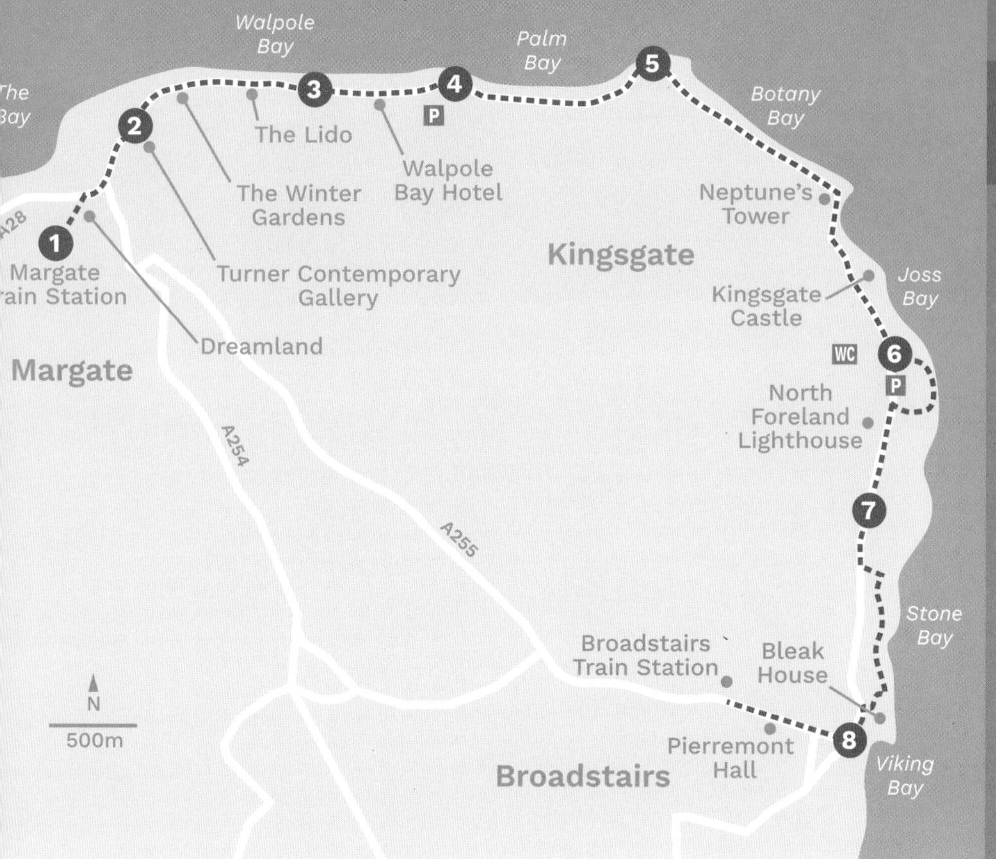

Interest on page 100) and ahead through the car park. Keep left onto the cycleway. You pass a derelict site that was once a crazy golf course and then continue on past the Viking Ship Play Park to reach the footbridge over Newgate Gap. If you prefer to avoid the ramp up to the Lido, you can keep on along the promenade as far as the Jet Ski Café and pick up these directions again at Waypoint 4 (skipping Waypoint 3 instructions).

3 This is Cliftonville, and you are on Queen's Promenade. Continue past the Oval Gardens, noting the elegant apartments built to match the existing buildings. In direct visual contrast, you will next pass the Thanet Indoor Bowls Centre which is in a tin shed. Just beyond, on the right, you will come to the stunning Walpole Bay Hotel, which is well worth a visit. Return to the cycleway and go right, keeping on across the bridge at Hodges Gap and past the Coastguard Station. You will reach the cannon standing looking over the sea. From here, either go down the steps to the Jet Ski Café, or simply keep on along the cycleway to the pumping station if you prefer to avoid the steps and pick up these directions again at Waypoint 5 (skipping Waypoint 4 instructions).

4 At the Jet Ski Café, keep on down to the right and onto the beach. Walk along to reach the low-level promenade at the Sacketts Gap Bridge. Continue walking past Friends Gap (by the boat club building) and around the headland to arrive at a fence ahead of you and the pathway up to reach the wastewater pumping station (which looks more pleasant

Notes of interest

★ The various 'Gaps' along the coast mark points where tracks have been driven down through the chalk cliffs to give access to the beach for various purposes, including smuggling.

★ Neptune's Tower was a folly built in flint and chalk around 1760 by Henry Fox, Lord Holland, in the style of Henry VIII's castles at Walmer and Deal. Apparently it used to contain a gothic tower, which lasted until 1970. The Captain Digby pub was originally also a folly, a chapel-like form nothing like its existing state.

★ Kingsgate Castle was built by Lord Holland, to serve as stables and staff accommodation, while he lived in the adjacent Holland House. Kingsgate was originally a gateway on the seashore designed to guard access to the houses. The name relates to a landing of Charles II on 30 June 1683, though other English monarchs have also used this cove, including George II in 1748.

★ North Foreland Lighthouse sits on the site of a light first exhibited at North Foreland in 1499, but the first real lighthouse was built here by Sir John Meldrum in 1636. The tower was destroyed by fire in 1683 and the present structure built in 1691. Originally the tower was 12m tall and constructed of brick, stone and flint. North Foreland was the last Trinity Lighthouse to be converted to automatic operation, in 1998.

than perhaps its name implies). At the top, turn left in front of the pumping station.

5 From here, keep on along the cycleway to reach the sandy Botany Bay. Stay on the cycleway past the modern Botany Bay pub to reach Neptune's Tower, a folly built by the owner of Kingsgate Castle which you can see ahead (see Notes of Interest, left). Follow the cycleway past the golf links to the children's playground (which is owned by the pub) and continue on to reach the road. Turn left to walk along the road, continuing past the flint-clad Captain Digby pub, the imposing Holland House, and then past the gate of Kingsgate Castle. Just after the stretch with no pavement, cut right through the hedge onto a wide pathway parallel to the road which brings you to Joss Bay, another attractive beach. After the pumping station, be careful if approaching the cliff edge as there is a sheer drop. Take care also passing Kingsgate Castle – the road is narrow and there are no pavements.

6 Cross the road to the car park. Ahead of you, improbably perched on the summit of a hill of brassicas, is the North Foreland Lighthouse, which you can visit later (see Notes of Interest, left). Bear left through the car park then follow the cliff edge along a sometimes muddy path to reach the corner of Crescent Road and Cliff Promenade. Turn right up the hill to the main road junction then turn left to reach the lighthouse. Keep on down North Foreland Road, passing the convent building which is almost hidden on the right, and then passing high flint walls. If you prefer to simplify the route, you can just go up the road from Joss Bay to the lighthouse.

7 Cross North Foreland Avenue then pass Lanthorne Road on your right. At the bottom of the dip in the road, you will reach a safety barrier (opposite Bishop's Avenue). Turn left here along the path leading down the steps to Stone Bay. Now follow the promenade along the base of the cliff, which is covered with cabbage plants and yellow-flowering Santolina in summertime, passing the café and beach huts. You will arrive at Viking Bay and Broadstairs Harbour. On top of the cliff is Bleak House (previously named Fort House) – this is where Charles Dickens stayed when he holidayed at Broadstairs in the 1850s and 1860s, and where he wrote David Copperfield.

8 Turn right up Harbour Street, go under the arch, then head left along Albion Street. After 170m take the second right into the High Street. 200m up on the left is Pierremont Park. At the far end of the park (the junction with Pierremont Avenue) you can either catch the 'Loop' bus back to Margate, or carry on for another 150m to reach Broadstairs Train Station, and return to your start point.

Kingsgate Castle on the cliffs above Kingsgate Bay, Broadstairs. Built in the 1760s, its name refers to a landing here by Charles II in 1683.

walk
18

Ditchling Beacon, South Downs

Time: **4 hrs** | Distance: **16.5 km (10.2 miles)** | Difficulty:

Exploring the South Downs is always enormously enjoyable, whatever the weather, but summertime is surely the most rewarding season of all for a walk here as the wildlife is at its busiest. Summer flowers bloom all across the downland, while ground-nesting skylarks pop up all over the place, singing as they fly, and butterflies bustle about. The rarely sighted silver-spotted skipper may be seen here too, as well as the green hairstreak and marbled white butterflies. This route leads across the Downs by way of Ditchling Beacon and Wolstonbury Hill, with glorious far-reaching views in every direction.

Start location

Hassocks Station, West Sussex BN6 8JD (grid ref: TQ303155).

Getting there

By car: There is a car park at Hassocks Station, just off the A273.

By public transport: Trains arrive at Hassocks from Brighton, Littlehampton, Bedford and London Victoria. Buses also stop at Keymer Road next to Hassocks Station. These include the 33 between Haywards Heath and Burgess Hill and two local services: the 331 and the 168. Check bus times online for further information.

Ditchling Beacon, in the South Downs National Park. This large chalk hill has a particularly steep northern face and, at 248m, is the highest point in East Sussex.

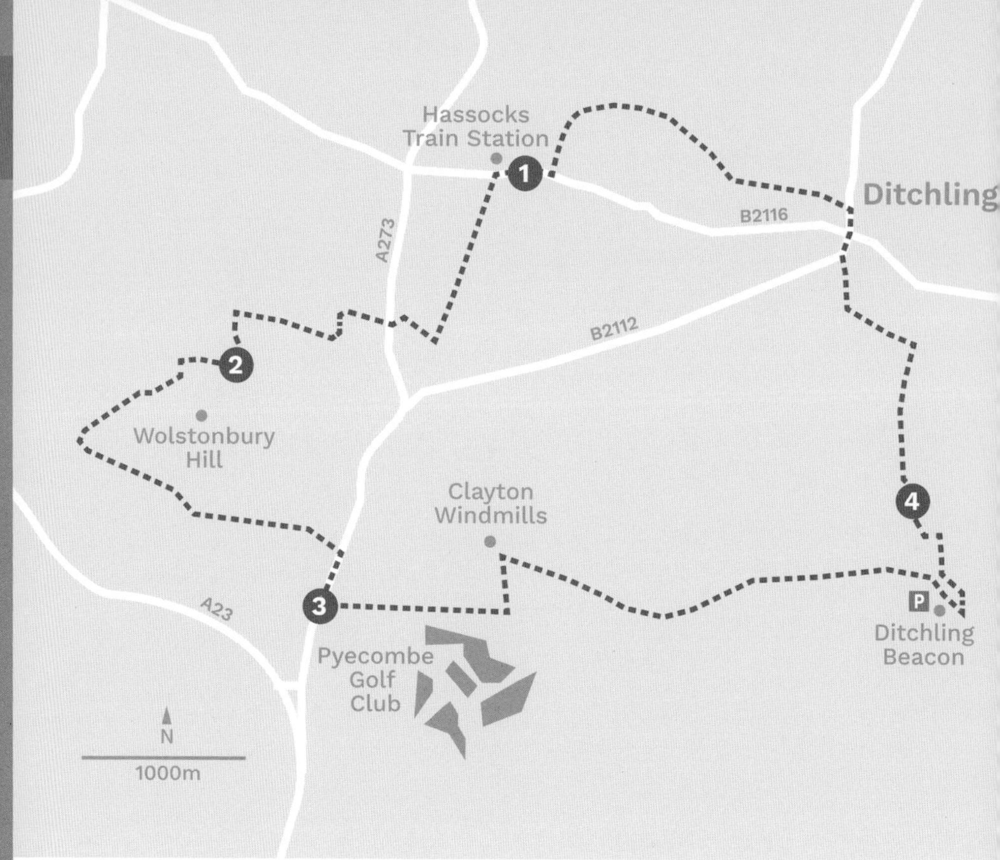

1 From the station car park at Hassocks, head down some steps towards Keymer Road. There is a public footpath on the right-hand side of Keymer Road that runs alongside the train line – head up the footpath here for approximately 850m. When you reach a bridge over the train line, cross the bridge and keep to the path past Clayton Wood natural burial ground, then out onto Brighton Road. Cross over Brighton Road to the public footpath and keep to the path until you reach a stile on your left. Climb over the stile, then follow the footpath through the woods. You will see another stile on your right that leads into some fields – cross over this as well. Now follow the path through the fields until you reach New Way Lane. Turn left onto the lane and keep walking until you reach the lane's end.

2 Here you will find a public footpath on the right – follow this path to the end where you will see a T-junction. Turn left onto the path that leads you into the woods, keeping right. There will be a stile on this woodland path – cross over. Follow the path around Wolstonbury Hill (this will be your first peek at some great views!). This is a very long path, so stick to it and enjoy the climb and the views, perhaps stopping somewhere along the way for a rest or a picnic. When you start heading down again, you'll come to a crossroads; turn left to continue your descent. Once you reach the bottom, either turn right onto Clayton Hill or take a little footpath just before you reach the road on the right.

The marbled white is an unmistakeable butterfly found in flowery grassland and often spotted on Ditchling Beacon. Here feasting on *Linaria vulgaris*, the common toadflax (also known as yellow toadflax or butter-and-eggs).

Notes of interest

★ Wolstonbury Hill is a 58.9-hectare biological Site of Special Scientific Interest in West Sussex. It is owned by the National Trust and part of it is a Scheduled Monument. More information about this, and about Ditchling Beacon, is available on the National Trust website (nationaltrust.org.uk).

3 Along Clayton Hill is the entrance to Pyecombe Golf Club. Go through the entrance and the car park, and make your way along the wonderful footpath through the golf course. Once you've enjoyed Pyecombe Golf Club, and especially the views, turn left onto Mill Lane and head through the farm. Here you can either take a short detour around the Jack and Jill Windmills at Clayton by turning left (retrace your steps once you've visited the windmills) or head straight for Ditchling Beacon by turning right. It's about 3km (1¾ miles) from here to Ditchling Beacon so take your time and soak up your surroundings. Once you reach Ditchling Beacon car park, turn left onto Ditchling Road and take the path that runs down the right side of the road.

4 Keep to the path and you will reach Underhill Lane. From here turn left onto the lane and then immediately right onto Nye Lane. Follow Nye Lane, keeping left at the fork in the woods to head towards Beacon Road. Turn right onto Beacon Road and on into Ditchling. Once through the High Street, keep an eye out for a little lane on the left side of the road called Boddingtons Lane. Turn up here. Along this lane, you will see some small steps on your left; head over these steps and follow the footpath for approximately 1.05km (0.65 miles). From this path you will have panoramic views of the walk you have very nearly completed (from right to left), and you will see how impressively far you have walked from the bottom. This path comes out onto Ockley Lane where you should cross over onto Grand Avenue. Then follow this road all the way back to Hassocks. Once in Hassocks town centre, turn right onto Keymer Road and follow the road along until you see the steps that lead you back to your start point in the Hassocks Station car park.

walk 19

The Tarka Trail, Devon

Time: 2 hrs | Distance: 4.7 km (2.9 miles) | Difficulty: ✪

The full length of Devon's Tarka Trail is 290km (180 miles), a long walking and cycling route winding in a figure of eight around Barnstaple and named for Henry Williamson's 1927 book *Tarka the Otter*. This walk is much shorter, covering a relatively small area around the River Taw close to and including parts of the Tarka Trail. Including stunning sea cliffs, interesting and varied countryside, wonderful wildlife and, of course, the beach, this walk makes the most perfect summer ramble.

Start location

The car park at Fremington Quay, Devon EX31 2NH (grid ref: SS516334).

Getting there

By car: Park at the car park.

By public transport: The 21 bus runs past the turning for Fremington Quay on the B3233 between Barnstaple and Bideford. Check online for more information.

1 Begin your walk at the car park 100m to the east of the Fremington Quay Café. Follow the path through the hedge and walk down the concrete former slipway onto the shingle beach. The currents in the Taw here can be mesmerizing, with several meandering rivulets bumping into one another. Continue onwards for 500m, with the sea on your left, until you reach the public bridleway on the right (signposted as 'No.25'). Walk slightly uphill and follow the path as it turns right inland.

Fremington Quay, where this walk begins, offers panoramic views of the River Taw. Fremington was once an important historic port, bustling and busy at the heart of the clay export trade.

2 This path may be very muddy following wet weather, but you will enjoy long views up the River Taw at Barnstaple. After 500m, in front of a bridge, descend the steps on the right to the paved track and turn left. This is the Tarka Trail, which at this point is shared by both cyclists and walkers.

3 Follow the Trail eastwards. You should now have lovely views of the flood plain and salt marshes, and the hedgerows brim with seasonal flowers, from primroses to bluebells and perennial ferns. On either side the Trail is bracketed by tiny streams smothered in bright green mosses.

Before you start

- Even if you are walking in the summer, parts of this walk may be muddy following wet weather. Remember to wear appropriate footwear, and watch your step.

- The route terrain includes beach, footpaths, farm tracks, some stiles and quiet roads. The brief stretch of beach walking is passable at all but the highest of spring tides.

This estuary boasts the third largest concentration of waders in Devon. You are likely to spot a European golden plover (left) and perhaps even the heron-like glossy ibis (below).

4 After 500m you will see a footpath sign off to the right – just by a culvert – here you should drop down a few steps. Then head directly inland along a farm track. Follow this track as it rises slightly uphill through two gates to meet a T-junction of paths. Turn right in front of the houses; ahead you will see magnificent views of the estuary and a surprisingly rugged and hilly hinterland on its northern side. Spare a thought here for Tarka the otter, who in the novel spends much of his time hiking up and down this landscape dodging rival dog otters and vicious hunting dogs.

5 The path now bends to the left, to reach a small road. Turn right here and walk for a few metres past Penhill Cottage. Then immediately turn left along the grassy footpath (signposted 'No.28'). Go through a gate and keep ahead along the field edge. Majestic cattle egrets often perch in trees here, keeping an eye out for prey.

6 The path now drops down to a stile and a paved road. Turn right here, and follow the road alongside Fremington Pill. In sunshine, the glistening mud can be dazzling. Look out for spoonbills – with their distinctive flattened

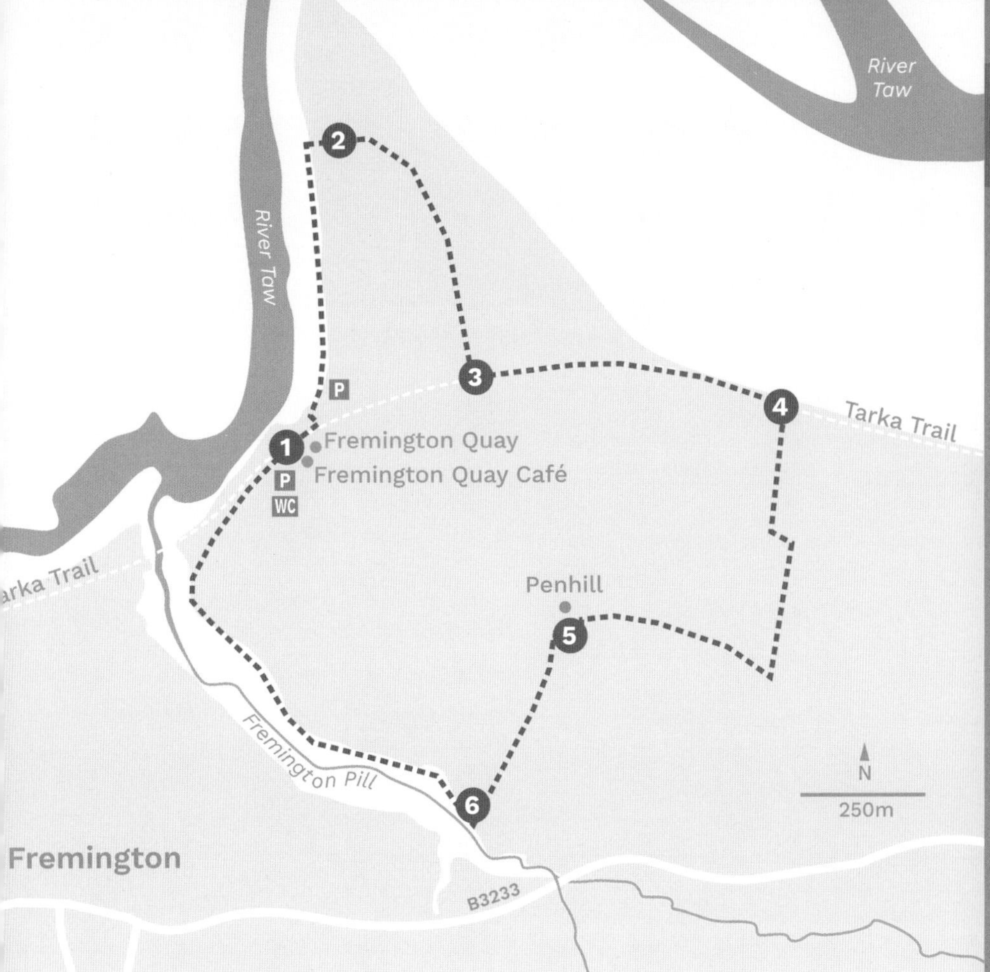

beaks, the birds seem exotic for Devon but they are a rare year-round visitor. Among plenty of other birdlife, it is also possible to spot glossy ibis here, as well as little egrets, spotted redshanks and shelducks. The road now quickly returns to the car park. It's worth popping into the café, not just for food but for the small historical display it houses on Fremington's industrial heritage. Climb the steps to the lookout for outstanding views right along the coast.

Notes of interest

★ The story of *Tarka the Otter* follows the fortunes of the eponymous otter growing up in North Devon. Published in 1927 and hailed as a children's classic, at the time this book was a landmark development in realistic writing about nature.

walk
20

Rhossili, Gower Peninsula

Time: **2 hrs** | Distance: **6.9 km (4.3 miles)** | Difficulty: ✪✪

Exploring a stunning coastal route, this walk displays some truly breathtaking views and strings together both of Rhossili's golden view points – the jewels in the Gower's crown. Your ramble will include sand and surf, a swim if you fancy it, a hill climb and the crest of Rhossili Down, just inland, which is studded with prehistoric cairns and burial chambers. Don't forget your camera – Rhossili was recently ranked 11th in a list of the most beautiful coastal locations in the world.

Before you start

- The terrain is mostly gentle seaside paths, with a short, sharp ascent and descent over stretches of bracken-covered moorland.

- If you are enjoying this fantastic walk during the summer months (or if you enjoy cold-water swimming year round) be sure to bring swimming gear: the beach is one of Europe's surfing hot spots. Adrenalin junkies might also be tempted to sign up for an accompanied parascending flight from the Down, which is a beloved destination for British flyers. Birdwatchers might prefer to visit in midwinter, when migratory purple sandpipers and other rarities – such as great northern and red-throated divers – flock to the beach.

Stunning Rhossili Bay beach is consistently ranked as one of the best: great for walking and picnics, a fantastic surf site, and brilliant for dogs.

Start location

The car park opposite Worm's Head Hotel, Rhossili, Gower Peninsula SA3 1PP (grid ref: SS415881).

Getting there

By car: This walk is most easily accessed by car using the car park opposite the hotel.
By public transport: There is a regular bus service from Swansea to Rhossili seven days a week. Check times online.

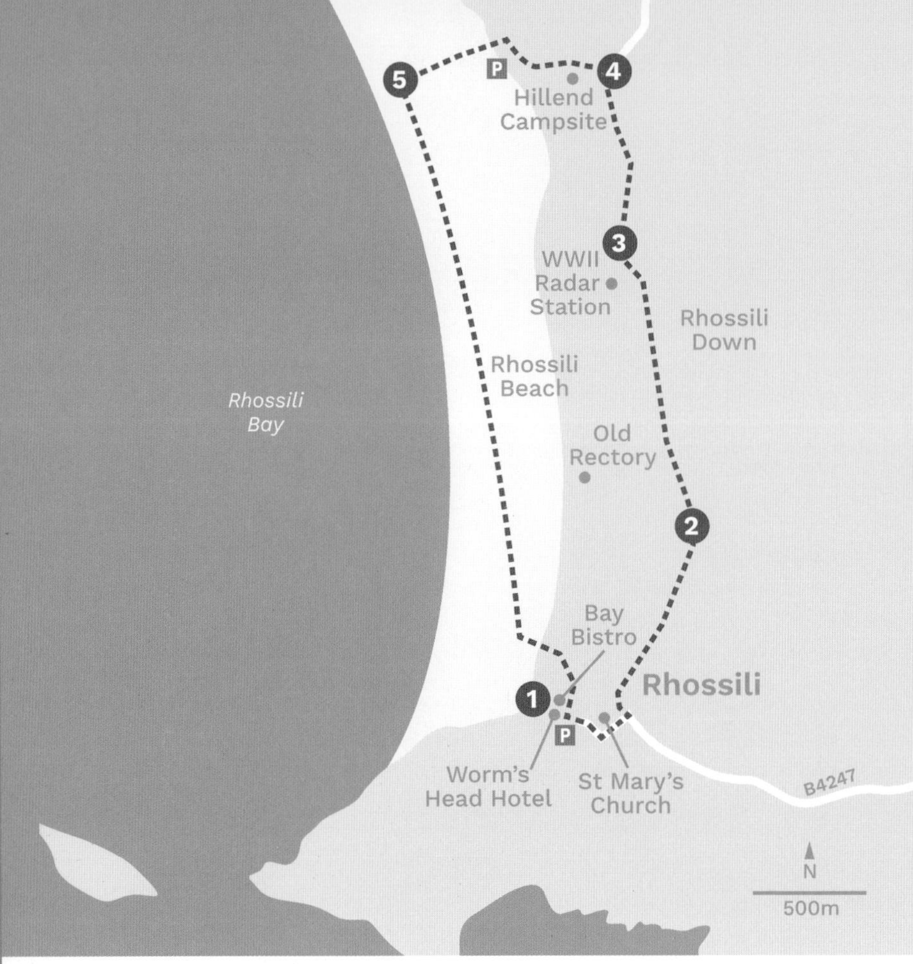

1 From your start point in the car park opposite the Worm's Head Hotel, walk back up the lane through Rhossili village, passing the church on your left, until you reach the sharp bend in the road. A lane peels away left and heads straight on before the curve; follow it to the end, where a gate leads on to National Trust access land. Bearing right, the path up the south flank of Rhossili Down is steep, but easy to follow, flattening off only as it approaches the trig point (193m).

The church of St Mary's stands at the start of the path up the steep, south side of Rhossili Down, which at 193m is the loftiest of the Old Red Sandstone ridges slicing through the Gower Peninsula. A glorious view over the beach and surrounding coastline extends from its spine, along which the area's Iron Age settlers buried their dead chiefs in a row of 14 chambers and cairns. The name of one group, Swayne's Howes, is of Norse derivation ('servants' village'), but the mounds predate the arrival of the Vikings by at least 2,000 years.

2 Keeping more or less to the highest strip of ground, follow the ridge-top path as it winds north through a mix of bracken and heather. Superb views extend in all directions, from Exmoor to the Brecon Beacons, and west to the Preseli Hills. Having passed the second of the ridge's three prominent peaks, the path falls slightly to a fork. Here you can either follow the track downhill (going left, to the ruined Second World War signalling post) or stay right and press on through the heather along the rocky ridge-top. Either way, you'll arrive after 10–15 minutes at the third and final high point of Rhossili Down.

3 The trig point marks the start of a steep, 150m descent to Hillend Caravan and Camping Park. Take extra care here if the grass is wet.

4 Ignoring the path that veers left/due south from the foot of the hill along the bottom of Rhossili Down (via the Old Rectory), head through the main gates of the caravan park and bear immediately right, past the front of the pub/café to the main reception and car park gate. From here, take a track that leads west, skirting the bottom side of the caravan park to a paying car park. Next, follow the fenced track through the dunes to reach Rhossili Bay Beach itself.

The house at the base of the hill, surveying the sands from the safety of a raised plateau along the bottom of Rhossili Down, is Rhossili's much-photographed Old Rectory, built in the 1850s. This exposed site was chosen because the resident priests used to minister to both Rhossili and the neighbouring parish of Llangennith. It is said that a ghost haunts the cottage, whispering, 'Why don't you turn around and look at me?' into the ears of visitors. Local superstition holds that the spirit is that of a sailor shipwrecked on one of the many vessels that have been blown aground here over the centuries, spilling their loads to create a grisly treasure-hunt. Whether villagers ever actively lured any ships onto the rocks using lanterns, as is sometimes suggested, remains a matter of debate, but there's no doubt that several locals made their fortunes from cargo salvaged here.

5 A steady, 45-minute plod along the tidal sand below Rhossili Down takes you south to the start of a short, steep ascent up the cliff. From these steps you will emerge next to the Bay Bistro – the perfect spot for refreshments to celebrate the end of the walk.

Notes of interest

★ The classic view of the beach, featured on countless tourist office brochures, is from the low cliffs at its far southern end, near Rhossili village. From this point the sands stretch north in an exhilarating arc, bounded on one side by ranks of foamy breakers and on the other by an elegantly sloping moorland ridge.

★ Before the last Ice Age, this stretch of coast formed part of a line of hills running 112km (70 miles) inland, overlooking a plain where the Bristol Channel now flows. Judging from the wealth of Mesolithic remnants uncovered in the area, the forest carpeting it provided a rich source of food for early Welsh hunter-gatherers.

★ Sea caves concealed in the cliffs of the southwest Gower have yielded a wealth of famous archaeological finds – most notably the 'Red Lady of Paviland', a skeleton stained with red ochre and adorned with shell necklaces and ivory rods, which the local curate who found it in 1823 believed to be the bones of a Roman-era prostitute. In fact, the 'Red Lady' was a 25–30-year-old male, who lived 29,000 years ago, making these the oldest remains of a modern human ever discovered in Europe.

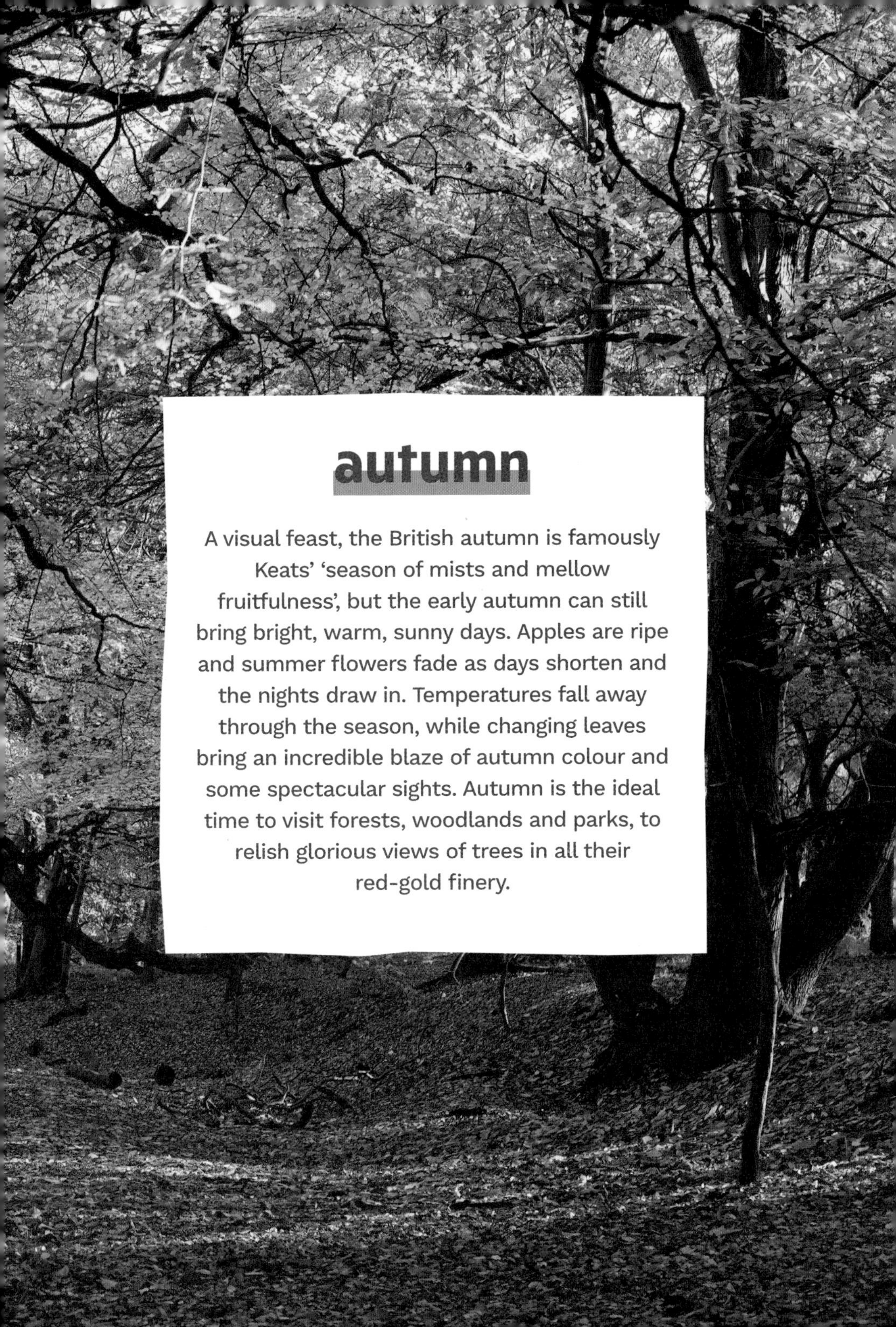

autumn

A visual feast, the British autumn is famously Keats' 'season of mists and mellow fruitfulness', but the early autumn can still bring bright, warm, sunny days. Apples are ripe and summer flowers fade as days shorten and the nights draw in. Temperatures fall away through the season, while changing leaves bring an incredible blaze of autumn colour and some spectacular sights. Autumn is the ideal time to visit forests, woodlands and parks, to relish glorious views of trees in all their red-gold finery.

walk 21

Pentland Hills, Edinburgh

Time: **5 hrs** | Distance: **12.5 km (7.7 miles)** | Difficulty: ✪✪✪

A superbly scenic circular route with wonderful panoramic views, which leads you up and over a chain of three hills – Scald Law, Carnethy Hill and Turnhouse Hill. Clear hill paths with stretches of stones or gravel make up most of this walk. There are a few steep climbs and descents to negotiate, but you will be rewarded with spectacular views.

Start location

Flotterstone car park, Midlothian nearest postcode EH26 0PW (grid ref: NT233631).

Getting there

By car: Flotterstone car park, 13km (8 miles) south of Edinburgh city centre, has ample parking.
By public transport: A regular daily Stagecoach bus (01) runs from Edinburgh and Dumfries to Flotterstone.

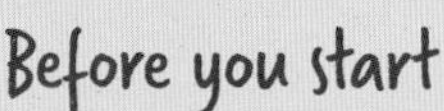

Before you start

- There are some steep ascents and descents during parts of this walk – take care as paths may be slippery, especially in wet or icy conditions.

1 Begin your walk from the Flotterstone Visitor Centre. Take the woodland path that runs parallel to the Glencorse Reservoir access road. This soon emerges onto the road. Make a right and continue, keeping an eye out for traffic. After a gradual rise the road levels off and passes Glen Cottage. Beyond a gate, follow the road as it continues alongside the picturesque Glencorse Reservoir then swings southwest. The steep slopes of Turnhouse and Carnethy rise ahead.

2 Once you have left Glencorse behind, the road continues alongside the Logan Burn. Pass through two gates beside cattlegrids, then you will find that the incline steepens a little on the approach to Loganlea Reservoir. This then levels off, and as you continue alongside the reservoir there are views of some particularly beautiful scenery to enjoy.

Allermuir Hill, Glencorse Reservoir and the Firth of Forth viewed from Carnethy Hill - the second highest peak in the Pentland Hills Regional Park.

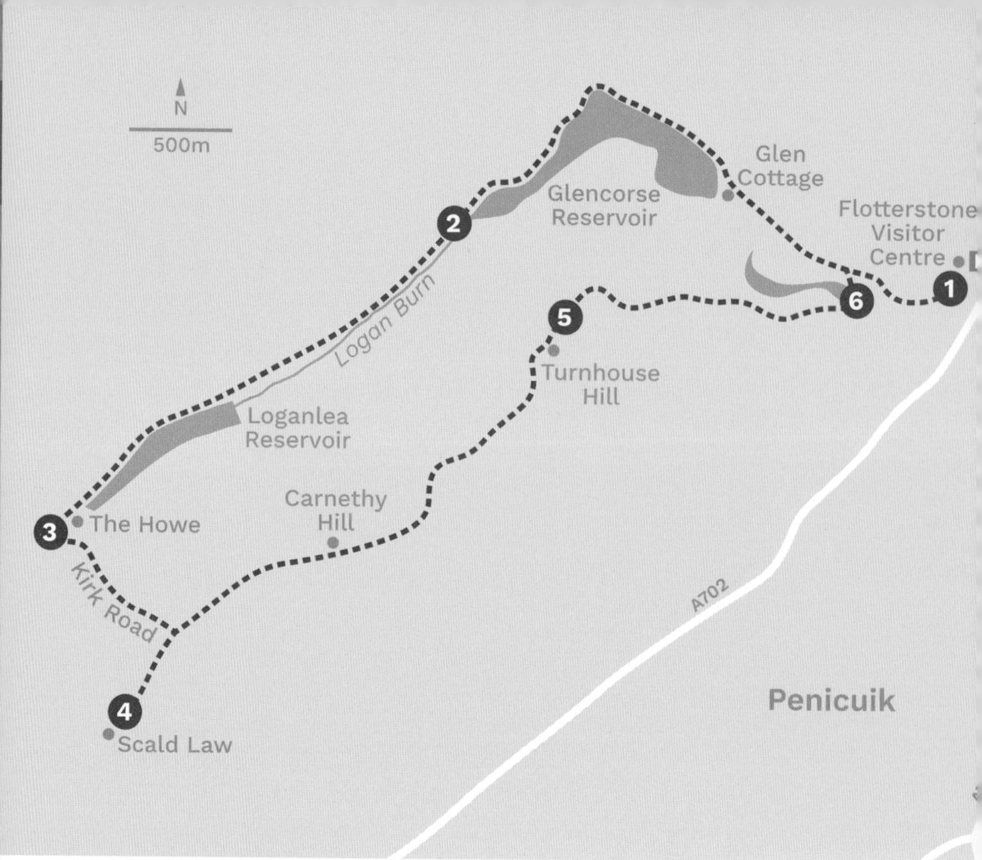

N
500m
Glen Cottage
Glencorse Reservoir
Flotterstone Visitor Centre
1
2
Logan Burn
6
5
Turnhouse Hill
Loganlea Reservoir
3
The Howe
Carnethy Hill
Kirk Road
A702
4
Scald Law
Penicuik

3 At the head of Loganlea go through a gate onto a track, then walk past The Howe – a large, beautifully located farmhouse. Follow the track as it swings left to cross a lovely old stone bridge over the Logan Burn. Bear right onto the old 'Kirk Road for Penicuik'. This climbs very steeply southeast up to a stile with superb views opening out across the park. Once you have crossed this stile, continue on the path to the left of a fence to cross the saddle, or low ridge, between Carnethy and Scald Law. Now turn right over another stile. From here, a sustained, steep pull up a good path will lead you up to the 579m summit of Scald Law from which you have an exceptional view – Carnethy Hill is especially prominent. Take care, as there are some steep ascents on this part of the route.

4 Return to the low ridge (the col), cross the Kirk Road and begin the steady climb northeast onto Carnethy. The gradient steepens as you near the summit, but once you reach the top another breathtaking panorama awaits. From there, make the steep descent from Carnethy along a good path through heathery slopes. This path drops down through a gate, from which point another steep climb continues. It rises over a crest and past a cairn before a final climb brings you to the summit of Turnhouse Hill. Here, fabulous views extending across East Lothian await you. Take care on the descent as the paths may be slippy, particularly after rain, or when there is snow or ice on the ground.

At Glencorse Reservoir you can find boat rentals for trout fishing, as well as a wonderfully scenic path enjoyed by walkers and cyclists alike.

Notes of interest

★ The Kirk Road is an historic right of way that was once used by residents of Bavelaw and Loganlea as a means of getting to church services in Penicuik.

★ A little to the south of Turnhouse Hill is the site of the Battle of Rullion Green, a skirmish that took place in 1666 between the government army and rebel Covenanters.

5 An excellent track now descends gradually northeast across glorious countryside. This track narrows to a path, which then drops steeply east (be careful in wet conditions especially, as this can be slippery). Once you are though a little pocket of woodland, another steady descent leads you down to a gate. Beyond this the path continues over an undulating and distinctive little ridge high above the Glencorse Burn. The path now drops down to a convergence of rivers and two bridges.

6 Take the left bridge over the Glencorse Burn and, once you have passed through a gate, you should turn right onto a track. At the end of this track, go through another gate, and turn right back onto the Glencorse access road. Now retrace your steps to make your way back to your start point.

walk 22

Tilberthwaite, Lake District

Time: 2 hrs 30 mins | Distance: 8 km (5 miles) | Difficulty: ✪

A pleasant, easy circuit starting from Tilberthwaite, which passes through woodland and slate-quarrying areas. This is a walk best enjoyed in autumn, when the leaves are falling, or even in winter after snow. The terrain is mainly good tracks and quiet tarmac lanes.

Start location

Tilberthwaite Gill car park, Cumbria LA21 8DG (grid ref: NY305011).

Getting there

By car: Leave the A593 Coniston to Skelwith Bridge Road at Great Intake just over 3km (just under 2 miles) north of Coniston and take the minor road heading northwest signed to Tilberthwaite. After about a mile you will reach a large parking area on the left just before the bridge over Tilberthwaite Gill. The postcode of Tilberthwaite Farm, a little further up the road, is LA21 8DG. Parking is free but do contribute some coins in the donation box if you are able to; the National Park uses the funds to help maintain the area.

By public transport: The 516 Langdale Rambler bus goes to Elterwater, although it is an hour and a half walk to the start location.

Before you start

- There are plenty of options for accommodation, eating and drinking available in both Ambleside and Coniston.

An ancient pedestrian bridge, Slater Bridge, crosses the River Brathay and connected the hamlet of Little Langdale with the many slate quarries in the Tilberthwaite area.

1 Starting from the car park, you should turn left along the road and carry on for about 400m. Immediately before the road heads into a farmyard, turn right through a wooden field gate by a footpath fingerpost sign. Follow the wall on your left, go through a gate and keep ahead on the track to another gate that leads you into trees. Now keep ahead on the main path until you reach a road.

2 Turn left along the road. There is a short steep section by Holme Ground Farm. The road levels off and then passes through a quarry area, with an impressively deep quarry on the right, to reach the buildings at Hodge Close. The quarry is a spectacular sight, but keep behind the fence and safely away from the edge. Do not attempt to descend into it or to swim in the lake at the bottom. The quarry is popular with divers wanting to explore the underground caverns but, even with their equipment and experience, this has proved to be an extremely dangerous dive site over the years. As the road now climbs steeply past Holme Ground, note the traditional and ingeniously designed Lakeland 'bank barn' on your left. Building a barn on a bank means that both upper and lower floors can be entered at ground level, avoiding the need for awkward ladders or pulley systems. Typically, livestock would be kept on the lower floor, with hay and feed passed down from the upper floor through trapdoors.

3 Now continue on the main tarmac road as it zig-zags through the buildings of Hodge Close. Then, immediately after the buildings, fork right on a stony track signed 'Oxen Fell ½ mile'. Proceed through a gate, ignore a bridleway going right, and keep straight on through another gate. The next gate leads to a small farmyard. Keep straight on along a tarmac lane, keep right when it forks, and continue to the main A593 road.

4 Turn left immediately before the road and follow the path running parallel to the road, which is over the wall to your right. This path eventually passes through a gate onto the road. Pass through the gate and immediately left down a short track that leads to a small tarmac lane junction with a National Trust sign.

5 Now take the right lane, which is signed to High Park and Halegarth, and follow it downhill keeping the trees on your right. The

Notes of interest

★ Tilberthwaite is a peaceful and unspoilt little hamlet at the end of a dead-end road. The name translates as 'the clearing by Tilba's fort', and slight remains of an early fortification have been found nearby. There are also the remains of a large slate-quarrying industry in this area – the quarry was busy during the 19th century but had mostly closed by the 1950s, with the last small-scale operations winding down in the 1960s.

Hodge Close Quarry was one of several historic slate workings in the Tilberthwaite Valley. Watch your footing if you decide to explore – there are many hazardous drops.

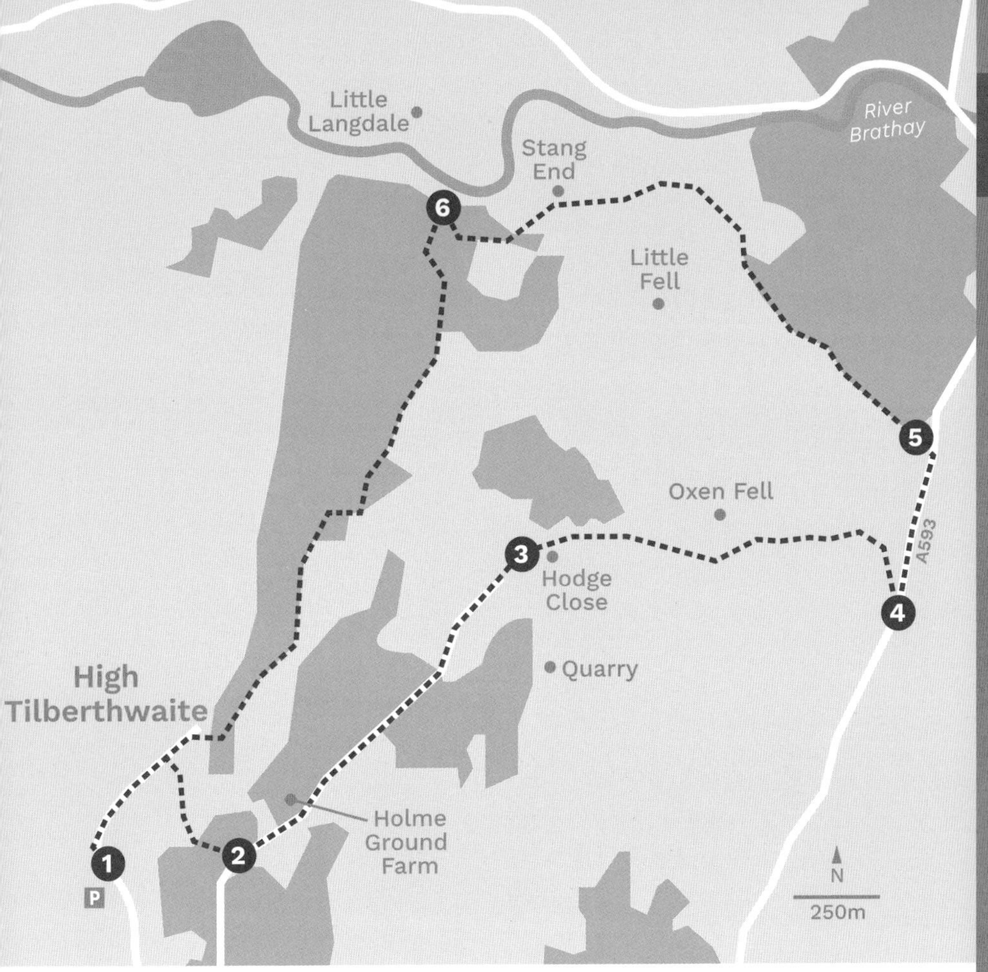

view to Wetherlarn dominates the first part of this section of the walk, then the lane runs along the side of the valley of Little Langdale. After a cattlegrid, stay on the lane and you will pass two farms, High Park and Stang End. The lane then crosses another cattlegrid. The road now descends again and the tarmac ends. The lane swings right at the bottom to reach a footbridge over the River Brathay. This footbridge is a pleasant resting place if you would like to pause before continuing. Before the bridge was built there was a deep ford here, and the road you have been following was a through route. Unwitting tourists used to try passing through the ford, and some locals amused themselves by sitting here watching their attempts. Although that pastime is no longer available, it does mean the road is now a peaceful and almost traffic-free route that walkers can enjoy.

6 Do not cross the footbridge, instead turn left along the track signed to Tilberthwaite and Coniston. Keep on the main track through woods. At the fork, keep right. The clear track continues on to the farm buildings at High Tilberthwaite. Keep straight on through these and retrace your steps back along the road to once again reach your start point at the car park.

walk 23

Strid Wood and Bolton Abbey, Yorkshire

Time: 2 hrs 30 mins | Distance: 9.6 km (6 miles) | Difficulty: ✪✪✪

Following a lovely loop, this route leads you on a relaxing wander through ancient oakland, passing the famous 'Strid', Bolton Priory and the Cavendish memorial. This walk is remarkably beautiful in autumn, particularly as the views in the woods and along the River Wharfe reveal a vibrant, blended blaze of foliage colours thanks to Strid Wood's mix of beech, ash and oak trees.

Start location

Strid Wood car park, Yorkshire BD23 6AN (grid ref: SE070556).

Getting there

By car: Driving is the best way to get to the Strid, though it is possible to walk from both Burnsall and Ilkley. There is a fee for using the car park, but the ticket is valid all day and can be used at the other two Bolton Abbey car parks as well (if you wish to explore further after your walk) so hold on to your ticket.

By public transport: There is an irregular bus service, the 74, running between Grassington and Ilkley on Mondays, Wednesdays, Saturdays and Sundays.

1 From Strid Wood car park, head down the gentle slope towards the river, bearing right until the path begins to run along the river. Follow the path past various art installations until it meets Cavendish Pavilion.

2 Continue past the Cavendish Pavilion and car park, following the path as it bends with the river and then continuing along the path up to the road on your right. Head along the road for a short while and, about 200m

Before you start

- Strid Wood was opened to the public in 1810 by the Duke of Devonshire and is still maintained by his estate. You may see otters, kingfishers, woodpeckers and roe deer during the walk.

- Bolton Abbey is an excellent location for fungi-spotting; there is an abundance of toadstools and mushrooms to be seen here during the autumn season.

- Cavendish Pavilion (opened in 1890) is the perfect riverside place to stop should you require quick refreshments while enjoying this walk.

- Please note that the Strid is dangerously strong; stay well back from the edge, and abide by any instructions on signs in the area.

The River Wharfe flows through Wharfdale, in the Yorkshire Dales National Park. Vibrant displays of glowing autumn foliage add warmth to the cooling days.

after the memorial fountain, turn left down towards the ruined priory. Carry on behind the priory before taking the main path left down towards the bridge and the stepping-stones.

3 Cross over the bridge, or use the stepping-stones if you are feeling adventurous, and then turn left. You have two route choices here: either take the lower, easier path or choose the higher, but more picturesque, path. For the lower path, take the left-hand fork and follow the slightly gentler path down, alongside the river until it meets the main path at the first bridge. For the higher path, take the right-hand path and follow it as it climbs through the trees and along. It will meet the other path to cross a beck at a small bridge. Now continue on to meet a road and then cross another bridge.

4 After crossing the second bridge, leave the road and simply follow the path along as it passes the bridge over the Wharfe opposite the Cavendish Pavilion. This path carries on, climbing away from the river before dropping back down again when the wood ends after roughly 3km (2 miles). Continue following the path before then crossing the river at the bridge (the first river crossing you'll meet after the Cavendish Pavilion bridge). Turn left and follow the path along again. Watch your step, as this section of the route is rather rocky and uneven underfoot, as well as quite steep.

5 After crossing the bridge, you should follow the path along to the left. Take the first right-leading path you meet to climb the hill past the Montessori school and then further up back to the car park where your walk began.

Notes of interest

* Strid Wood is one of the largest remnants of sessile oak trees (also known as Cornish oak, Irish oak or durmast oak) in the Dales. The word 'strid' itself comes from the Anglo Saxon *stryth* – meaning 'turmoil' (also the root of the word 'strife') – but the word in this instance is corrupted to describe the point where the river dramatically narrows to a central point, creating a stretch of great pressure so narrow it almost looks like you could stride over it.

* The Cavendish Memorial Fountain, situated between the Priory ruins and the Cavendish Pavilion, was erected as a memorial to Lord Frederick Cavendish in 1882. It was paid for by public donations and designed by Thomas Worthington and John Elgood.

* Bolton Priory was founded in 1154 by the Augustinian order and has a tumultuous history. Abandoned and damaged during the 1300s due to attacks by Scottish raiders, the abbey was terminated in the Dissolution of the Monasteries. The nave of the abbey remained in use as a parish church and some renovation was carried out in the Victorian era including windows designed by Augustus Pugin – the same architect who designed the Palace of Westminster.

Bolton Priory closed in 1539, but the tower was left half-standing. Its base was later converted into an entrance porch with a bell-turret. Most of the remaining church is Gothic, some Victorian.

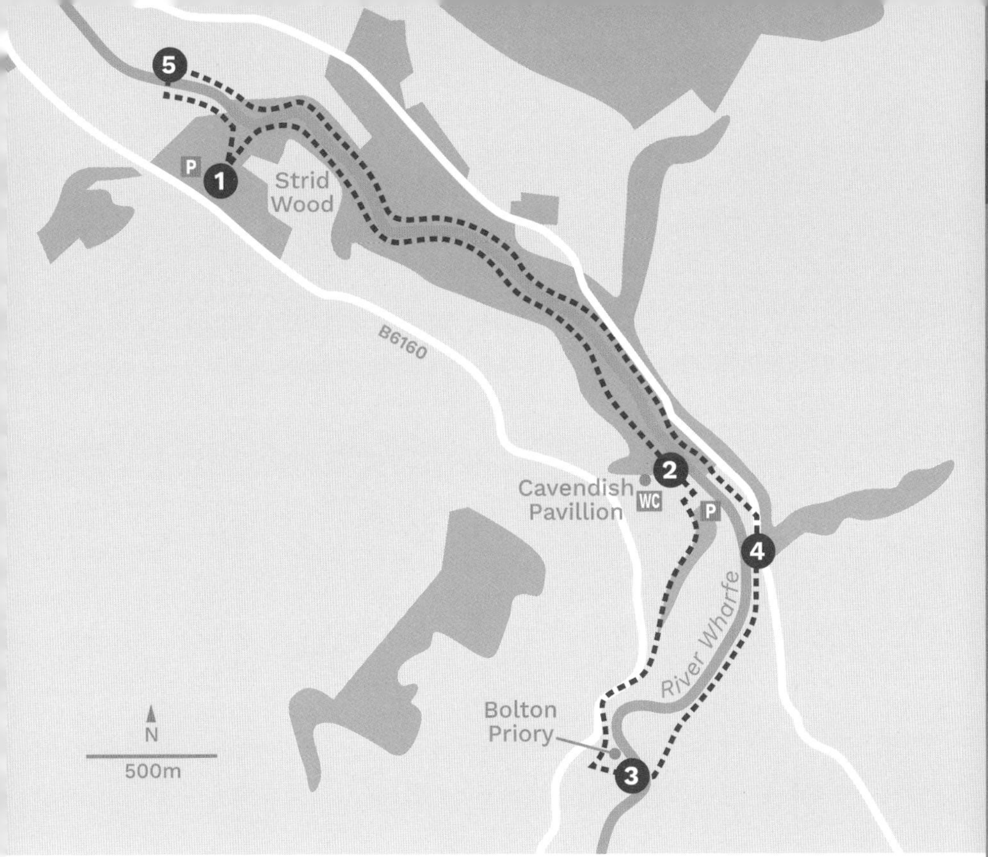

5
P
1
Strid
Wood
B6160
2
Cavendish
Pavillion
WC
P
4
River Wharfe
Bolton
Priory
3
N
500m

walk
24

York's Walls

Time: 2 hrs 30 mins | Distance: 7.7 km (4.8 miles) | Difficulty: ✪

A short walk along the banks of the River Ouse leads to an elevated walk along York's historic city walls, which used to guard the then much smaller city. Many of these walls survive from the 12th to 14th centuries.

Before you start

- The River Ouse is prone to flooding in winter. If the grassy area or parts of the cycleway at the beginning of this route are under water, then do not attempt this walk.

- The walls are not a right of way; at times sections may be closed for maintenance. While the walls are kept open as much as possible for visitors to enjoy, sections may also be closed for safety reasons if there is snow and ice in the winter.

- Although the walls are wide and easy to walk on, some sections do have a sharp drop to the left with no barrier, so take care with children. Dogs, other than guide dogs and assistance dogs, are banned from this route.

- This might be a walk to avoid if you are nervous about heights.

Start location

York Youth Hostel, Water End, York YO30 6LP (grid ref: SE591529).

Getting there

By car: The Youth Hostel is about 1.5km (1 mile) northwest of York city centre just off the A19. You may find parking on nearby streets, or consider using the park & ride service.
By public transport: The 30, 30x, 31, 31x, 19 and 29 local suburban bus services all pass the Youth Hostel and go to the city centre. The 2 service from the Park & Ride at Rawston Bar on the A19 will take you to Clifton. From there it is a short walk along Water End to the Youth Hostel. For train travel, York is a major station with numerous connections in all directions. This walk passes the station just after Waypoint 2. From the front of the station, you will see the city walls opposite. Cross the road and go left a little to find the steps up onto the walls.

1 From the end of the YHA's driveway turn right along the main road, cross at the lights and continue in the same direction then cross a large road bridge over the River Ouse, descending the steps to your left. Carry on straight ahead, following the river to your left. At the far end of the grassy area it narrows, joining a footpath and cycleway that comes in from the right. Stick to this path, now next to the river. Pass under the green steel bridge, and walk on ahead.

2 Immediately before the next bridge, go through an arch and turn right up steps that will bring you onto the city walls at the Barker Tower. Continue past the large war memorial on your left, then the railway station to your right. The walls turn left and continue to cross a road at the Micklegate Bar. In the gatehouse buildings you will find the Henry VII

Most of York's medieval walls are still standing and, 700 years later, they offer a wonderful elevated walk around the city. York's Roman walls are mainly hidden within the ramparts.

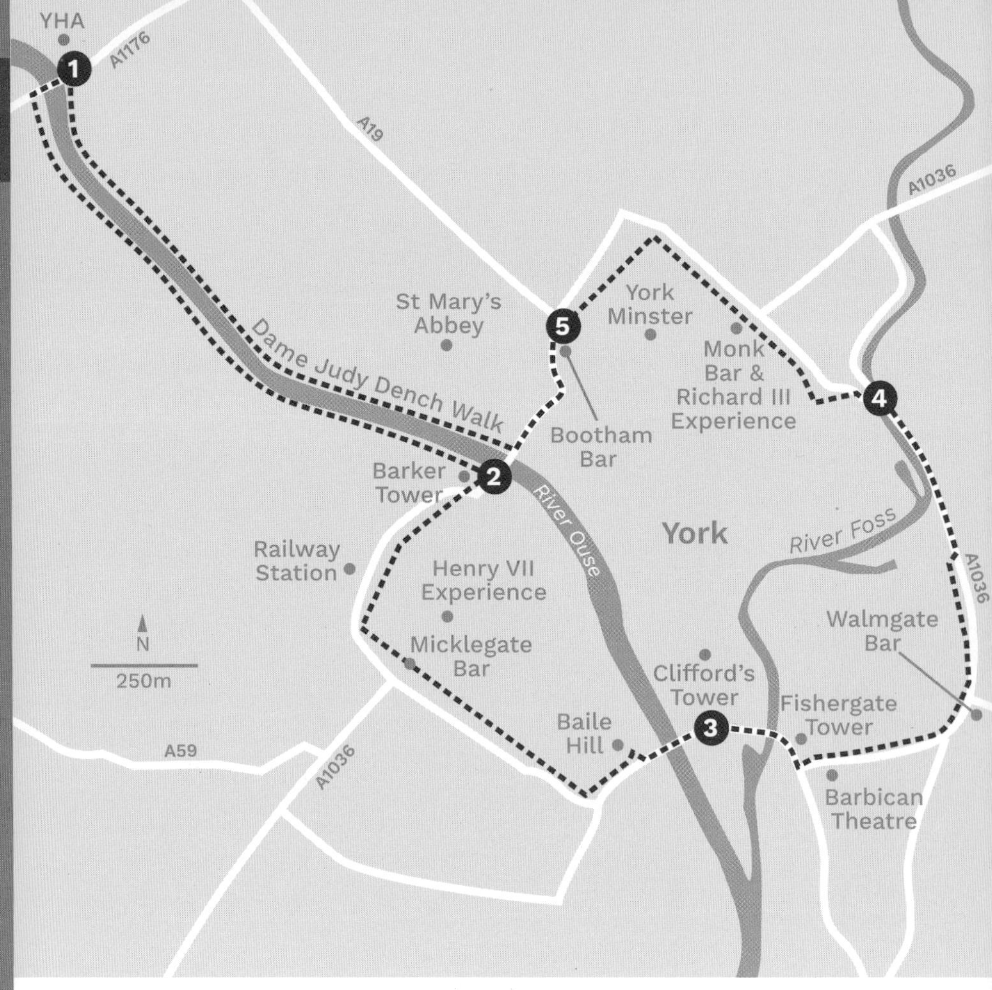

experience (a joint ticket will also allow entry to the Richard III experience, which you will pass later). Climb the steps and continue along the walls, noting the pleasant residential streets. Eventually the walls turn left again. Continue past Baile Hill, the motte (or mound) of an old castle, and descend steps to the road at the site of the old Skeldergate Postern. Proceed to cross the River Ouse via a large bridge, turn left at the roundabout and after about 30m cross the road at the pedestrian lights.

3 You have two options for the next section.

Option A: To continue on the main route around the walls, turn right back to the roundabout and go left on the road to cross a bridge over the River Foss. Another section of the city walls lies ahead of you. At the left end, go through an arch at the Fishergate tower and immediately right up steps to take you back onto the ramparts. Continue until you have to descend to the road at Fishergate Bar, ascend the steps on the other side and continue on the walls, passing the Barbican Theatre to your right. Steps lead down to the road again at Walmgate Bar. Here cross at the lights and continue up the steps on the opposite side. Carry on along the ramparts until they end at the red tower (made of red bricks). Walk clockwise around the tower then turn left along the ring road; soon you will be alongside the River Foss to your left. Go straight across at the traffic lights to find the next section of the walls.

Option B: Look to the castle on its mound ahead, and walk anticlockwise around it. As you pass the steps up to the top it is worth pausing a moment to read and reflect on the dreadful story on the plaque just to the left of the steps. On the other side take the road, Castlegate, passing to the right of the Hilton hotel for about 20m then turn right in front of a church to reach Saint Mary's Square. Turn left up Coppergate Walk, passing the entrance to the Jorvik Viking Centre. At the next road go right, and straight on over a crossroads. Pass a small stone chapel then immediately turn left up York's shortest street, Whip-ma-whop-ma Gate (a plaque on the chapel explains the name!). Almost immediately turn right along Saint Saviourgate, passing the methodist church and the York Dig centre. At a T-junction turn right then go left along Peasholme Green. Turn left at the traffic lights to find the walls on the left again at Layerthorpe Bridge.

4 Go up the steps through an arch to climb back onto the walls. Pass some Roman ruins on the left and continue, descending steps down to the road at Monk Bar. Cross the road, but before crossing the cycle path go right through a door and climb the steps through a tunnel back onto the walls. To your right here is the Richard III experience. Continue along the ramparts, now with wonderful views across to the impressive York Minster. Walking in autumn, you will also see from here the historic Gray's Court hotel adorned in splendid finery as its cloak of Boston ivy changes colour through the season. The walls go left again, then steps lead down inside a tower to the road at Bootham Bar, opposite the art gallery.

Micklegate Bar, guarding the main road south, is the place where monarchs are traditionally greeted when entering the city and where the remains of those punished as traitors were once displayed.

5 Turn left along the road. At the next junction, turn right down Museum Street. On approaching the bridge follow the fork right and go down a cobbled street alongside the main road that leads down to the river bank. Turn right along Dame Judi Dench Walk. Continue with the river to your left and pleasant parks to your right. Pass back under the green railway bridge and continue on the riverbank. Immediately before the next road bridge a brown sign points right up to the YHA. Go up the short steep road and right along the main road a short distance, crossing at the lights again, to return to the Youth Hostel.

walk
25

Wendover, Buckinghamshire

Time: **4 hrs** | Distance: **11.5 km (7.2 miles)** | Difficulty: ✪✪✪

Perhaps it is because the Chilterns are close to London and surrounded by dormitory towns that they are cherished by so many people. Their eye-catching escarpments are steeped in history, with echoes of a countryside now disappeared in many other parts of the UK. This circular walk strikes out from Wendover, heading along the edge of the Chilterns, encompassing some of its loveliest views and the iconic and anciently enigmatic Ridgeway. This route includes fields, good footpaths, one steep climb, and the monument on Coombe Hill marks the highest point in the Chilterns (280m). Bacombe Hill, towards the end of this route, is a spectacular nature reserve with willow warblers and green woodpeckers amid the hazel and dog rose.

Start location

Wendover Station, Wendover, Buckinghamshire HP22 6BN (grid ref: SP866078).

Getting there

By car: There is paid car parking available at Wendover Station.

By public transport: Wendover is served by Chiltern Railways from London Marylebone Station.

View from the Ridgeway Path across the Buckinghamshire Chilterns. The gently rolling hills are cloaked in woodland and chalk downland, and provide a home for plenty of wildlife.

Before you start

⁕ Sleeping, eating and drinking options are all available in Wendover should you need them.

Notes of interest

★ Chequers has been the retreat of British prime ministers since the 1920s. The imposing 16th-century mansion blends in with a landscape of solitary oaks and yews, thanks to its façade of local stone and bricks.

★ Bacombe Hill Nature Reserve is an ancient site of chalk grassland, scrub and woodland. Spindle, buckthorn and wayfaring tree grow in the scrub, all with berries that ripen in vibrant, striking colours during the autumn. Another shrub to be found here is juniper, beloved of a number of rare insects but sadly in decline across the Chilterns.

1 From the station approach road, turn right across the bridge and then left, following the footpath sign over a stile under pylons. Cross the stile and head gently right across the field. Cross the stile at the top of the field, turn right along the lane and then take the first left turn, following a bridleway signpost and a narrow path between fences. Go straight ahead through a metal gate, then downhill and over a stile, after this continuing slightly right to Coxgrove Wood. A glance over your shoulder will reveal picturesque views of Wendover Woods, the Vale of Aylesbury and Halton House – a former residence of the Rothschild family.

2 Follow the main path through the wood, with beautiful mature beech and holly trees. After passing a yellow arrow on a tree, take the right-hand path to eventually pick up a blue waymarker to the village of Dunsmore.

3 Turn right at the crossroads by the duck pond and its black and white signpost. After 100m, turn left over a stile and take the right fork downhill to Cobnut Farm. Continue ahead through Godmerhill Wood. Eventually the Ridgeway joins the path and you should head west towards Chequers.

4 Cross the road to enter Chequers' grounds (you can't miss the CCTV cameras), then pass over the driveway and follow the path to Maple Wood. Bear right along the path skirting the wood to a gate. Follow the right edge of the field, with some of the Chilterns' characteristic hidden valleys lying on your left. Proceed through another gate and cross the

The Coombe Hill Monument, overlooking Aylesbury Vale, is an iconic Buckinghamshire landmark. It sits on one of the highest spurs of the Chilterns.

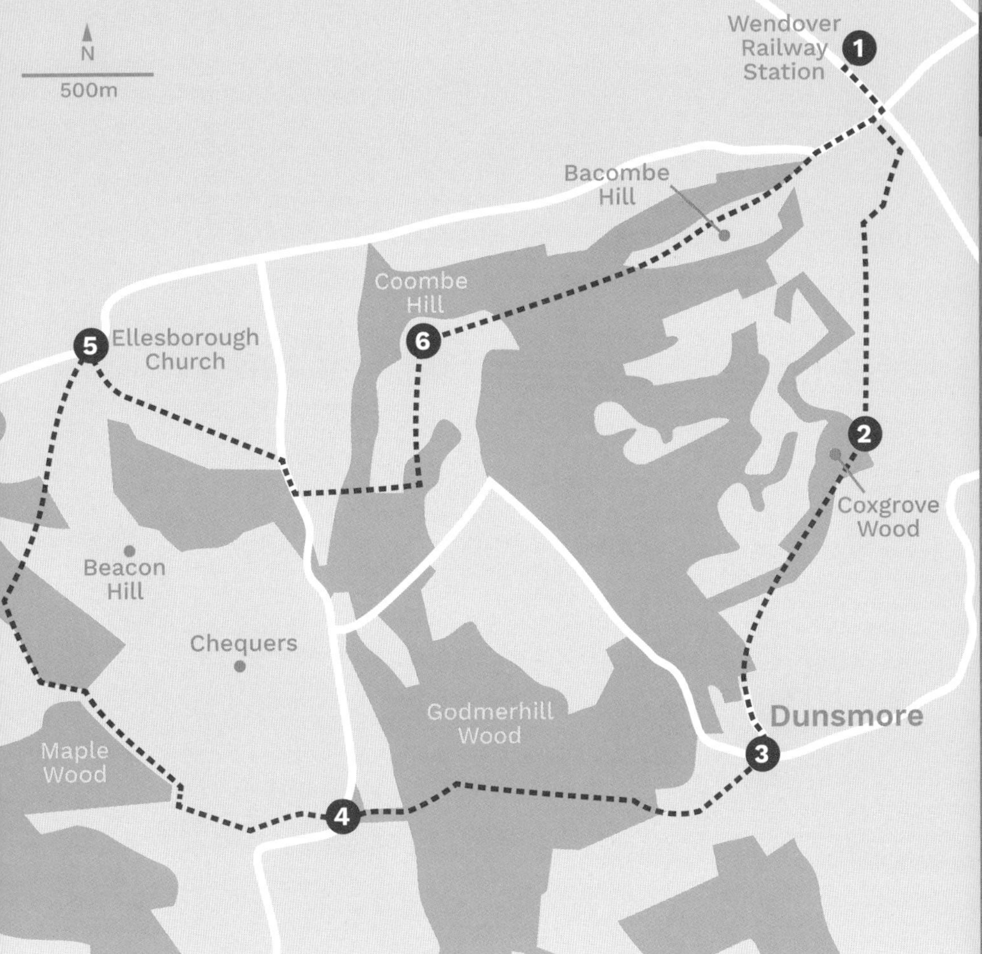

lane, contouring around Beacon Hill and enjoying the glorious views across the Vale of Aylesbury. Exit the gate opposite the pretty Ellesborough church.

5 Turn right and immediately right again. After 300m turn left, the direction signposted for a circular walk. At the road, turn right, walk 100m and cross the road, following the footpath sign. At the fork in the woods, bear slightly left following the National Trust sign up a steep hill. Near the brow of the hill, bear left to make for Coombe Hill and its monument. This is the highest point of the Chilterns.

6 From the monument, follow the grassy track that lies parallel and to the left of the gravel track to a gate. Here you should cross a ditch and pick up the Ridgeway again. Return to Wendover via Bacombe Hill. Now, rejoin your outbound route just before the railway bridge, and make your way back to the start point.

nature in autumn

Autumn is a particularly mindful walking season, as you can't help but notice all the changes around you, the lower light and the shorter days, the shifting colours in the leaves and the crisper, fresher edge to the cooling air.

Autumn runs through September, October and November. The beginning of September often feels as balmy as late summer, but usually within a few weeks the days start to shorten and the temperature dips away. While the weather may be mixed, of course – ranging from easy, mild days to rainy and windy – the dark dropping into the evenings always comes as something of a surprise. Autumn brings vast new colour vistas, as the leaves change hue and set the landscape ablaze with tones ranging from gentle golds and warm ambers through to unforgettable reds. These spectacular displays reach their peak in October, lit up by the lowering glow of the liquid-golden autumn sunlight. Then the trees begin to shed their leaves, uncovering the starkly beautiful skeletons of branches and revealing the bones of last season's nests, now abandoned.

There is also much wildlife activity to witness, and wherever you decide to walk there is plenty to see as animals embark on pre-winter feeding missions, especially in the woods. From all sorts of birds, to deer and badgers, red squirrels and even seals if you are heading for the coast, autumn is a great time to see our favourite creatures.

Early autumn is perfect for owl-spotting, especially if you are walking at dawn or dusk. Owls are crepuscular, so this is when they are most active. Look for open habitats, where owls will be easiest to see as they hunt for mice, shrews and voles, and try to head out just before or after a clear, dry night with plenty of moonlight. Temperatures may be on the chilly side, so wrap up warm – and don't forget your binoculars, preferably a pair with wider lenses suitable for low-light viewing. Organised owl-spotting walks may be a good option, depending on where you are, so keep an eye out for one of these if you fancy owling in company.

October sees migrant birds arrive back in the UK, looking to settle down for the winter months. Walking the coast path in Norfolk is a great way to spot some fascinating birds, especially if you explore the Blakeney Freshes area. Look for flocks of golden plover along the coast, and spot wigeon and brent geese getting their fill of salt-marsh grazing. Large groups of stunning and distinctive lapwings may also be found in wetlands, mudflats, meadows and open farmland at this time of year. Looking up, you may well catch a glimpse of geese and swans making their way methodically across the skies, stretching out in the most beautiful flight patterns. Siskin finches and bramblings will also be pottering about all over the country, easy to spot in woodland and farmland. As the hawthorn and rowan berries ripen, they attract ravenous flocks of fieldfares, the large and colourful winter thrush. Focused on filling their bellies, the fieldfares can be found feasting in hedgerows, parks and woodland and often move about in groups of up to 200 birds.

The deer rut also takes place in autumn, a spectacular sight – although it goes without saying, one to watch from a distance. As the males compete, displaying their strength and dominance, they charge about, bellow and may even clash and lock horns, putting on a magnificent and awe-inspiring show. There are plenty of walking routes that take in deer-rut locations – find a trail in Suffolk, Carmarthenshire, Shropshire, Devon, West Sussex, Exmoor, Dartmoor, the New Forest or North Yorkshire.

Seal pupping takes place as early as late August in Cornwall, but further into autumn for the rest of the country. Walkers in Wales may start seeing pups in September through to October, and down the east coast of England and in Scotland pups arrive through November and sometimes into December. The ice-white pups of grey seals can be spotted on the breeding-ground beaches. Do remember to keep to a safe distance so as not to disturb the pups or worry their mothers.

Naturally a time of slowing down, autumn walks are the perfect opportunity to notice the calmer, quieter transformations of plants and trees, quite apart from the theatrical displays of vibrant leaf colour.

Stocking up isn't just the preserve of wildlife; this season brings plenty of opportunities for us to forage for nutritious wild foods too. Rosehips redden on rose plants and sloes from the blackthorn trees darken and ripen. Young nettles may be (carefully!) collected and used for teas, smoothies, soups and stews, and sorrels, dandelions, blackberries, apples and crab apples are all ready for gathering. Mushrooms spring up in fields, meadows and on the forest floor, although (as with any foraging) it is important you are completely confident you can identify them accurately before you fill your basket.

Enjoying this most beautiful of seasons on foot is the very best way to relish its stunning combination of vibrancy and calm stillness, as we look forward to the winter months ahead.

Fungi flourish in the cooler, wetter days of autumn. There are over a hundred edible species growing in the UK, but you must ensure you know what you're picking.

walk 26

Walthamstow Wetlands, London

Time: **3 hrs 30 mins** | Distance: **11.7 km (7.3 miles)** | Difficulty: ✪✪

A gently flat circular walk along canals and marshes, taking in the wildlife of the Walthamstow Wetlands. The route follows well-marked, hard-surfaced footpaths and towpaths. Autumn offers opportunities to enjoy beautifully colourful wildflowers – including white campion, purple knapweed and yellow gorse – as well as the chance to spot numerous different birds, such as herons, goldfinches, pochards, shoveler ducks, gadwalls, Cetti's warblers and peregrine falcons.

Start location

Walthamstow Wetlands car park, Forest Road, Walthamstow, London N17 9NH (grid ref: TQ350893).

Before you start

- This route should be suitable for compact wheelchairs and pushchairs, however the footbridges over the canal are steep and there are a number of sections of uneven towpath and raised cobbles that may prove tricky.
- Refreshments are available at the start/end of the route at Walthamstow Wetlands Engine House or The Ferry Boat Inn on Forest Road. There are also two cafés on the towpath between Waypoints 4 and 5.
- As Walthamstow Wetlands is primarily a nature reserve with nesting birds, dogs are not permitted.

Getting there

By car: Park in the Walthamstow Wetlands car park halfway between Tottenham Hale and Blackhorse Road Stations. Parking charges start at £2. Check car park opening hours online, and allow yourself plenty of time as it can be busy on holidays and weekends.

By public transport: You may commence this walk from Tottenham Hale (Victoria Line and National Rail) or Blackhorse Road (Victoria Line) Stations. Simply walk along Forest Road to the entrance of the north side of the Wetlands and begin the walk there. If you are travelling by bus, services 123 and 230 stop on Forest Road. Alight at The Ferry Boat Inn stop. Check online for specific travel information.

Walthamstow Wetlands, part of the London Wildlife Trust, is a 211-hectare site comprising ten reservoirs. The locally-listed Engine House (here in the background) is now home to a café.

1 To begin your walk, leave the car park and cross Forest Road, turning right and entering the north side of Walthamstow Wetlands on the left. Follow the path straight ahead, with Low Maynard Reservoir on your right, crossing a wide outlet.

2 When you reach the southern end of Lockwood Reservoir, follow a left fork to go up steep steps to the reservoir embankment. Turn right, then proceed along the bank till you reach a wide gate that prevents further access. Head back down the embankment on the right to join the wide concrete path again. On windy days, or if you find that the steps are too steep, continue to follow the wide concrete path between Low Maynard Reservoir and the bottom of Lockwood Reservoir embankment.

3 Cross the inlet at the top of High Maynard Reservoir, following the path around to the left to cross the bridge over the River Lee Flood Relief Channel. Once you have gone through the nature reserve gates, turn immediately left. Follow the footpath past the allotments and houses on the right, until the path splits. Then turn left away from the housing, signed towards Tottenham Marshes.

4 Turn left and follow the path back over the relief channel, following the path as it forks right just after the bridge. Continue along this path to cross the green bridge and arrive on the canal towpath. Turn right for 200m then veer off to the right to cross the canal via a footbridge. Continue straight ahead, heading away from the canal and keeping the field on your left, then taking the left fork where the path splits. Continue following the path along the top of the field, ignoring two paths on your left. After walking through a small woodland, choose the left fork and follow it back towards the canal. Turn right where the paths merge, then walk through a gate next to a boatyard, arriving at The Waterside Café.

With ten resevoirs, the Walthamstow Wetlands offers an important site for waterfowl who come to spend the winter. Breeding birds, as well as summer visitors, also enjoy safe haven here.

5 Continue along towpath for 2km (1¼ miles), passing a bridge on your left at Riverside Café and Rowing Club. Take the next bridge over the canal, halfway along the side of Springfield Park. After crossing the bridge, turn right to walk along the edge of Walthamstow Marshes (which is on your left). Walk under the railway bridge and continue along the path, ignoring paths leading off to the left, until you reach a footbridge over the canal. Don't cross the bridge, instead turn left just after to take the path along the edge of the field, emerging through the hedge onto a raised, wide concrete trail. Here, turn left.

Notes of interest

★ Coppermill Tower is a Grade II-listed building on the site of a 14th-century mill. It is now a public viewing tower and houses an interesting historical timeline of the wetlands.

★ The original pumping station dates to the 1890s. The Engine House is now managed by London Wildlife Trust and Waltham Forest Council as a visitor/ exhibition centre, café and shop.

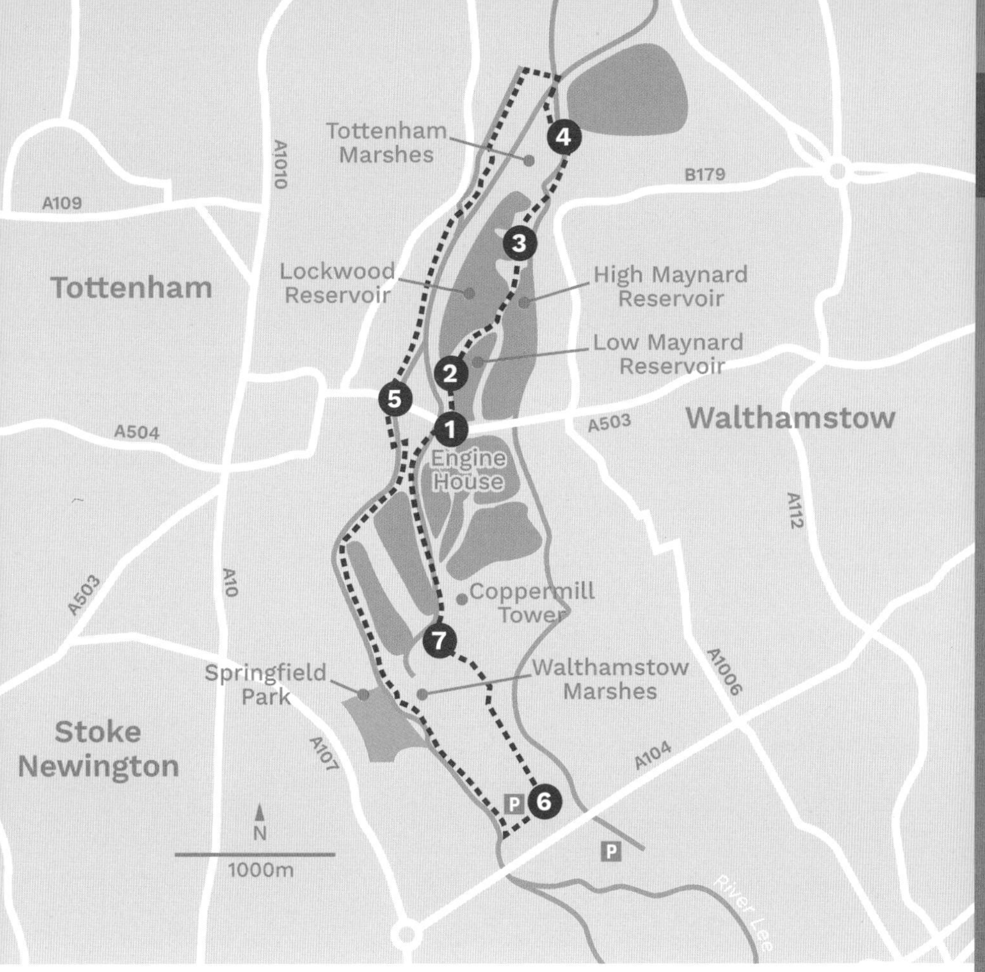

Possible shortcuts: At this point, your walk can be cut short by taking an alternative route back to the start. Walk up the slope to Ferry Road and turn left back to the Wetlands car park. Alternatively, you may turn right to reach Tottenham Hale Station.

6 Follow this trail for about 1.5km (1 mile), passing under a railway line until you reach a car park. Walk diagonally right across the car park. Then follow the grassy path for a few metres – this will lead you to a gate from which you emerge onto Coppermill Lane opposite the entrance to the south side of Walthamstow Wetlands.

7 Now enter the Wetlands and follow the wide concrete path past Coppermill Tower (see Notes of Interest on page 142) on your right. There are steps on the left; climb these up to the reservoir embankment. Turn right and proceed along the bank till you reach an outlet tower, where the path bends round to follow the reservoir to the left. Here, leave the embankment and proceed down the slope to join the original concrete path heading forward towards the Engine House building. Passing the building on your right, head under the railway line and then up to the right to emerge back in the car park where you started this walk.

walk 27

Odiham Castle, Hampshire

Time: **1 hr 45 mins** | Distance: **5.6 km (3.5 miles)** | Difficulty: ✪✪

A peaceful circular walk along quiet lanes, footpaths and the canal, taking in castle ruins, pond life and bats along the way. There are some inclines. A beautiful old village start/end point and a lift road bridge add to the interesting points. Autumn is a particularly special season to enjoy this walk, with the trees along the Basingstoke Canal path erupting in a blaze of gold, bronze and orange.

Start location

Odiham High Street, Hampshire RG29 1LP (grid ref: OS144 7425).

Before you start

* If walking with children or dogs, take extra care by the canal. It is also possible to use the edge of the field by Deptford Lane instead of walking along the lane itself, although this short detour may not be suitable for wheels.

* If you wish to add pond-dipping to the experience for children, continue a few metres beyond the lift bridge instead of turning onto the canal path between Waypoints 3 and 4. The small pond there is a perfect spot for investigating pond life.

Getting there

By car: M3 Junction 5. Parking may be available on the High Street (time limits may apply), in the pay and display car park in Deer Park View or in Basingstoke Canal car park (London Road, Odiham RG29 1AL).
By public transport: Travel by train or bus to Hook Station, the closest station. From here, the 13 bus service runs to Odiham High Street, the start point of this walk.

1 Start in Odiham High Street, then head west and downhill. You will pass Deer Park View on your right. Continue to the roundabout. You will see a petrol station to the right and across the road. Cross this road and continue straight on between bollards through the pretty houses in the cobbled West Street. At the end, veer left and continue towards Robert May's School.

2 Carry on until you are just past the main school entrance and turn right, up a few steps onto a narrow, signed footpath between the school (on your right) and a cow field. Continue forwards on the footpath, passing Laurel Close on your right, until you reach North Warnborough Street. Turn right here, then continue forward through the pretty village towards The Anchor Inn. A short alternative route from the school is more suitable for pushchairs, although the tarmac path does end with a track: just before the school entrance turn right onto the tarmac path. The school sports courts are soon on your left. Follow the path past new housing and a play area and keep straight ahead onto a narrow gravel track. Go across Laurel Close to continue on the gravel track which ends at the quiet North Warnborough Street and opposite The Anchor Inn. Turn right to rejoin the main route at Waypoint 3.

Basingstoke Canal, Odiham in Hampshire. The canal is considered by Natural England as one of the finest waterways in England.

The now-ruined 13th-century Odiham Castle was built long before the canal existed – the canal runs through part of the castle's bailey.

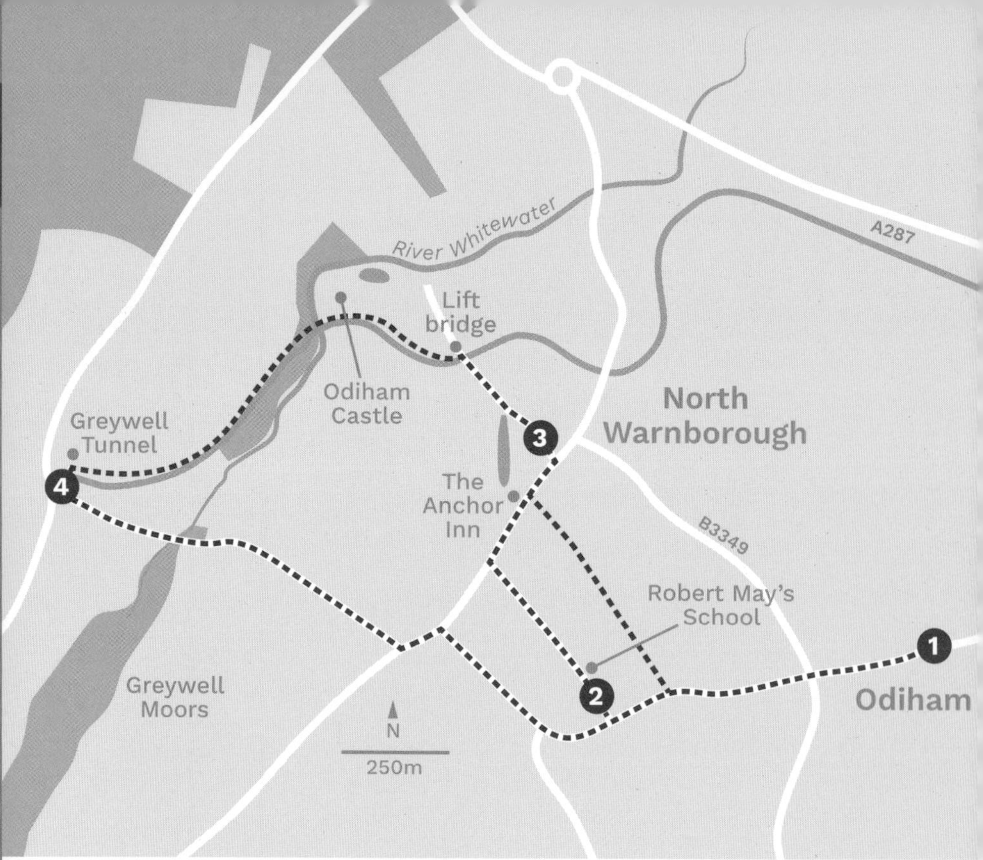

walk
27

River Whitewater
A287
Lift bridge
Odiham Castle
Greywell Tunnel
North Warnborough
The Anchor Inn
B3349
Robert May's School
Greywell Moors
Odiham
N
250m
1
2
3
4

3 Turn left into Tunnel Lane before the small roundabout and immediately after the fence to your left with posters advertising local events. Continue down the peaceful lane to the canal and lift road bridge. Cross the bridge, then turn left to follow the towpath with the canal on your left. Keep an eye out for ducks, swans and pond life. The towpath runs right past the ruins of Odiham Castle (known locally as King John's Castle), a fortress built in the early 1200s. There are few visible remains, just the octagonal keep and earthworks around the edge, but the castle was witness to more than a few significant events in its time. Shortly after passing the castle, the canal crosses the River Whitewater. Follow the towpath to the entrance to Greywell Tunnel; springs inside this tunnel provide a significant source of water for the canal. There is no public access to the tunnel anymore, and it now provides a home to a significant and protected bat colony – the largest in Britain, in fact. As a result, it is now designated a biological Site of Special Scientific Interest.

4 At the tunnel entrance the towpath ends at a short incline. Turn left there to cross above the tunnel entrance. Follow the short footpath that drops down onto Deptford Lane. Turn left, leaving the junction of Hook Road and The Street behind you. The route is uphill now until you get back to Robert May's School. Continue along Deptford Lane past an interesting mix of old and new houses. You will pass Greywell Moors on your right and then find yourself surrounded by fields. You also cross the River Whitewater again. (From here, you may choose to take one of the footpaths on the left to head back across fields to the other side of the towpath, then from the lift bridge retrace your footsteps back to the start). When you reach the end of Deptford Lane, turn left onto The Street (take care on the bend) and very soon turn right (both turns are signposted for Odiham). The path runs past the cow field on your left, and levels out as it passes the school again. You are now back on the outward route (at Waypoint 2). Continue until the path/road curves left; here you should cross to take the right fork onto West Street again. Continue forward, crossing the road near the small roundabout opposite a pub. Carry on to the left of the pub, to retrace your footsteps to Odiham High Street where this walk began.

An opening bascule bridge (a moveable bridge with a counterweight) on the Basingstoke Canal near Odiham Castle.

Notes of interest

★ If you find yourself with a little extra time once you return to the High Street at the end of this walk, you may wish to take a right turn into Church Street, just before the shops begin, to see some of the very old and beautiful architecture. Here you will also find the All Saints Church, some parts of which date to the 13th century, and the grim but interesting original punishment stocks and whipping post, thought to date from the 18th century.

★ The lift bridge is opened for boats to pass through in the summer – a fascinating sight.

★ The canal towpath ends near the closed Greywell Tunnel, which is now a haven for protected bats. Unless you are a night walker, you won't see them but species living here include Natterer's bat, Daubenton's bat, the brown long-eared bat, the whiskered bat and Brandt's bat.

walk
28

Westonbirt and the Arboretum, Gloucestershire

Time: 4 hrs | Distance: 13.8 km (8.6 miles) | Difficulty: ✪✪

Sherston, on the edge of the Cotswolds, is the starting point for this ramble. A number of fascinating 15th-century buildings line its broad High Street, so be sure to build in a little extra time to explore. Focusing on the famous Westonbirt Arboretum, this easy, mainly level walk will lead you over pasture and parkland, along paths and country lanes. Autumn brings the most spectacular and diverse blaze of gold, flame orange and scarlet to this world-famous tree collection. Particularly interesting in autumn are the katsura trees, the acer glade and the National Collection of maple trees.

Start location

High Street, Sherston, Wiltshire SN16 0LH (grid ref: ST853859).

Getting there

By car: Leave the M4 at Junction 18, take the A46 north, then turn right onto the A433. 2.4km (1.5 miles) beyond Didmarton and, just after The Holford Arms pub, take the minor road on the right to Sherston.

By public transport: The C62 bus runs between Mamesbury and Sherston, bus 69 runs from Stroud to Westonbirt and bus 620 from Bath connects with bus 69 to Westonbirt. Direct trains run from London, Reading, Swindon and Cheltenham to Stroud.

One of the finest international tree collections is to be found at Westonbirt Arboretum. It is home to more than 2,500 different species from all over the world.

1 The start of the walk takes you north, out of the High Street into Church Street, passing the Church of the Holy Cross on the left and the Rattlebone Inn on the right. The pleasingly evocative name of this pub is in fact in recognition of John Rattlebone, who defeated King Canute's army at the Battle of Sherston in 1016. Stay on the left side of the road and carry on past two small lay-bys. Opposite the second lay-by, look for a gravel drive leading to houses with the name 'Hunters Field' on a stone gatepost. Go up the drive keeping to the wall on the right which will guide you to a footpath and then, via a kissing gate, into a field. Keep on in the same direction across the field to pass through a second gate. A few metres ahead, cross over a stile to the road. Here, turn left onto a bridleway signposted for Knockdown Road and carry on for 200m. The bridleway enters a field, and you should walk ahead with the hedge on your right. Continue along a second field.

2 On entering the third field, walk for 50m then turn slightly left at a white post to walk across the field (not waymarked), heading for the farm gate on the far side. Here, exit to the road. Turn right and walk for 500m until you are just past a farm; now the road swings sharp left. Leave the tarmac here and proceed straight ahead along a track following the left boundary of the field; eventually, this track takes you past boarding kennels and onto the main Tetbury road. Cross the road with care, to reach a metal field gate. Pass through, and walk up the field keeping to the left boundary until you reach the entrance to Westonbirt Arboretum.

3 Continue on the public footpath as it follows the broad drive ahead for 1km (½ mile). There are many interesting tree species to see without any need to deviate from this route. At the north end of the drive, you will reach a T-junction. Cross over and proceed ahead along a well-marked grass path into trees where almost immediately you reach a waymarker post. Turn right here and look for the next waymarker post slightly right of centre; aim for this, then follow the broad, winding path through mixed woodland, veering to the left slightly. Although away from the 'tourist' paths, and indistinct at first, the strategically placed waymarker posts will keep you on track. Where the path makes a definite curve to the right, you will reach cross-paths. Turn left here and look for bird box 33 attached to a larch tree on your left to confirm you are in the correct place. Now go ahead downhill, following an indistinct path to a squeezer stile. Cross this into downland.

4 Now climb the well-worn path up the hillock in front of you, passing under a stand of beech trees and continuing with the wall to your left until you reach a wooden gate. Here, go through the gate to exit the park. Keep walking in the same direction over a succession of fields, keeping the low, moss-covered walls of the arboretum on your right. As you cross the third field, you will notice on your right a broad avenue stretching across the arboretum. Beyond this you can see the tower of Westonbirt School; this is no coincidence as the grand-looking school was once the home of Sir George Holford (see Notes of Interest on page 153). As you climb the stile to leave the fifth field, you part company with the arboretum wall. Go ahead now along the edge of a large paddock, keeping the wall on your left. Leave the paddock via a stile at a road junction.

Before you start

* If you wish to add a visit to Westonbirt House and Gardens to your walk, be sure to check opening times online. Visiting is only possible on particular days, and both house and garden visits are guided tours which must be pre-booked.

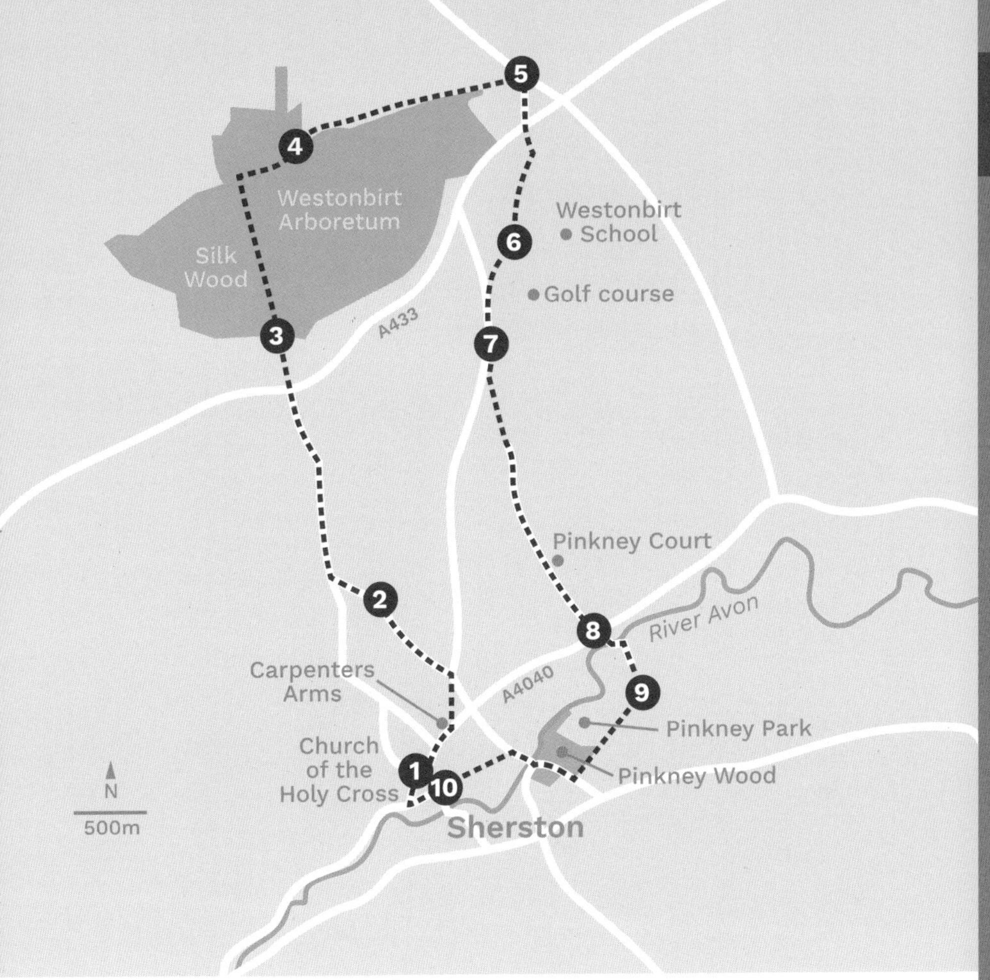

5 Turn right now, with the paddock wall to your right, and walk the short distance to the main road. Take care as you cross this busy road and go through a wooden gate into a field. Here, bear very slightly right, passing under power lines and keeping the nearest pole to your left. Head towards the right edge of the clump of trees on the horizon, passing a water trough to your right; ahead, you will see a gate in the fence. Follow the waymarker sign there directing you slightly to the right of the woodland ahead. When you reach a tarmac driveway, look left to enjoy a view of the imposing structure of Westonbirt School. The historic Westonbirt House, with its 120m façade, is now part of the school which was founded in 1928.

6 To the right, the drive curves away to the entrance gate. Your route lies ahead, along another driveway that crosses the parkland leaving the school away to the left. The drive carries you onto a lane by cottages, where you should go ahead through the wooden gate next to a metal farm gate. The path beyond climbs gently with a wire fence on the right and a copse on the left, which soon gives way to a golf course. At the end of the path, pass through the wooden gate and turn right for a few metres to meet the road. Walk left along the

Historic Westonbirt House is open to the public only on certain days. Since 1928 it has been occupied by the independent Westonbirt School.

road, passing Park Farm on the right; ignore a fork off to the left, but immediately after, look for a footpath sign. Here, climb the stone stile on the left. After 200m and several stiles, you will come to a stone stile offering you a return to the road; ignore this but instead climb the low wall on your left into a field. This 200m section can sometimes be overgrown. If it is impassable, carry on along the road for 200m to join the path via a stone stile on your left. Walk diagonally over the centre of this field, aiming for the left end of a row of trees crossing the field from the right. This field may be cropped in summer and is frequently muddy in winter.

7 The trees follow the line of a driveway. When you reach this, continue ahead on the driveway keeping to the right and entering the yard. The right of way is narrow, running between the green metal fence and the hedge. At the end of the metal fence, climb a low, wooden barrier and continue to the stone stile next to the farm gate, which gives access to the road. Walk left along this road for about 1.3km (3/4 mile), passing the fine old buildings of Pinkney Court on the left. The road descends gently to a junction.

8 Cross the junction and follow the lane ahead down to the Sherston branch of the River Avon. Walk over the bridge, then up the lane alongside old stone walls. The lane climbs past farm buildings, then degenerates into a track. Keeping the stone wall to your right, follow the track ahead up the hill until you reach a metal gate into a field. Walk on, with a fence and then a wall on your right, which you follow round to the right to pass through the high, iron gate into Pinkney Park.

9 The track ahead runs in a roughly straight line for 700m, passing Pinkney Wood on the right, before emerging onto a lane. Turn right here and follow the lane down to a junction by the river. Go right, crossing the river bridge and climb the road passing a buttressed wall on the right. Soon after, opposite the entrance to Lower Farm on the right, look left for steps which you climb to a kissing gate. Go slightly right across the pasture, passing the back corner of a stone barn on your right, to climb a stile in the wooden fence ahead. Continue, picking up the stone wall on the right to reach the field corner. Here, ignore the kissing gate on the right leading to a lane, but take a similar gate ahead and walk along the edge of the next field, with the backs of houses on your right. At the far end of the field carry straight on along a tarmac footpath and go ahead between the houses, ignoring the short path to your right. You should emerge onto a residential road.

10 Cross the road and continue on the footpath which soon descends via steps to a road. Cross and climb the steps on the far side to reach a lane and go ahead to the methodist chapel on the right. Here, turn left along the lane until it meets a road junction. Now turn right and walk up Brook Hill, which in a few metres brings you to the southern end of Sherston High Street. You have now reached the end of your walk.

Notes of interest

★ The Westonbirt Arboretum tree collection was started in 1829 when Robert Holford began planting oaks, pines and yews in open fields close to what is now the visitors' centre. His son, Sir George Holford, took up the work from 1875 and extended the planting of exotic trees into the established woodland. Sir George's nephew, the fourth Earl Morley, carried on the collection from 1926 and the arboretum continued to expand, but the war years and subsequent neglect through shortage of labour saw a decline in the park's fortunes. In 1956, the Forestry Commission acquired Westonbirt from the fifth Earl Morley with the objective of establishing a specialist scientific collection. There are now over 14,000 trees and shrubs spread out over 200 hectares of woodland.

walk 29

Tintern and Offa's Dyke, Wye Valley

Time: 3 hrs 30 mins | Distance: 10.8 km (6.7 miles) | Difficulty: ✪✪✪

This beautiful walk gives you a taste of the tremendous beauty to be found in the Wye Valley. The route follows woodland tracks and paths – some are rough underfoot, and the riverside stretch can be muddy. There are a couple of steep ascents and a little road walking.

Start location

Tintern Abbey car park, Tintern, Monmouthshire NP16 6SE (grid ref: SO530008).

Getting there

By car: Tintern is on the A466 road up the Wye Valley between Chepstow and Monmouth. The car park is well signed off the main road, right next to the extremely prominent Abbey ruins. If the car park is full, or you prefer to park for free, there is a second car park to be found up Forge Road next to The Wild Hare in the village. (This is on the site of the old wireworks and there are interesting plaques along the wall explaining the site.) If starting here, take the path from the bottom of the car park down to the main road, turn left to Abbey Mill and pick up the instructions from there.
By public transport: Bus service 69 from Chepstow to Monmouth, which passes close to Chepstow Railway Station, stops in Tintern. There is a stop at the Abbey ruins. The service runs seven days a week with a reduced service on Sundays – check online for details.

1 From the Tintern Abbey car park, take the riverside path with the River Wye on your right and continue along a lane between cottages, turning left to reach the main road. Turn right and walk past Abbey Mill, then immediately turn right again towards the river and cross over the steel pedestrian bridge (the Wireworks Bridge).

Not always a pedestrian bridge, this once carried a tramway from the local ironworks situated along the Angidy Valley that runs into Tintern from the west.

2 Beyond the bridge, follow the old trackbed into woodland to a path junction. Go right, along a path to the left of a wooden gate with a private sign, and then continue ahead, parallel with the riverbank down to your right. On reaching a path junction, look to your left to locate a tunnel entrance. It is here that the Wireworks line joined the main Wye Valley Railway. Turn right along the old trackbed, which you will now follow for some distance. It eventually begins a long, gradual ascent through a cutting and arrives at a fork. Turn left at the fork, following a broad track that runs up to the left, leaving the railway. Keep on the main track as it doubles back on itself round a sharp left bend and continues climbing to reach a T-junction with a broad track coming downhill from the right.

3 Take a couple of paces right and look for the start of a small path on the opposite side of the track. Follow this, and you will start climbing through woodland. The path is easy to follow and leads directly up the hill, veering right before meeting an obvious cross-path. Go left at this point, keeping on the main path, to reach a junction where a path goes right up wooden steps. Unfortunately, there may no longer be any waymarking on this section, but

Tintern Abbey, roofless but resplendent amongst hills of spectacular autumn foliage. The Abbey sits on the Welsh bank of the River Wye.

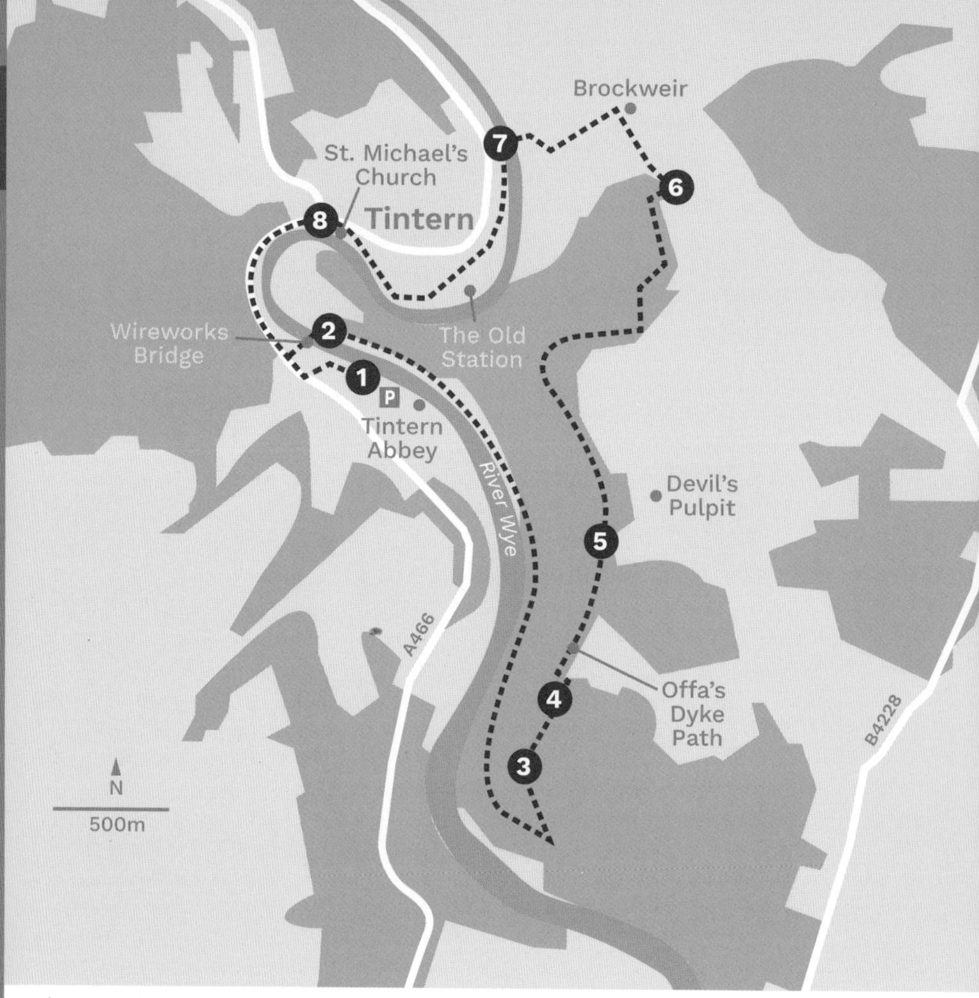

the paths are clear and if you concentrate on the instructions all should be straightforward.

4 Take this path up to the right, climbing up rough steps and then doubling back left, after which you should go right again with views of the river ahead (as long as the trees are bare). Continue to a further waymarker post, this one bearing the acorn symbol of the Offa's Dyke Path (see Notes of Interest on page 159). You will follow this route for a while. Turn left and follow the clear, well-made path. Pass through stone pillars into a wood. By a waymarker post you will reach an amazing view point down to the Abbey ruins below.

Continue on the path to a second view point, where a plaque on the rock informs you that you have arrived at the Devil's Pulpit. Legend has it that the devil taunted the monks from this rock pinnacle, which overlooks the Wye and the Abbey. On the right of the path is an extraordinary old yew tree growing around a large rock.

The Abbey was founded in 1131 by Cistercian monks, and it was the subject of alterations and additions that continued into the 14th century. The Cistercians were often known as 'white monks' because their habits were woven from coarse, undyed wool – a visible reminder of their

North of Tintern sits Brockweir, a beautiful small village nestled alongside the River Wye on the Gloucestershire side of the river.

vow of poverty. Monastic life ceased here in 1536 with the Dissolution of the Monasteries.

5 Continue on the main path to reach a path junction and metal kissing gate, where a wooden signpost gives directions to Brockweir, Tintern and St Briavels. Follow this route, easy walking now, to a junction where the Tintern path descends left. Go ahead here, signed 'Brockweir and St Briavels'. Eventually you come alongside a field on the right, then the path veers away down to the left. Continue, descending to cross-paths. Here, go on ahead, then turn right at a field corner to climb a stile a little further ahead.

6 A short distance further, at the next Offa's Dyke acorn sign a few feet beyond a stile on the right, leave the Offa's Dyke path and take a small path (not waymarked) down to the left. This soon emerges from trees into the top of a field. Below, you can see Brockweir and its bridge, with a whitewashed house standing alone to the right of the village. Head down the field towards the house, picking up the field boundary on the left. Go through some undergrowth in the bottom corner and cross a stile by a gate under a tree. Continue down the following field, keeping to the hedge on the left to a gateway at the bottom. (When last seen, the gate is off its hinges, lying on the grass.)

Turn left onto a track and follow this to a lane at the bottom – here you turn right and walk down to the road. Turn left here, then carry on ahead to cross the river via the road bridge.

7 On the far side, before the main road, descend concrete steps on the left to the railway path. Follow this to reach Tintern Station.

The Wye Valley Railway passed through Tintern in the 1870s, with the plan that the picturesque line would attract tourists. Unfortunately, the tourists never arrived in the droves that had been hoped for and, although this station had two platforms sharing three tracks, plus a goods yard and sidings, the Wye Valley Railway succumbed to the inevitable and closed in January 1959. In recent years however, the old station has taken on a new lease of life as a bustling café, with displays of the line's history and other items of local interest in some old carriages, as well as plenty of play areas and things of interest for children (should you happen to have some in your company).

Leaving the station behind, continue along the walkway as far as the river, where you will see a turntable for the miniature railway. Here, you have to descend to the riverbank down steps on the right. (The railway crossed an old bridge here, then plunged directly into a tunnel.) Pass through a pair of gates at the bottom of the steps and walk on with the river on your left. Take care here after heavy rain or if the river has been in flood, as the path can be extremely muddy. Follow the footpath to reach St Michael's Church at Tintern Parva (meaning

'little Tintern'.) Continue through the churchyard to a lane and fork left between cottages to reach the road. Turn left.

8 The remainder of your walk lies along this road. This last kilometre (½ mile) leads you past some interesting buildings, shops and opportunities for refreshment, and with the river always in sight it makes a fitting end to this excursion into the Wye Valley. Narrow footpaths at some points mean that you must cross the road with care on a couple of occasions, but you will soon find yourself back at Abbey Mill (now on your left), beyond which you take the lane down to the riverbank again and on to your original start point at the car park.

Tintern's Grade II listed former Wireworks Bridge, which crosses the River Wye from Monmouthshire into Gloucestershire. Originally built as a railway bridge, it is now only for pedestrian use.

Notes of interest

★ Tintern was not always the rural setting that one might imagine. In the 1560s engineers looking for a site for the manufacture of iron and brass for ordnance purposes found that the village offered all that was required; water power, fuel, minerals and the Wye for transportation. Britain's first brass was produced at Tintern, but the brass works soon became the wireworks with around 100 local men working there. For 300 years the valley was full of wireworks and forges. But the Industrial Revolution heralded the end of all this business, and by the close of the 19th century all the works had shut their doors.

★ The Offa's Dyke Path is the only National Trail to follow a man-made feature. Most historians believe the construction of the dyke was ordered by Offa, King of Mercia, between 757 and 796 CE, although there is a recent theory that the work extended through the reigns of more than one Mercian ruler. The dyke is a large earthwork that formed a rough boundary between the Anglian kingdom of Mercia and the Welsh kingdom of Powys, either for defence or simply to show the dividing line between the two kingdoms. It stretched 240km (182 miles) from Prestatyn in the north to Sedbury, near Chepstow, in the south. Men from the border country along the Mercian side were all required to contribute to its construction in one of two ways; they had the option to send food for the workers or to build a section of the earthwork themselves.

walk 30

Strumble Head, Pembrokeshire

Time: 4 hrs 24 mins | Distance: 14.2 km (8.8 miles) | Difficulty: ✪✪✪✪

A glorious circular route, heading out from one of the Youth Hostel Association's (YHA) most spectacularly located properties at Pwll Deri. You will be walking in a hamlet named Harmony and visiting the site of the last invasion of Britain, before returning along one of the finest stretches of the Pembrokeshire Coast Path.

Start location

Pwll Deri Youth Hostel, Goodwick, Pembrokeshire, SA64 0LR (grid ref: SM893388).

Getting there

By car: Take the Pwll Deri road out of Goodwick, and keep following signs for Pwll Deri. From the St David's–Fishguard Road, approach via St Nicholas. The hostel is near the end of a dead-end road. Parking there is limited and only for those staying at the hostel. There is a good parking area on the right side of the road a couple of hundred metres before the hostel, opposite a view point with some benches. Alternatively, there is plenty of parking at Strumble Head, from where you can begin the walk from Waypoint 6.

By public transport: The YHA is not reachable by bus, but in summer you can use the 404 Strumble Shuttle service to reach Strumble Head, from where you can begin at Waypoint 6.

Strumble Head, within the Pembrokeshire Coast National Park, marks the southern limit of Cardigan Bay. This rugged, rocky section of coast was formed by volcanic activity.

1 From the top of the hostel's driveway, cross the road and take the most left of two driveways opposite, to Pwll Deri holiday cottages. Immediately after passing a white cottage on the left, go left to a wooden gate on the right that leads you onto the open hillside. Go slightly right, uphill, on a path for about 30m then turn right by a wooden marker post. Follow the small path which climbs gradually through bracken to a stile. Cross it and continue on the clear path to another stile. Cross this and follow the wall on your right to a stone stile in a corner. Climb this as well, then go downhill, keeping in the same direction you have been following. You will reach a stile in a wire fence on the right. Cross this, then go through the wooden gate immediately beyond and follow an enclosed path that passes left of a cottage to a T-junction. Now turn left and follow the grassy path running between hedges up to a road.

2 Turn right and follow the road downhill to a T-junction at the hamlet of Harmony, named for a large Baptist chapel that was built here in 1913. (You can see the chapel, and an interesting graveyard, if you carry on round the bend in the road for a short distance where the route turns left up the track.) Go left for about 100m, then take the good track you will see going left at a right bend. Keep on this, ignoring a right turn you see soon and continuing uphill. Ignore a track going left to a house and campsite at the end and keep straight on, squeezing along the right side of a garage with blue doors to reach a wooden gate into a field.

3 Follow the hedge on your right for a short distance to reach a track coming through a gate on the right. Turn left on this. After about 20m go straight over a cross track and keep straight on along a smaller path. When this splits, after about 30m, take the left branch.

Before you start

⁂ This area of the coast is a fine wildlife-watching area, so do take binoculars along if you have them. An old wartime lookout post at Strumble Head has been converted to a bird hide where you can spend some time watching comfortably. There is a good chance you will see some seals on the coastal section of the walk, and maybe dolphins further out. As well as the usual array of sea birds on the cliffs, look out for choughs (pronounced 'chuffs'.) These look like small black crows but have bright red legs and beaks. You may see them on the path ahead of you as they hop around looking for insects on rocks. Until a few were recently reintroduced to the Cornish coast, this was the only place on the British mainland where you could see them.

One of the top birding sites in Pembrokeshire, more than 200 species have been recorded at Strumble Head, including the red-billed chough (below), storm petrels, gannets and various skuas.

Soon you will reach a bridleway fingerpost sign on your right. Keep straight on to a second marker post; this directs you straight on along a track between hedges. Follow this track to a gate with a T-junction immediately beyond. Turn right on this pleasant grassy path and continue along it. After a while, this turns left then goes through a gate on the right into open country. (The area to your left here is called the North Pole! Legend has it that a cottage here was built from the timbers of a ship called the 'North Pole' that sank off Strumble Head.) Keep straight on alongside the boundary on your left to reach a T-junction by a marker post. Go left through a wooden gate and follow the good track downhill. When you reach farm buildings, go slightly left to a gap between stone barns then right down to a road.

4 Turn right along the road for about 400m then go left through a white gate and down the driveway to Tre-Howel. At the bottom turn right through another white gate then keep straight ahead, following the footpath signs, through cattle pens. (If there are cattle in the pens, do be patient and co-operate with any instructions from the farmers. There is a way through without having to come into direct contact with the cattle if you follow the waymarkers precisely.) Follow the track beyond which soon turns left. Ignore a right turn and keep straight on through a gate and downhill

Porthsychan is one of many small inlets that lie along the Pembrokeshire Coast Path, north of Strumble Head. Seals are often spotted here.

A memorial stone to poet Dewi Emrys at Pwll Deri on the coast of North Pembrokeshire. His poem 'Pwll Deri' is an ode to this precise landscape.

along a wide, hedged track to reach three metal gates. Take the right-most one and continue on the track; it soon swings right. A bit further on the hedges give way to wire fencing. Go through the left-most of two metal gates ahead and keep straight on with the hedge on your right for nearly 100m to a fingerpost sign. Head diagonally left here, keeping a large clump of gorse just to your right. You will see a large standing stone ahead, aim for this. On getting close to the stone, you will see an impenetrable wire fence ahead. Just before this, head right a little to find a wooden gate in the fence. Go through this and up to the stone, which is a memorial to the last foreign invasion of Britain (see Notes of Interest, right).

5 You will now be following the coast path all the way back to the start. Turn left on this and follow it with the sea to your right. It is well waymarked with the National Trail acorns and easy to follow. Just ignore all paths turning left to head inland. At Porthsychan (the dry harbour) you will see a small path going right for a short distance, down to a small, pebbly beach. This is a wonderful place for a rest, and maybe a paddle if the mood takes you. After just over 4km (2.5 miles) of wonderful walking you will reach a road, turn right here and carry on along to where it ends at Strumble Head.

6 At the end of the road there is a large car park on the left and at the back of it a signpost indicates where the coast path continues. Again, this path is very easy to follow. Having rounded a headland, the sea below is often rougher here than on the other side of Strumble Head. After another 4km (2.5 miles) of glorious coastal walking the huge cliffs beyond Pwll Deri come into view and the path makes a left turn to begin a long ascent back to your start point at the Pwll Deri Youth Hostel.

Notes of interest

★ Strumble Head is one of the famous beauty spots on the Pembrokeshire coast. It is also an excellent location for observing wildlife. This has long been a dangerous area for shipping – the lighthouse, built in 1908, sits on a small island that is connected to the mainland by a footbridge. The lighthouse was automated in 1980 and is now a Grade II-listed building.

★ The memorial stone you see during Stage 4 of this walk marks the place where, in February 1797, French soldiers landed. This is regarded as the most recent invasion of Britain by foreign troops. It was one of three planned landings, though only this one actually took place. The plan was supposedly to stir Celtic grievances against the English and provoke uprisings, but the locals here were not interested in taking part. On landing, the soldiers set up headquarters at Tre-Howel farm and were told to live off the land. Discipline soon broke down as many of the conscripts went off to loot local settlements where they got drunk and then deserted their posts. The French commanders soon had to surrender, and the invasion was over.

★ The coast path is part of the Pembrokeshire Coast Path, a National Trail created in 1970. It runs for 299km (186 miles), with about 10,600m of ascent, along the length of the county's coastline, which is one of the finest stretches in Britain. In 2012 the path was incorporated into the Wales Coast Path.

winter

Don't let the short winter days trap you indoors – spending as much time out in nature as you can is key to enjoying this stunning season. Weather can be unsettled, wet and windy, and temperatures drop, but frosts make the landscape glitter in low morning sunlight and some of Britain's most wonderful wildlife can be spotted on winter walks. Remote or high terrain may be more challenging for less experienced walkers during winter, and days are shorter, but there are plenty of opportunities to get out and see something new.

walk
31

Birnam Oak, Perth and Kinross

Time: **3 hrs 30 mins** | Distance: **10.4 km (6.5 miles)** | Difficulty: ✪✪

A pleasant stroll from Birnam along the banks of the River Tay, past ancient trees including the Birnam Oak (a survivor from the Birnam Wood Shakespeare refers to in *Macbeth*), which has an incredible 5.5m girth. This route leads through The Hermitage at Dunkeld, past Ossian's Hall and Cave, before looping back round through woodland to Birnam. The walk begins at Beatrix Potter Garden, which is decorated with the famous characters from the beloved children's books. Beatrix Potter was inspired to write the books by the wildlife she saw during her summer holidays to Dalguise with her parents.

Start location

Beatrix Potter Garden, Birnam, Perth and Kinsross PH8 0BN (grid ref: NO030417).

Getting there

By car: By road Birnam is just off the A9 north of Perth. There is limited parking at Birnam Arts Centre.

By public transport: Birnam Station is on the railway line between Perth and Inverness. Check Scotrail for train times. There is also a bus service to Birnam from Perth – for information, check online.

1 This walk commences at Beatrix Potter Garden, by the Arts Centre in Birnam. Cross the road towards the Birnam Hotel then head down the road, on the right of the hotel, signposted 'Birnam Path (to Birnam Oak)'. Go left and follow the footpath down to the River Tay. Turn left again and walk along the river past the famous Birnam Oak tree. Follow the path by the river under Thomas Telford's Bridge. Turn right at the path junction, following the sign to Inver and Fiddler's Paths, then walk on under the A9.

2 Turn right and cross a footbridge over the River Braan, which is signposted to Inver. Keep left and follow the path until you reach the single-track road, turn right following the sign 'Inver Paths to Hermitage' – this will take you through Inver and back up to the A9. This path now runs parallel to the A9 for a short distance. Go left into the lower Hermitage car park and follow the lower path, which is signposted 'Braan Paths', up to Ossian's Hall (a folly built in 1782–3 to enhance the view of the falls in the River Braan). After a short stop to admire the view, you should carry on up the path past the Coin Tree – a tree stump embedded with coins – to Ossian's Cave. This is another folly, which was added by the Duke of Atholl. Continue walking up the path through the trees until you reach a gap in a wall. Turn left here, following the signpost to the Rumbling Bridge which spans a gorge over the River Braan. Go through the gate and then turn left down the single-track road.

3 Now cross the Rumbling Bridge and, after 50m, go left on a path through the trees signposted as the 'Braan Path'. This path goes through the trees, and you will pass a car park on your right and an information sign. Keep left

The frosted beauty of bare, wintry branches is a splendid sight as you make your way along the path through the woodland near Birnam.

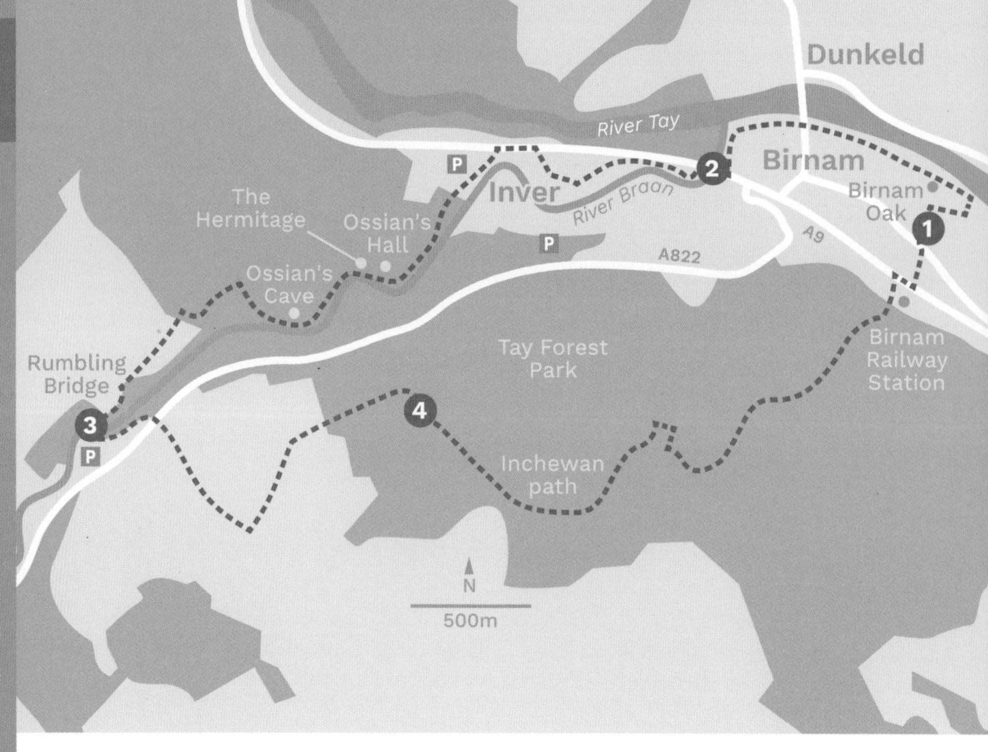

and continue straight along this path until you reach a road. Cross over this road and continue up the farm track opposite to a turning on your left signposted for Braan and Inchewan paths. Go left here and follow the path, forking right at waymarker signs to a T-junction just after crossing a bridge and going through a high gate.

4 Go right at the T-junction following the Inchewan path and the waymarker signs. The track climbs up and bends round to the left before descending down to a large junction of forestry tracks. Go right here, following the Inchewan path sign. After a short while look out for the waymarker arrow and bear right on a small path below the forestry track. Follow this path through the woods to a path junction. Now turn left and follow the track down towards Birnam. Go through a gate, bearing left and looking out to your right for the sign towards the railway station. Join the path here to head under the railway line and A9, then turn sharply right to take you between houses and the A9. Go left at the end of the path and continue down Station Road, and then left to reach your start point at Beatrix Potter Garden once more.

Notes of interest

★ Thomas Telford's Dunkeld Bridge was a revolutionary design when it was built in the early 19th century. The bridge replaced the ferries, which were dangerous way of crossing when the river ran high.

Spanning the River Tay, Thomas Telford's famous Dunkeld Bridge carries both pedestrians and traffic over its seven arches. The bridge was built between 1805 and 1809.

The iconic Birnam Oak, sometimes referred to as 'Macbeth's Oak', is thought to be around 600 years old. The lower three metres of its trunk are hollow, and the lower branches supported.

walk
32

Loch Trool, Galloway

Time: **5 hrs** | Distance: **8.9 km (5.5 miles)** | Difficulty: ✪✪✪

A pleasant and enjoyable walk around Loch Trool, one of the highlights of the Galloway Forest Park. You will follow waymarked hard-surface paths and tracks, with some walking through the trees. Early on the route, you will pass the site of the Battle of Trool, where Robert the Bruce defeated the English Army in 1307, despite being outnumbered by five to one (see Notes of Interest on page 174). Plenty of fine views of the loch and surrounding countryside can be enjoyed from the Southern Upland Way (SUW), and you will see and hear burns and waterfalls flowing down from the hills into the woodlands. Keep an eye out for redstarts and roe deer in among the oak trees.

Start location

Glen Trool car park, Galloway DG8 6FA (grid ref: NX397790).

Getting there

By car: From Newton Stewart take the A714 to Girvan, turning right at Bargrennan to Glen Trool village. Follow the signs to Glen Trool Visitor Centre. Go past the visitor centre and continue to follow the road for 3km (1.5miles). Take the first tarred road on your right to reach a car park just before a bridge.

A patchwork of stunning colours surrounds Loch Trool during the day, but at night it is reportedly the darkest place in the UK – the perfect spot for stargazing.

1 From the Glen Trool car park, head out along the road across the Water of Trool bridge and almost immediately you will pick up the green waymarkers of the SUW, which comes in from the right. Follow these waymarkers to turn left past Caldon's House and continue uphill along the SUW into conifers on the steep southern side of Loch Trool. There are view points along the way that offer views over Loch Trool to the Fell of Eschoncan and Buchan Hill, foothills of The Merrick. Near the head of the loch you pass the site of the Battle of Trool.

The beautiful old trees you will see as you pass Caldon's House are the remnants of ancient woodlands with which Glen Trool was once covered.

2 Once you have crossed the bridge at the head of Loch Trool, leave the SUW on a path that goes left and takes you up to a track back along the northern shore of the loch to the turn-off to the car park. The route winds up through Buchan and Glenhead Woods back to your start point at the car park. If you fancy a little bit extra, from the car park at Buchan Bridge, a short detour towards the lake brings you to a view point and the Bruce's Stone, a massive granite boulder commemorating Robert the Bruce's victory at the Battle of Glen Trool.

Bruce's Stone is a cairn erected in 1929 on the 600th anniversary of Bruce's death. It is inscribed: 'In loyal remembrance of Robert the Bruce, King of Scots, whose victory in this glen over an English force in March 1307, opened the campaign of independence which he brought to a decisive close at Bannockburn on 24 June 1314.' Bruce's Stone sits at the view point looking out over the loch, which is believed most likely to have been the battle site.

Notes of interest

★ Some historians slightly dismissively describe the Battle of Glen Trool as being a skirmish rather than a battle, but regardless it was one of the early victories for Robert the Bruce in the First Wars of Independence against Edward I and the English. Bruce had crowned himself King of Scotland in 1306, but there were plenty (especially the English) who violently opposed this claim, and Bruce and his supporters were forced into hiding. In 1307 they established a base at Glen Trool, taking cover in the hills and launching surprise attacks. Bruce's precise location was a mystery to the English troops, but in March 1307 at Glen Trool he and his small army of 300 managed to lure the force of 1,500 English heavy cavalry along the steeply sloping banks of the loch. Bruce's army climbed up above, and they ambushed the English soldiers by hurling boulders down onto the them, knocking them into the water and forcing those remaining to flee.

★ A trail from this walk also leads up to the highest summit in southern Scotland – The Merrick. It takes roughly another 4–5 hours to reach this peak of the Galloway Ranges, from where one can see out all across the Galloway Forest as well as over to the Isle of Man and Northern Ireland.

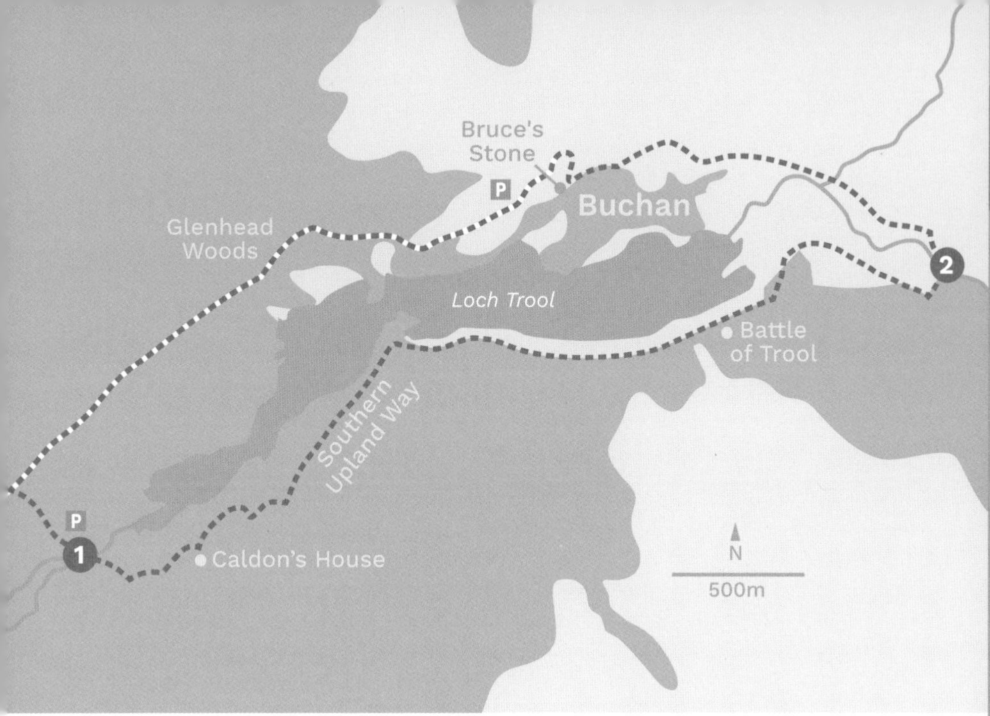

walk
32

Bruce's Stone
Buchan
Glenhead Woods
Loch Trool
Battle of Trool
Southern Upland Way
Caldon's House
N
500m

Bruce's Stone perches in a fantastically serene vantage point overlooking the gleaming waters of the loch and the rolling hills further on, surrounded by woodland, streams and waterfalls.

The Wirral, Merseyside

Time: 2 hrs 15 mins | Distance: 7.3 km (4.6 miles) | Difficulty: ✪✪

This varied circular walk from West Kirby takes in Grange Hill and Caldy Hill. There are spectacular views of Liverpool Bay, across to the Pennines and over to North Wales before dropping down into Caldy village, onto the Wirral Way and around the Marine Lake.

Start location

West Kirby Railway Station, West Kirby, Wirral CH48 4DZ (grid ref: SJ213868)

Getting there

By car: Pay and display parking is available behind the railway station in the concourse car park. Also next to Morrisons supermarket in Dee Lane (postcode CH48 0QA), which is on the route. Turn right along Dee Lane for a short distance to reach the station.

By public transport: West Kirby Station is at the terminus of the Wirral Line on the Merseyrail network. Trains to Liverpool are every 15 minutes during the day and every 30 minutes at quieter times. West Kirby is served by numerous local bus services. Check online for details.

Before you start

* West Kirby has a range of pubs, shops and cafés, should you be in need of refreshment.

1 Facing the railway station, turn right along Grange Road. Soon you will pass the entrance to the Wirral Way and the Wirral Country Park on your right. Continue on the road up the hill past Brookfield Road on your right, then carry on up the hill passing Darmond's Green, Ashburton Road, Heatherdene Road and Gerard Road on your left. Soon after passing a fifth road on your left, Homestead Mews, go left on the public footpath signed to the War Memorial. Follow this path, turning left at the top of the sandstone steps, then continue to the War Memorial to enjoy some spectacular views. Continue on the path around the memorial and remain on the level path as you continue, leaving the memorial behind you. This leads onto the narrow path around Grange Hill House. This all-accessible wheelchair-friendly path will bring you to Grange Old Road.

2 Turn left along Grange Old Road for a short distance and follow it round a right bend back to the main road, Column Road. Using the central reservation crossing points, cross over the start of Blackhorse Hill, and continue on Column Road. Immediately beyond Village Road, turn right just before the end of a wall onto a paved footpath that runs parallel to Column Road and leads straight up to the Mariners' Column.

The Mariners' Column was built in 1841 by the trustees of Liverpool docks to replace an old windmill that had been a useful navigation aid for mariners entering the Mersey Estuary, but had been destroyed by a storm in 1839. Note the old millstone at the base of the column which is a relic from the old windmill.

Caldy Beach offers long views out across the River Dee estuary. Keep an eye out for high tide if you venture down onto the sand.

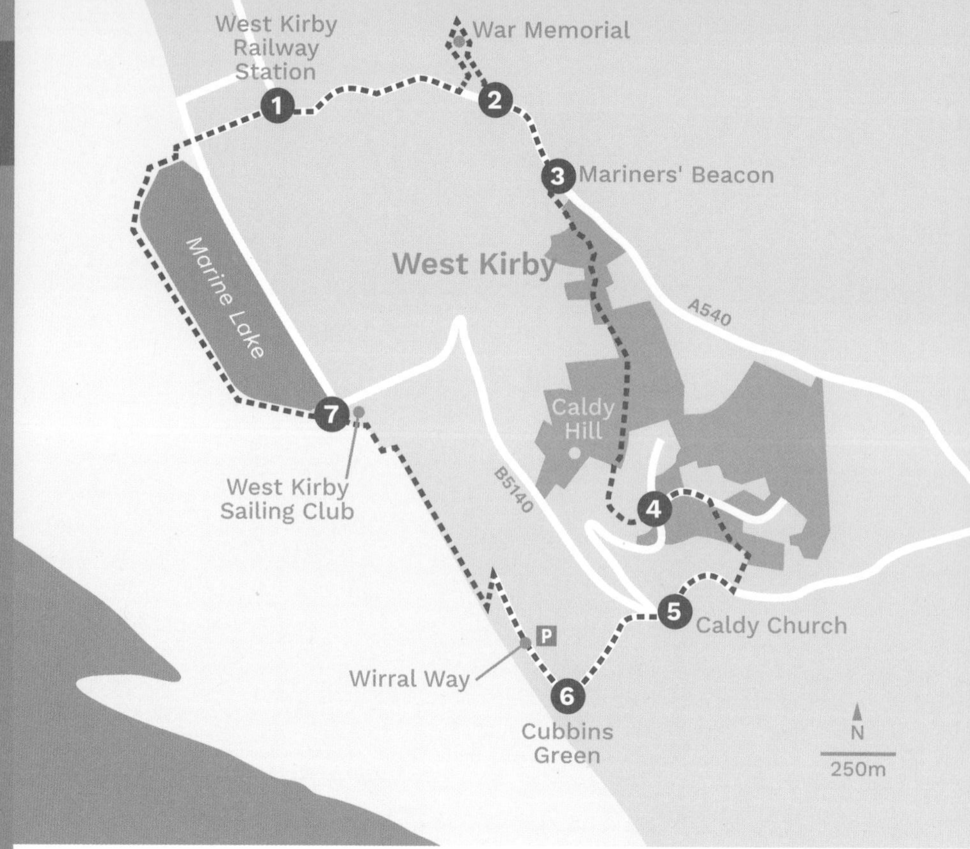

3 Follow the public footpath straight on. There are numerous small paths leading off the main path. Continue on the natural main path ahead along the length of Caldy Hill, past a set of old gate posts and over a rocky outcrop. Take the right fork past the fenced white house on your right, past the yellow fire hydrant on your left and over the brow of the hill to where the hill opens out onto managed heathland. There are some great views from the seats along here, particularly the seat by the Peak and Northern Footpath Society fingerpost sign. Continue along, again following the main natural path ahead for some distance until you pass through a gap in an old sandstone wall. Continue past the pine trees, through another gap in the wall to a gate and walk straight ahead to reach a road junction with Thorsway to the left and Kings Drive straight on.

4 Go straight on along the verge of Kings Drive. After about 150m, immediately after the white buildings of Pine Ridge, take the public bridleway (locally known as Fleck Lane) on the right and go down the hill. At Caldy Road be sure to take particular care due to lack of visibility. Turn right and walk along past the old hospital on the right into Caldy village.

5 Pass the church and go round a right bend. Then, on reaching the War Memorial on the right, fork left down the short bridleway to a road, Croft Drive, at a bend. Turn right (effectively continuing straight on) and walk along Croft Drive to the entrance to Wirral Country Park.

At high tide on the Dee estuary this wooden jetty provides access from the Marine Lake to moored yachts

6 Turn right immediately before the abutments of an old railway bridge and follow the Wirral Way along the old railway until you reach a small bridge on the left. This takes you over a ditch and onto Cubbins Green with delightful views across the Dee estuary and West Kirby Marine Lake. Walk along the cliff-edge path past the bench and picnic area. At the end of Cubbins Green you will come to Macdona Drive. Take to the beach here and head towards West Kirby Sailing Club. If the tide is high or the sea is rough, it is possible to avoid the beach by heading down Macdona Drive and turning left to the promenade at Sandy Lane.

7 At the promenade, go left and take the path clockwise around the Marine Lake. At the far end of the lake you will reach the bottom of Dee Lane, which you should follow to return to the start. If the sea is rough, or you want a slightly shorter alternative, follow South Parade along the right side of Marine Lake to reach Dee Lane.

Notes of interest

★ The Wirral Way follows the line of the old railway route to Hooton. Built in 1866, the railway was closed in 1962 and developed in the early 1970s as Wirral Country Park. There was a Caldy Station near the old bridge abutments. It was a little inconvenient for the village but a local landowner objected to the original intended course of the line; this resulted in the station being much closer to the coast than was planned.

walk
34

Bradgate Country Park, Leicestershire

Time: 2 hrs | Distance: 6.6 km (4.1 miles) | Difficulty: ✪✪

This circular walk leads you through Bradgate Park, which offers wonderful views of Leicestershire. Bradgate Park covers an area of over 300 hectares and, during the Middle Ages, was a deer-hunting park for the Lord of Groby Manor. You may well glimpse red and fallow deer among the abundant flora and fauna, as well as seeing some of the oldest and youngest rocks in England, which were created by volcanic activity. The estate was owned by the Grey family and Lady Jane Grey was born in the now-ruined Bradgate House. In 1928 Charles Bennion gifted the park to the people of Leicestershire, for them to enjoy in perpetuity.

Start location

Bradgate Road car park, Newtown Linford, Leicestershire LE6 0LN (grid ref: SK511059)

Getting there

By car: Car parking is available for a fee at Bradgate Park's Newtown Linford car park. Use postcode LE6 0HB for satnav. There is limited on-street car parking.

By public transport: Roberts Coaches operates service 120 from Leicester to Coalville (no Sunday service). Check online for further details.

Before you start

- The car park is closed at sunset (no later than 8.30pm during summer, but considerably earlier in winter), and vehicles will not be allowed in after this time.
- Be aware that cyclists and horse-riders also use this park.
- Red and fallow deer roam freely in Bradgate Park. Be aware that they are wild animals and therefore may be unpredictable. Follow the rules and guidance provided. Visiting during winter is safest, as you will avoid both birthing and rutting seasons, when tensions run highest in the herds. Detailed safety advice is available on the website, bradgatepark.org.

1 Exit the car park and turn right onto Bradgate Road. Pass the cricket ground on the right and, after a short distance, take the footpath on the right by house number 19. Continue forward up the hill on the grassy footpath. Take care on grassy footpaths and tracks into and through the park as they may be slippery, especially if there is snow or ice on the ground. Also be careful on the uneven, rutted and rocky paths.

2 Towards the top of the hill pass through the large wooden swing gate in the wall to enter Bradgate Park, then go ahead a few paces to a cross track. Turn left, then bear right to

Leicestershire's shortest river runs through the Lower Park. The River Lin feeds into the Cropston Reservoir, and the shallow waterfalls were designed to keep the water clear.

pass the small plantation called Tyburn. Continue uphill and follow the path to the Leicester Yeomanry War Memorial.

The War Memorial stands on a consecrated area of holy ground and commemorates the men of the Leicestershire Yeomanry who died in the Boer War and the two World Wars. Built just after the First World War, it is made of concrete and granite chip, and stands about 10m high.

Continue, following the path through the plantation to reach the folly known as Old John Tower. There are great views from this view point (212m) across to Leicester (10km/6 miles away) and the toposcope points your attention to many places of interest.

Old John Tower was built on Old John Hill in 1784 for the fifth Earl of Stamford. The tower was used during the 19th century as a viewing point for the horseracing practice circuit laid out by the seventh Earl of Stamford.

Notes of interest

★ Bradgate House was completed in 1520 by Thomas Grey, second Earl of Dorset. Lady Jane Grey, the nine-day queen, was born here in 1537. The house was raided by Prince Rupert in 1642 and later housed arms and ammunition moved for safety from the magazine in Leicester before it was taken by royal forces during the Siege of Leicester in 1645. The house was abandoned after the death of the second Earl of Stamford in 1719 and by 1790 it was lying in ruins.

★ Local legend has it that Old John Tower was built to commemorate a servant who was accidentally killed by a bonfire held to celebrate the 21st birthday of the sixth Earl of Stamford.

The earliest record of Bradgate referred to as a deer park was in 1241. The park is home to a herd of about 550 red and fallow deer.

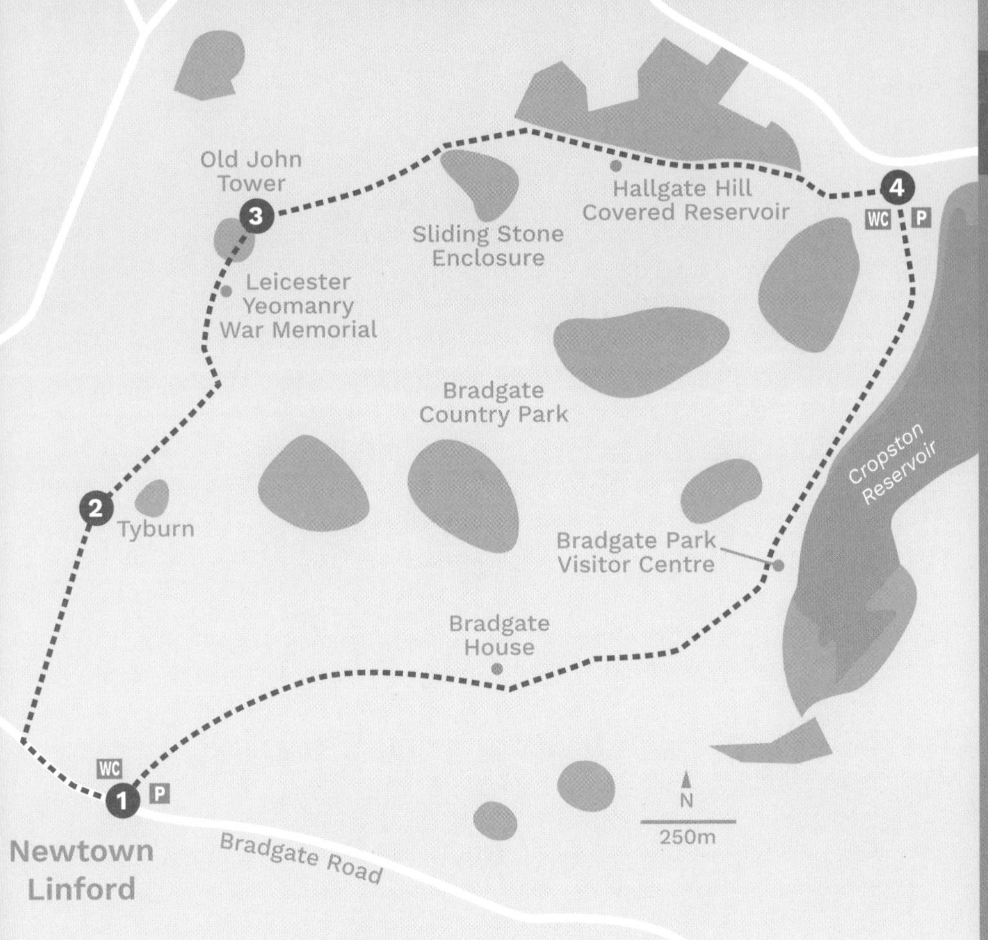

3 Take the path straight down the hillside to the small circular pond. Follow the track to skirt around the left side of the walled Sliding Stone Enclosure. Ignore the path leading to the gated park entrance and continue along the track to the park boundary wall. Carry on past the underground reservoir to follow the path along the wall. Just past the house on the left, take the path that leads through the gate towards the Hallgates car park.

4 Turn right onto the tarmac drive and follow it all the way through the park, passing the Deer Barn Café and Visitor Centre on the left and the ruins of Bradgate House on the right. Towards the end of the park is an area with rocky outcrops, wooded valley and the River Lin, known as Little Matlock. Continue ahead to reach your start point at the Newtown Linford car park. The main drive can be very busy and it is also used by cyclists, so do take care.

walk 35

Cley-next-the-Sea, Norfolk

Time: **4 hrs** | Distance: **12.3 km (7.6 miles)** | Difficulty: ✪✪

The first half of this route is, strictly speaking, a coastal walk. All the ingredients are here: quays, jetties, boats and general maritime gear, but you will barely glimpse the sea. Instead this section of the Peddars Way and Norfolk Coast Path navigates a course along the top of the sea defences, through the wide salt marshes and creeks left behind when the sea turned its back on this once-prosperous port over a hundred years ago. The second half of this route retreats inland through the low-lying fens of the Glaven Valley, before climbing onto Blakeney Esker for panoramic views of north Norfolk from a rare vantage point high above sea level. This tapestry of golden marshland stretches north to the shingle spit of Blakeney Point, and from the raised ridge of the esker you finally catch a glimpse of the elusive North Sea, as you descend on the final leg of your journey back to Blakeney harbour. This area is a twitchers' paradise, and the seal colony out on nearby Blakeney Point welcomes newborn grey seal pups in November/December each year.

Start location

Blakeney Quay, Blakeney, Norfolk NR25 7NE (grid ref: TG027441).

Getting there

By car: There is paid (free to National Trust members) parking available at Blakeney Quay. It is important to note though that the car park is subject to tidal flooding.
By public transport: Norfolk County Council's Coasthopper Bus (CHOP) provides an hourly service all year leaving from the Sheringham Tourist Information Centre, calling at Cley, Blakeney, Morston and Wells-next-the-Sea; search online for details. Sheringham is the nearest railway station with a frequent service from Norwich.

Before you start

* Walking in winter, you are almost certain to experience a 'snitern', a 'biting wind'. Blakeney's original name, Snitterley, is thought to derive from this term, and, appropriately enough, sniterns regularly blow in from the North Sea, across the flat salt marshes, to buffet the quay at Blakeney.

* Places to eat may be found in both Cley and Wiveton.

* The coast path can become very muddy, but mostly you'll be walking on good, surfaced lanes and bridleways.

* Boat trips to view the seals head out from Blakeney and Morston Quays.

Wrecks of abandoned fishing boats on the Blakeney salt marshes. This stretch of Norfolk coastline offers enormous skies and wide-open views.

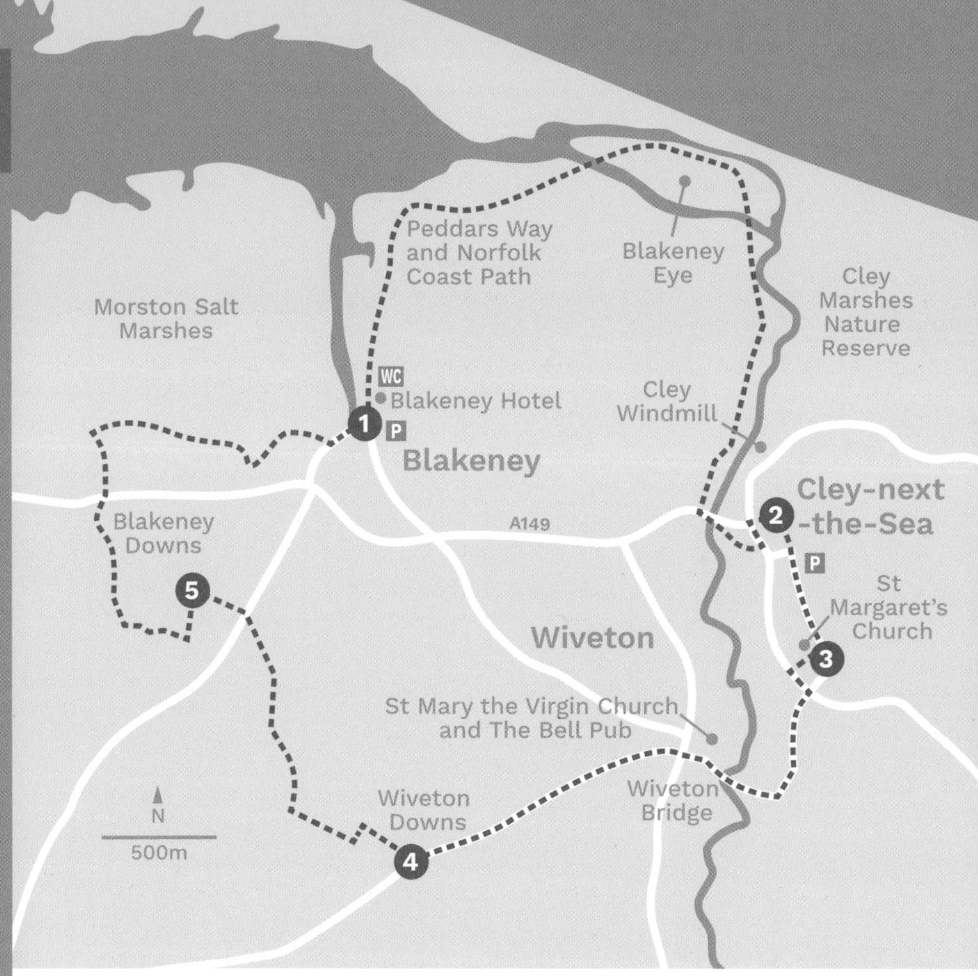

1 Facing out to sea from the old quay in Blakeney, turn right, passing the Blakeney Hotel on your right, to join the Peddars Way and Norfolk Coast Path, which heads out to into the salt marshes towards Blakeney Point.

The seal colony at the western tip of this shingle spit forms part of a larger population at the Wash: together they're home to 40 per cent of Europe's common seals. Grey seals have also used the spit to rear their young, and since the 1980s their population has been increasing steadily. The common seal (Phoca vitulina), also known as the harbour seal, gives birth to a single pup between June and July, and the grey seal (Halichoerus grypus, or 'sea pig with a hooked nose') to a single white pup between November and December.

Follow the Peddars Way and Norfolk Coast Path for about an hour (4km/2.5 miles). The path passes Blakeney Eye (an 'eye' is an area of higher ground in the marshes, dry enough to support buildings) and arcs round to bring you towards Cley-next-the-Sea. When you meet the A149 Coast Road, turn left along the footpath near the road towards the village, with the unmistakable form of Cley Windmill on your left.

Blakeney Quay is a tidal creek linking the North Sea, Blakeney Point and Blakeney Harbour. In medieval times, this village was a commercial port.

This part of Cley-next-the-Sea (pronounced, and originally spelled, 'Cleye') initially served as the harbour, with the town centre sited about a kilometre (½ mile) south at Newgate Green (Cley Green on OS maps) by the church. But in 1612 a fire destroyed over a hundred buildings, and this, coupled with the gradually receding tide, provided an opportunity to move the town further upriver to this place so that it could be more 'next-the-sea'. As with all prosperous ports, smuggling was rife and pirates were never far offshore. There were numerous tunnels used to smuggle contraband in and out of Cley, right under the noses of the Customs and Excise Men. Even today at least two local houses are said to have smugglers' tunnels connected to their basements.

You'll soon come to a small road bridge over the river which leads into Cley. (If you wish shorten your walk there are buses back to Blakeney or to Sheringham which leave from outside Picnic Fayre Delicatessen.) Walk left round the far corner from the delicatessen into the High Street and turn left down an alley opposite the phone box. Walk past the Old Town Hall and follow the path that takes you behind the houses on the main street, along an old jetty and straight to the windmill. Here you have to turn right through a small alley. Then walk up some steps to emerge on the main street outside Crabpot Books.

2 To continue, take the public footpath to the left of Crabpot Books which slips down the centre of the village behind The George & Dragon pub to emerge on a surfaced lane (Church Lane). Continue along this lane in a southerly direction past the village hall, ignoring the road on your right, until you reach a long flint-cobbled wall and Knoll House. Turn right into St Margaret's Church. Go through the gate into the churchyard and round to the far side of the church where there is a large picnic area. Exit right onto Newgate Green ('Cley Green' on OS maps).

3 Cross over to the far (south) side of the large triangular green, ignoring the first road left (Three Swallows pub is back to your right). Take the road opposite, to the right of the houses. Follow this road south, with the river on your right, to a crossroads where you turn right across Wiveton Bridge up to Wiveton, with St Mary the Virgin Church and the Wiveton Bell pub on the green. On the side of the green opposite the church, take the centre road marked with a picnic spot signpost (not the main Holt road left or right) and continue uphill to Wiveton Downs (approximately 15 minutes).

4 Here you'll come to a fingerpost sign pointing left to Wiveton Downs and right to Blakeney. It's worth a short detour left through the kissing gate onto the common to admire the views south, but then retrace your steps and take the right path marked 'Blakeney' onto Wiveton Downs/Blakeney Esker.

Created by meltwater flowing through a tunnel beneath a glacier, Blakeney Esker was formed during the last Ice Age, 15,000 years ago, and is one of the finest examples of this geological process anywhere in England, which has earned it SSSI status. The height of the esker provides a perfect vantage point to survey the Glaven Valley.

Upon entering Wiveton Downs, follow the path bearing left, passing a small bump, and circle round left past a gate to exit on Saxlingham Road. Cross the road and walk up the bridleway

signed towards Blakeney. Follow this bridleway through New Farm to the next road crossing (approximately 15 minutes' walk), where you cross over onto a surfaced path (through white gates) and up to some houses.

5 Turn left here to follow a well-worn path at the side of fields and make your way across Blakeney Downs. When the path cuts through a gap in the trees, you should bear right towards the house on the small hill (or bluff). The path skirts the left side of the bluff until you reach the main road. Turn right on the road, crossing carefully near the brow of the hill and then almost immediately left onto the bridleway, which drops down to meet the Peddars Way and Norfolk Coast Path. Turn right to follow the coast path back to Blakeney, returning to the point where this walk began.

The unique ecosystems of the Norfolk saltmarshes provide a haven and significant conservation area for wildlife of all sorts. Migrating birds, such as the Brent goose, come and go.

Notes of interest

★ The harbours at Blakeney, Cley and Wiveton were known collectively as the Glaven Ports, and together formed one of Britain's most important trade hubs from the 13th century until the sea finally abandoned them over 600 years later. Gathered closely around the mouth of the River Glaven, they specialized in the export of wool, flour, corn and fish, and the importation of coal from Newcastle and stone quarried in Northamptonshire. They were also among the few English ports trusted to carry gold and silver, and had a special licence to 'export' pilgrims during the 15th century.

★ The marshes have created a haven for salt-loving plants and migratory birds. Brent geese from Siberia and pinkfoot geese from Iceland arrive here in the winter months. In summer, the explosive 'teu-he-he' of redshank taking flight from the higher grassy areas blends with the 'seep' of tiny reed buntings perched on the shrubby sea-blight bordering the path.

★ Thousands of bird-lovers from all over the world make the annual pilgrimage to the coast during the summer and winter migrations. The coast path winds through a network of nature reserves littered with the shells of abandoned fishing boats, and crisscrossed with boardwalks and birdwatching hides. On the approach to Cley-next-the-Sea the broad landscape and wide open skies are neatly punctuated by the silhouette of the village's 18th-century windmill, one of Norfolk's defining landmarks.

nature in winter

While getting out the door might require a little more preparation (and determination) in the winter in the UK, braving the cold will certainly reward you with increased vitality, improved moods and the most beautiful views you can imagine. A walk is always worth it.

Winter in the UK reveals the most magical transition, as the natural world slowly sheds anything it no longer requires for the next few months and draws back, conserving energy and retreating inwards. The winter months are December, January and February, with the shortest daylight hours falling on midwinter solstice, the longest night of the year, on 21 December. From this point, the days begin to lengthen out again, almost imperceptibly at first, with slighter lighter mornings and evenings more noticeable from late January.

Days may be windy and wet, or chilly and clear, but either way walking out in nature is a wonderful way to experience the glorious sparkling vistas and exciting extremes of our winter weather. Lower winter sunlight sets the scene, playing across ground-hugging mists and shimmering frosts to cast a beguiling spell over our views of familiar landscapes, refreshing our perspectives as though we are gazing on these natural marvels for the first time. For the loveliest landscape views over the winter, head for the hills – or at least aim high. The coldest months encourage us to shelter indoors, but the best antidote to winter claustrophobia is the opportunity to drink in some long, wide vistas from a good height. Try walks on clifftop pathways and wide-open heights like the Yorkshire Moors and the South Downs, where you can see for miles. Explore the wild coast of Northumberland, the Lake District and the breathtakingly bleak beauty of the Peak District. Confident walkers will enjoy the views and more challenging mountain trails at Beinn Eighe, Wester Ross, Britain's oldest National Nature Reserve, winding through pastures, woodland, past pine trees and water, through heather and deer grass on the way up.

Migratory birds, visiting to escape colder climes at home, remain busy with their hunt for food through these months. Bramblings, having arrived in the autumn, feast on nuts and berries in the wintery woods. Redwings, attracted to fruits such as hawthorn berries, may be spotted in open fields and along hedgerows – often travelling with the fieldfare flocks. More common in the east of the UK, waxwings gather to gorge on their favourite foods – hawthorn, cotoneaster and rowan berries.

One of winter's most memorable sights, and one you will only see while walking, must surely be the mountain hares, resplendent in their blueish-white winter camouflage by November. For the best opportunity of a sighting, pull on your boots and some good warm gear and head for the Highlands, Snowdonia, the Upper Pennines or the Peak District. Starling murmurations are another mesmerising and much-photographed British winter spectacle, usually hitting peak numbers in December and January with European visitors joining in with the birds resident here year-round. The best time to see them is late afternoon/early evening, just before dusk, as the enormous dark clouds of birds wheel through the skies before settling down to roost for the night. Murmurations can be viewed in various rural locations all over Britain, as well as over Brighton Pier in East Sussex and Gretna

Green in Dumfries and Galloway. An online search will provide the most up-to-date information about murmuration-sighting spots closest to you. And another opportunity to marvel, or even pull out your camera, is surely afforded by the sight of red squirrels in winter. Although increasingly rare in the UK, they can still be found in some areas such as the Isle of Wight, Abernethy Forest and on Anglesey.

Late in the winter, especially walking in Wales and southern Scotland, keep your eyes peeled for goshawks. These stunning but elusive birds have returned from the brink of extinction, with population numbers now gradually increasing. Watch for them in dense woodlands, and particularly woods planted with conifers; these areas provide the greatest likelihood of seeing goshawks as they perform their remarkable display flights over the trees, hoping to attract a mate. The RSPB recommends a walk to the top of Acres Down in the New Forest, on a fine day, for a good chance of spotting goshawks on the wing.

Towards the end of February, as thoughts turn to the possibility that spring might be just around the corner, listen for the song of woodlarks on heaths in eastern and southern England, and for the hammering of green woodpeckers in woods and forests. If walking near ponds, look for frogspawn from January onwards.

For the most spectacular winter landscapes, and varied views, look to knit together a number of different walks in places like Dartmoor, Devon, the Chilterns, Derbyshire, Northumberland, Pembrokeshire, Penzance, the Sussex coast, Wiltshire, Monmouthshire and the Yorkshire Dales.

During the winter, red deer usually prefer to take shelter on lower ground. Groups of deer in woodland areas tend to be lower in numbers than those in open-hill habitats.

The robin red-breast is one of only a few garden birds to sing throughout the winter. They live all across the UK, in parks, gardens, woodlands and hedgerows.

walk
36

Windsor to The Savill Garden, Berkshire/Surrey

Time: **3 hrs** | Distance: **11.6 km (7.2 miles)** | Difficulty: ✪✪

A beautiful walk, which loops through Windsor Great Park passing the Savill Garden. See the deer and enjoy a wonderful view from the Copper Horse statue which overlooks Windsor Castle and the Long Walk.

Start location

Old Windsor Memorial Hall, Straight Road, Windsor SL4 2RN, (grid ref: SU984747).

Getting there

By car: Old Windsor Memorial Hall is on the A308 Straight Road directly opposite the Toby Carvery.
By bus: First Berkshire Buses, routes 8 and 8A.

Before you start

- More information about Windsor Great Park and the Savill Garden may be found on the website: windsorgreatpark.co.uk
- Remember to keep a safe distance from the deer. You are also likely to encounter horse-riders in the Park; always stand aside and allow the horse to pass.

Originally planted by Charles II, Windsor Long Walk is a tree-lined avenue, three miles long. It begins at the George IV Gateway and ends at the Copper Horse statue.

1 Starting at the Memorial Hall, use the crossing to cross over the main road. Turn right and walk past the Toby Carvery and then left into St Luke's Road. Just past The Jolly Gardeners pub, where the road curves round to the left, turn right into Crimp Hill. Continue past two pubs and a junior school, until you come to a sharp bend in the road. Continue along the track, passing a cemetery and a couple of estate houses on the right, to a secured gate which leads into the Deer Park.

2 Enter the Deer Park through the kissing gate to the side of the main gate. The track forks twice; take the left fork each time. You will find yourself on a wide, sandy track which winds its way uphill through woodland for about 1.5km (1 mile). The track eventually bends to the right to join a paved road near Bishopsgate – turn left and exit the Deer Park once again using the kissing gate adjacent to the main gate. You are still within the boundary of Windsor Great Park. Take a track to the left which heads towards Bishopsgate. Shortly before you reach Bishopsgate, cross the road and follow a track to the right (the Rhododendron Ride) adjacent to a ranger's house. This is signposted towards the Savill Garden. About 800m along the Rhodedendron Ride, you'll see the Cow Pond through the bushes on the right. This has a magnificent display of waterlilies in summer, and is a good place to take a break any time of year. You can extend your walk a little by walking all the way round the Cow Pond if you like.

3 After visiting the Cow Pond, continue along the Rhododendron Ride for a further 800m approximately and you will come to the Savill Garden Visitor Centre – refreshments are available here. Continue straight past the visitor centre, then bear right when you reach the picnic area and skirt the borders of the Savill Garden, passing on your left the Cumberland Obelisk and subsequently the Polo Ground. After 500m, you will come to Queen Victoria's Avenue – turn right and pass through Cumberland Gate.

Notes of interest

★ The Savill Garden was commissioned by George V and created in 1932 by Sir Eric Savill under the careful guidance of the Keeper of the Gardens and a team of horticulturists – it as majestic today as it was then. The original weeping willow tree still stands today.

★ The Guards Polo Ground at Smith's Lawn was used as an airfield during the Second World War.

The magnificent Copper Horse statue is a bronze monument to George III, created by Richard Westmacott and erected on its stone plinth at Snow Hill in 1831.

4 Now take the first turning on the left (after about 300m) towards Cumberland Lodge; turn right as you near the lodge to follow a path that skirts it. A number of tracks and paths converge at the top of Gravel Hill – cross the road and head downhill on a track opposite. This track descends to the Ox Pond. Keep going along a grassy track with hedges on either side. At the end, you should pass through a kissing gate into the Deer Park with the statue of King George III (the Copper Horse) directly in front of you. Continue over the crest of Snow Hill, passing the Copper Horse, and down the other side to join the Long Walk, with views of Windsor Castle in the distance.

5 About 600m along the Long Walk, turn right (the first track on your right) onto a horse trail. Continue straight for a further 500m to reach Bear's Rails Gate at Waypoint 2. Retrace your steps now to the starting point via Crimp Hill and St Luke's Road.

walk 37

The Seven Sisters, South Downs

Time: 4 hrs | Distance: 13.2 km (8.2 miles) | Difficulty: ✪✪✪

One of the few linear walks in this book, this route takes you from East Dean to Seaford, along the tops of the stunningly sheer, white chalk cliffs of East Sussex with sweeping sea views and a beautifully preserved smugglers' beach. There are good paths with springy turf underfoot but dangerous cliff edges.

Start location

The Tiger Inn, East Dean, 5km (3 miles) west of Eastbourne, East Sussex BN20 0DA (grid ref: TV557978).

End location

Martello Tower, Seaford, East Sussex BN25 1BU (grid ref: TV485985).

Before you start

- The crash of invisible surf rising from the shingle far below may well entice you to take a peek over the edge, but such temptation should be resisted, especially after heavy rain or rough seas, when the Seven Sisters become notoriously crumbly and unstable.

- Buses link Exceat with Eastbourne and Seaford for those wanting a shorter walk of 7.3km (4.5 miles) (see the end of Waypoint 3).

Getting there

By car: From the west, take the M4, then cut down to the A27 and carry on. From the north, take the M23/A23, then turn left when you see signs for Eastbourne. Follow signs for Beachy Head. There is ample parking available in East Dean.

By public transport: Both Eastbourne and Seaford are easy to reach by train, and regular bus services run between Eastbourne and Seaford via East Dean and Exceat (The Cuckmere Inn). Check online for details.

1 From your start point outside The Tiger Inn at East Dean, cross the village green to the Frith & Little Deli and turn left, then fork right down the road marked 'No Through Road'. Follow this surfaced road past a few houses until you reach a gate. Go through the gate and head steeply uphill, ignoring a cross-path, and then through two smaller gates onto the access land at National Trust's Crowlink. Follow the path through the woods up to the crest of Went Hill – here you will see a barn with a red roof in the distance. Head for the barn, in the direction of the sea, keeping to the right of the barn and following the bridleway down to a gate at the bottom of the field. Go through this gate, then through another gate before turning right onto the South Downs Way (SDW). Birling Gap is two minutes to the left downhill and further east still is the decommissioned lighthouse Belle Tout (pronounced 'toot') which was completed in 1832.

Until then, the only reliable warning light for ships had been provided by Jonathan Darby, vicar of St Jude's Church in East Dean. Darby became so concerned about the danger to sailors that he excavated a makeshift lighthouse and rescue centre 6m up the face of the cliffs at Birling Gap. He spent night after night in this

Cuckmere Haven is a chalk grassland, rich in flowers and wildlife. This beach lies at the mouth of the Cuckmere River, watched over by the Seven Sisters.

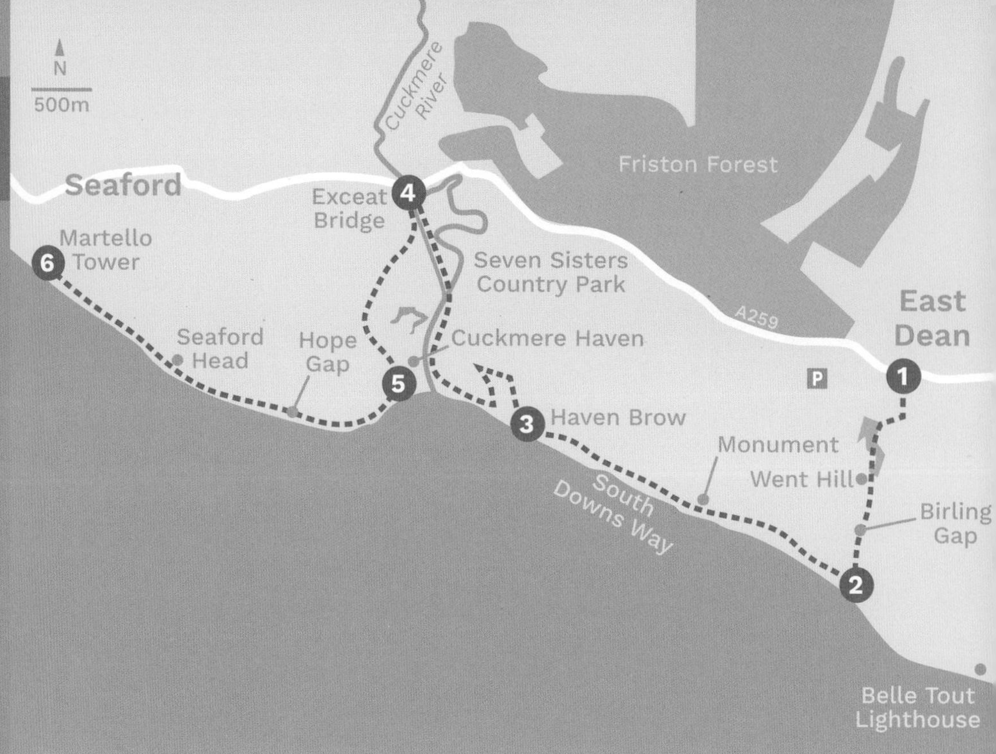

cave and saved many lives until 1726, when he died from exposure. Parson Darby's cave still sits beneath Belle Tout lighthouse.

2 Here is where the 4km (2.5-mile) rollercoaster of the Seven Sisters starts: it will take approximately 45 minutes to traverse all Seven Sisters. Cross Went Hill Brow (Sister number 1); descend into Michel Dene; ascend Baily's Hill (Sister 2); and down into Flathill Bottom; briefly up Flat Hill (an uncounted Sister!) and down to Flagstaff Bottom; up to Flagstaff Point (Sister 3); down to Gap Bottom; up to Brass Point (Sister 4); down to Rough Bottom; up to Rough Brow (Sister 5); down to Limekiln Bottom; up to Short Brow (Sister 6); down to Short Bottom; and finally up to Haven Brow (Sister 7). High above the beach the rollercoaster ride of ups and downs reaches a crescendo at the top of Haven Brow. The reward for surmounting the highest Sister is the magnificent view across the tranquil Cuckmere Valley from 78m. The only inhabitants of Cuckmere Haven moved into the coastguards' cottages on the far side of the beach in 1818. The navy built these cottages to provide a permanent base for Customs and Excise Men to tackle the prolific trafficking of gin, brandy and tobacco up the Cuckmere River to Alfriston.

One notorious smuggler lived at the Manor House in East Dean. James Dipperay amassed a large fortune from the supply of contraband and, when he was finally arrested, betrayed his fellow local smugglers in return for his own freedom. His colleagues were deported to Australia, and Dipperay retired a wealthy man.

3 Here take the left fork leading steeply down and away from the SDW. Continue along the cliff and over a stile. The path skirts the edge of Cliff End to the right, descending to Cuckmere Haven. From Cuckmere Haven you need to double back along a path at the base of the cliff to reach the beach. Cross the beach to the mouth of the Cuckmere River.

The wild meanders of the Cuckmere River were first tamed in 1846 by cutting a straight channel from the shoreline to Exceat Bridge. The channel was built to improve drainage, prevent flooding and create land for pasture. Today the valley is further protected by earthbanks along the river's course and the extensive maintenance of shingle banks to the west of its mouth. But climate change and rising sea levels have placed an impossible burden on resources, and there are plans to allow the valley to return to its natural state. It is hoped that if the process is managed carefully, it will result in a self-sustaining tidal estuary of salt marsh and mudflats.

Follow the path tight against the river's canalized bank, which makes a beeline to Exceat (about 20 minutes). Exceat is home to the Seven Sisters Country Park Centre and, on the far side of the bridge, the Cuckmere Inn. It also marks the departure of the South Downs Way from the Vanguard Way. Our route follows the latter, which skirts the western edge of Cuckmere Haven and climbs past the coastguards' cottages to Seaford Head. When you reach the road, cross Exceat Bridge towards the Cuckmere Inn and turn left into the car park. Buses link Exceat with Eastbourne and Seaford for those wanting a shorter walk of 7.3km (4.5 miles).

4 At the far end of the Cuckmere Inn's car park go through the gate and follow the Vanguard Way south for 20–30 minutes, ignoring paths to left then right, before emerging on the west side of Cuckmere Haven with the coastguards' cottages in front of you, and a great view of the Seven Sisters from Seaford Head.

5 Passing the coastguards' cottages on your left, continue uphill to Hope Gap and then right following the cliff edge through Seaford Head Nature Reserve. Walk for a further 30 minutes past Hope Bottom and along the esplanade to the Martello Tower, where this walk ends. You will find Seaford Station if you head ten minutes further down the esplanade, then take a right up Dane Road.

There are 74 Martello towers lining England's coast, from Folkstone to Seaford. Seaford's tower was the last link in this defensive chain built to repel the French during the Napoleonic Wars.

Notes of interest

★ Locals often profited from sailors' misfortune and wreckers hung false lights from the Seven Sisters to lure cargo ships to their doom. One unfortunate vessel to strike the cliffs was a three-masted clipper weighing 633 tonnes, which was en route from Adelaide laden with wool and copper ingots when she ran around in the early hours of 21 February 1876. Inquisitive wreck hunters can find the ship off Flagstaff Point (grid ref: TV537966) during spring low tides, when the large teak and iron frame of its hull protrudes from the foreshore.

★ Seaford town was first recorded in 788 AD as 'Saeford' but there were earlier Roman and Celtic settlements here at the mouth of the River Ouse. The town became an important port and was granted membership of the Cinque Ports Federation. But the gradual silting of the Ouse coupled with a great storm in 1579 caused the river to burst its banks, diverting its course further west. A port was built at the new river mouth and Seaford's influence was gradually eclipsed by the 'New Haven'. Today the town is unremarkable but for the moated Martello Tower on the seafront which houses Seaford Museum. 'Martello' is believed to be a corruption of Mortella in Corsica, the location of a round fort.

walk
38

Richmond, London

Time: 2 hrs 15 mins | Distance: 7.3 km (4.5 miles) | Difficulty: ✪✪

This circular route explores the historic Richmond Green area, follows the River Thames and then crosses Petersham Meadows before climbing through Richmond Park to King Henry's Mount view point. You will return to your start point via Richmond Hill, with its famous protected views, and the Terrace Gardens.

Start location

Richmond Station, Richmond, London TW9 1DN (grid ref: TQ180751).

Before you start

✲ If you want to shorten or lengthen your walk, options are given within the route instructions.

✲ Be aware that part of the route through Richmond Park is on a well-trodden country path with rough steps and some unevenness, which may be muddy or slippery after rain or snow.

✲ Please note that dogs are not permitted in Pembroke Lodge Gardens.

Getting there

By car: There is a car park at the station.

By public transport: Richmond is at one end of the District and the London Overground lines and is also served by National Rail trains on the Waterloo to Reading Line. It is also well served by bus routes, with the following all stopping here: 33, 65, 371, 490, 493, 969, H22, H37, N22, R68 and R70. Check online for further details.

1 Leave Richmond Station at the main Kew Road exit. Turn left and cross at the zebra crossing towards Oriel House, then turn right on the far side and almost immediately turn left into Old Station Passage, signposted 'Capital Ring'. At the end, turn left and go across the railway. Go past Richmond Theatre on your left, with Little Green on your right. Cross Duke Street and almost immediately turn right and cross the road to the corner of Richmond Green.

2 Fork left and take the left path, along the edge of Richmond Green. At the end, turn right along the pavement. As the road narrows, cross to the left side and very soon turn left through Richmond Palace Gateway. Go clockwise round the green to pass the old Wardrobe buildings and Trumpeters' House, then leave along the path between white bollards in the far right corner. Turn left into the road (Old Palace Lane) and go past the The White Swan pub to the River Thames, by the White Swan sign and Asgill House.

Option: To extend the walk by 1km (½ mile) and visit Richmond Lock, turn right here. Go under the railway and road. Continue along the path (actually a raised causeway) with the Old Deer Park on the right. At Richmond Lock you can avoid steps by retracing your steps back to Asgill House, otherwise go across the bridge and turn left on the far bank to head alongside

Richmond Park on a crisp winter morning. One of London's eight Royal Parks, it covers an area of 2,500 acres and provides an important habitat for wildlife.

Pause at Terrace Gardens – originally formed from three separate 18th-century estates and opened to the public in 1887 – for a wonderful view out over the Thames.

the river (Raneleigh Drive). At the road bridge (Twickenham Road Bridge), go up the steps, cross the river and then go down the steps back to riverside. Retrace your steps under the road and rail bridges, back to Asgill House.

3 Turn left to go past Asgill House and continue straight on along the riverside, past the Old Deer Park Information Board. Go along Cholmondley Walk, onto a cobbled road. At The White Cross pub, keep to the riverside, passing the Slug & Lettuce pub and onto Richmond Riverside. Walk under Richmond Bridge and continue on for some time along the river. Shortly after the Canoe Club and just after the path bends, look out for a grotto and tunnel under the road, leading into Terrace Gardens.

Option: For a shorter walk of about 5–5.5km (3–3½ miles), missing out Richmond Park, head left down the steps to the Terrace Gardens. Go through the tunnel under the road and then up steps into the gardens at the Grotto Gate (to avoid steps, go back a few metres and cross the busy Petersham Road into the park). Turn left and then right to go past The Glasshouse. Ahead is the café and to its right the River God statue. As you get near the café turn left, keeping the grass on your right. Keep left and then follow the path round to the right

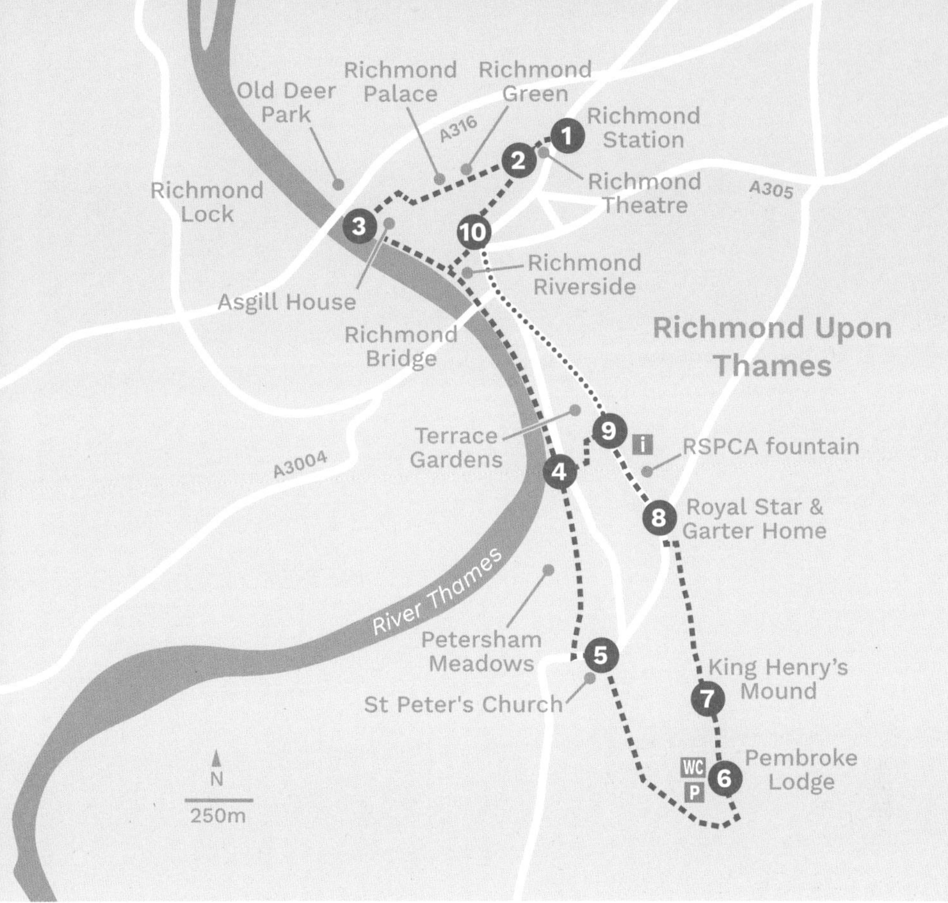

towards the wooden summerhouse. At the summerhouse turn left; almost immediately, keep right and go past the Spring Well. Shortly after turn right, continuing uphill. Continue straight on at a Y-junction, until you reach the lower terrace. Go past the Fishmarker Stone until you reach the Aphrodite Statue terrace. Go up the steps and behind the statue, up more steps on the left and along a winding path that takes you to the top terrace. Turn right along the Upper Terrace and, shortly opposite Friars Stile Road, turn left and go up a few steps to the road (Richmond Hill). Turn right along the road and shortly turn right and walk along the terrace to the protected Richmond Hill view point. To return, retrace your steps to Friars Stile Road and then continue at the end of Waypoint 8 where you will probably wish to take the alternative route directly down Richmond Hill.

4 To reach Richmond Park, continue straight along the river and then follow the path as it turns away from the river through Buccleugh Gardens (passing toilets). Go ahead through a kissing gate and cross Petersham Meadows. Continue straight on across the meadows and through a second kissing gate. Continue straight on past St Peter's Church and come out on the main Petersham Road. Turn left and continue to The Dysart.

The famous tree-lined view south, across Richmond Park to the dome St Paul's Cathedral, from King Henry's Mound. This is one of London's protected sightlines.

Option: For a short diversion to the centre of Petersham village (with its attractive houses), before you pass St Peter's Church, turn right towards Petersham Nurseries Café and just by its entrance take a narrow footpath between brick walls. This will eventually bring you out on a road (River Lane) where you should turn left. At the main Petersham Road, turn left and continue past Petersham House, and The Dysart, where you rejoin main route.

5 At The Dysart, cross at the pedestrian lights towards Richmond Park. Go through Petersham Gate into Richmond Park then go straight on gradually uphill, along the main gravel path (this is also a cycle path, so look out for bikes). Pass a children's playground. At the brow of the hill, by a seat and just before the brick wall on the right ends, branch left uphill, along a well-used dirt path. Follow the path round to the left, then right as it climbs up to go parallel to a wire fence. Continue straight on at the junction with Capital Ring path, following the fence. Then go up about 36 rough path steps. Just after the steps, go through a gate on the left and follow the path ahead to the white house, Pembroke Lodge – a café. Through the main lodge gates on the right by the car park are a refreshment kiosk, toilets and visitor centre. The climbing is now over, so this is a good spot for a break.

6 Follow path past the front of the lodge. Turn right at a road, signposted 'King Henry's Mound' and then shortly fork left on a tarmac path keeping the lawn to the right. Go between seats and the Rose Garden, then shortly go left, to the first view point. Turn right at the main path and, at the next junction, fork right alongside a hedge. By a gate, turn left uphill to King Henry's Mound view point and proceed to the upper level by the telescope. (Note the iron 'window' in the hedge behind; it frames the legally protected vista of St Paul's, which sits 16km/10 miles away.)

7 Leave the mound, and go down a slope keeping views to the left. Turn right at a Y-junction and go through the arches of the John Beer Laburnum Walk. Go through a kissing gate into the main park and fork left along metal fence. Continue along the path until you reach a roundabout and Richmond Gate. Cross to the other side of the road before the gates (keep an eye out for traffic leaving and entering the park) and leave the park. You will come out opposite the Royal Star & Garter Home. Keep right and continue to a roundabout.

8 Use the zebra crossings at the roundabout to cross to the RSPCA Fountain and the Royal Star & Garter Home. Turn right and go down Richmond Hill. Cross Nightingale Lane and continue along the terrace, with magnificent views to the left. After the view points, continue along the pavement and go down steps into Terrace Gardens.

Option: To return directly to the station and avoid the steps, continue down Richmond Hill and follow the road until you pass Water Lane on the left. Rejoin the main route at Waypoint 10.

9 Inside the gardens, go along the upper terrace, down steps on the left and follow the path to the Aphrodite Statue. Go to the front, down a few steps and turn right along the lower terrace. Look for the Fishmarker Stone on your left and follow the tarmac path downhill (not the steps) as it leaves the rockery. Keep left at all junctions until you arrive at the Spring Well on the left and shortly after the summerhouse. At the front of the summerhouse turn right and follow the path downhill, round the edge of the lawn. As you approach the café, note the River God statue ahead but go right, continuing downhill past The Glasshouse. At the exit gates turn left. (For a step-free route, go directly across the road to the riverside.) Shortly, turn right to go down steps and under the road through the flint-lined Grotto Gate tunnel. At the riverside, turn right and retrace your outward route back under Richmond Bridge. After Richmond Riverside Terraces, turn right by the Slug & Lettuce pub, into Water Lane. At George Street turn left.

10 Continue straight on and across the pedestrian crossing. Turn left along King Street. Turn right into Paved Court to emerge at Richmond Green. Continue straight on with the Green on your left, past The Cricketers pub. Cross Duke Street and continue past the theatre. Immediately after the railway, turn right into Old Station Passage by the 'Capital Ring' sign. At the main road use the zebra crossing, on the right, to cross back to your start point at the station.

walk
39

Abbotsbury and Chesil Beach, Dorset

Time: **4 hrs** | Distance: **12.7 km (7.9 miles)** | Difficulty: ✪✪

This circular route leads from Abbotsbury via Abbotsbury Castle, West Bexington and Chesil Beach along grassy chalk downland and a level path alongside Chesil Beach. Situated amid gently rolling downland behind Chesil Beach, Abbotsbury is one of the most picturesque and historically interesting villages in Dorset. Its 600+-year-old Swannery is unique: the only place in the world where you are able to walk through the heart of a colony of nesting mute swans. The outward leg of this walk leads along a ridge-top path to the northwest of the village via an Iron Age hillfort called Abbotsbury Castle. It then heads down to the coast and returns alongside Chesil Beach. A short detour at the end to climb Chapel Hill to St Catherine's Chapel affords one of the loveliest view points around.

Before you start

- The Swannery and Children's Farm, near the start of this walk, are both excellent venues for a family day out.
- There are places to stop for food and drink in Abbotsbury, at the Swannery and the Subtropical Gardens.

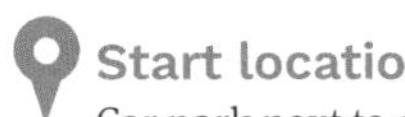

Start location

Car park next to church, Abbotsbury, Dorset DT3 4JL (grid ref: SY578853).

Getting there

By car: Head for the car park in Abbotsbury, reached via the B3157.

By public transport: The regular Jurassic Coast bus service X53 between Exeter and Poole stops at Abbotsbury.

Golden hour sets St Catherine's Chapel at Abbotsbury aglow, with Chesil Beach and the Isle of Portland on the English Channel's Jurassic Coast behind.

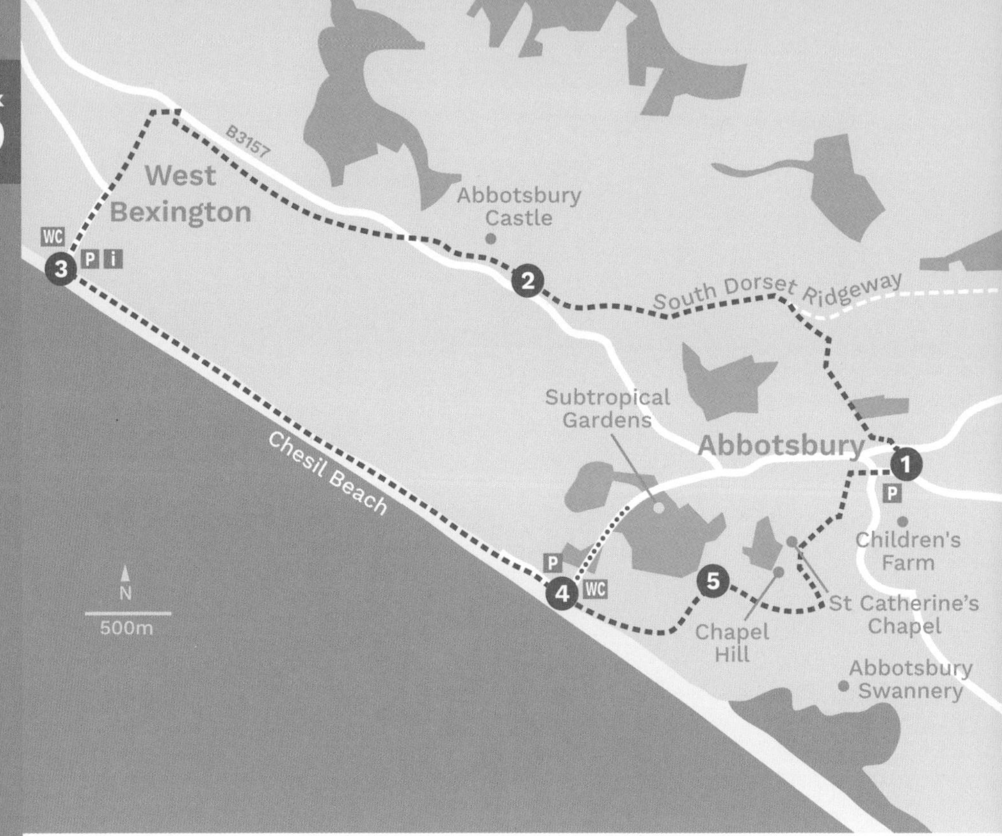

1 From the car park head down Rosemary Lane opposite, and turn left along Back Street for a very short distance. Turn right along a track which is signed for Blind Lane. Follow the bridleway uphill and bear left at the first junction (signed for Hillfort). The ridge-top path, which is also part of the inland route of the South West Coast Path (SWCP), is signed as the 'South Dorset Ridgeway' and links West Bexington with Osmington Mills, providing excellent views over the coast, Chesil Beach and the Fleet Lagoon. St Catherine's Chapel, situated on Chapel Hill just to the south of Abbotsbury, is a prominent landmark. Continue along this path for some distance.

2 The earthworks of Abbotsbury Castle soon become clearly visible. Just beyond this, you should reach and then cross the B3157, continuing in the same direction for 1.6km (1 mile). The path then turns left; follow it downhill to the village of West Bexington, where you join a lane that leads to the coast and a car park. An information panel in the car park provides some interesting details about Chesil Beach.

3 Now turn left and follow the coast path alongside Chesil Beach – an easy, flat stretch of walking.

Chesil Beach runs 28km (17 miles) from West Bay to the Isle of Portland. Its name derives from the Old English *ceosel* or *cisel*, meaning 'gravel' or 'shingle'.

4 Soon you will reach a car park with a sign to Abbotsbury's Subtropical Gardens. Follow this if you would like to take a detour to visit this 8-hectare garden, which is filled with rare and exotic plants from all over the world. To continue the onward route, about 500m beyond the car park, the SWCP heads inland from the coast.

5 The most direct way back to the village is to carry straight on along the bridleway which takes you around the west and north of Chapel Hill. However, it is well worthwhile following the short, waymarked path up to St Catherine's Chapel – a lovely view point – before heading down into the village. You may wish to end the walk by exploring around Abbotsbury itself, including the Swannery. Return to the car park where you started, and your walk is complete.

Notes of interest

★ Chesil Beach is a 28km (18-mile) shingle bank that is one of the finest barrier beaches in the world. As a result of tidal action the pebbles are graded in size, the smallest being at the western end.

★ The Swannery was established by the Benedictine monks who built the monastery and farmed the swans as food for their lavish banquets. Apart from the Swannery, you will also see the great thatched tithe barn which, together with the chapel, were left unharmed when Henry VIII dissolved and demolished the monastery in 1538.

walk
40

Penderyn, Mid Glamorgan

Time: 5 hrs | Distance: 13.5 km (8.4 miles) | Difficulty: ✪✪✪

A pleasant walk through the countryside to four beautiful waterfalls followed by a return to a welcoming pub, with crackling log fires in the winter. The perfect day out.

Start location

The Red Lion Inn car park, Church Road, Penderyn, Mid Glamorgan CF44 9JR (grid ref: SN 945 086).

Getting there

By car: From M4 junction 32, then A470 towards Merthyr Tydfil, turn left onto A465 towards Hirwaun. Then A4059 to Penderyn. On passing Penderyn Distillery on your right, you will then come to the Lamb Hotel on your left, turn left here – Lamb Road – and then left at the end of the road, going uphill where you will find The Red Lion Inn on your left. If you plan to leave your car at The Red Lion, contact the pub in advance to request permission to use the car park.

Before you start

* Bring waterproofs, or a change of clothes.

1 With your back to the pub entrance, turn left and walk along the road with the church on your right. Follow the road around behind the churchyard, pass Pantcefnyffordd Farm on your right and continue along the road. At the left bend in the road go straight ahead to a metal gate which is signposted 'Craig y Ddinas and Pontneddfechan'. Follow the track straight ahead. Continue straight along the track via a wooden gate to a metal gate with rocks on the left and continue straight along the track; ignore the left-hand fork. On reaching the metal gate with large rocks across it, go through the wooden gate on the left of the metal gate and continue straight on, following the blue sign for 'Public Bridleway'. The track now descends more steeply, and to your right are the peaks of the Brecon Beacons. Further on you will come to a marker post on your left with a yellow waymarker and a blue waymarker. Follow the blue waymarker heading straight on. The path then curves round slightly to the right and then to the left, following the line of a fence. You will reach another marker post on your left: ignore this and go straight ahead where the path rises slightly and bears left. Once at the top of the slight incline there is a marker post on your right – ignore this and follow the path straight ahead along the fence on your left.

2 You will now come across a steep descent where the path is very rocky and can be slippery. There is a handrail on your left – this place is known as Craig y Ddinas (Dinas Rock). At the bottom, the footpath continues on the right side of a car park. On reaching the road turn right across the bridge, then turn left, carrying on straight ahead to the children's playground signs. Turn right in front of the small row of houses and the footpath continues straight in front of you. At the end of the houses follow the path up into the wooded area; the

Water rushes between mossy rocks on this famous walk exploring the Four Falls in the Brecon Beacons. The views are captivating, but remember to watch your footing.

Bridge on the Afon Sychryd. In Welsh, the limestone cliff is called Craig y Ddinas: 'Fortress Rock'. The name comes from the Iron Age earthworks on its summit, ddinas meaning a defensive site or 'city'.

path zig-zags to the top. At the top of this steep climb there is a stile to climb over, then you are on the golf course. On the golf course keep close to the bracken on your left and then follow the power lines briefly, and you will see a marker post. At the marker post to the left of the electricity poles you will see another post – head for this. At this marker post follow the tree line on the right of the fairway. On the opposite side of the fairway is a stone wall. At the end of the first tree line follow the edge of the fairway, keeping the fairway on your left. Passing the green on your left you will see a path in front of you with a waymarker post on your left. Here it tells you to turn right along the hedgerow (which necessitates crossing the tee-off point for hole number 4 – stand quietly aside if anyone is teeing off). Following along the edge of the fairway on hole 4 you will see marker posts in the scrubland on your left; keep walking on the left side of the fairway. The fence on your left gets nearer the edge of the fairway and you will see the waymarker post on the corner. Continue ahead. You should come across a red disc sign on the edge of the fairway, but if this is not visible continue to the green ahead and at the back of the green turn to the left though the ferns to find the stile in the corner. There is a yellow cap on the stile's upright. Here the footpath leaves the edge of the fairway. You should head towards the waymarker post on your left. Look out for small ponds on both your left and right.

Continue on and cross a stile in a corner on your left. Continue straight in front of you keeping the fence on your left. As you get almost level with the tree on your right and the corner of a fence on your left there is a track on

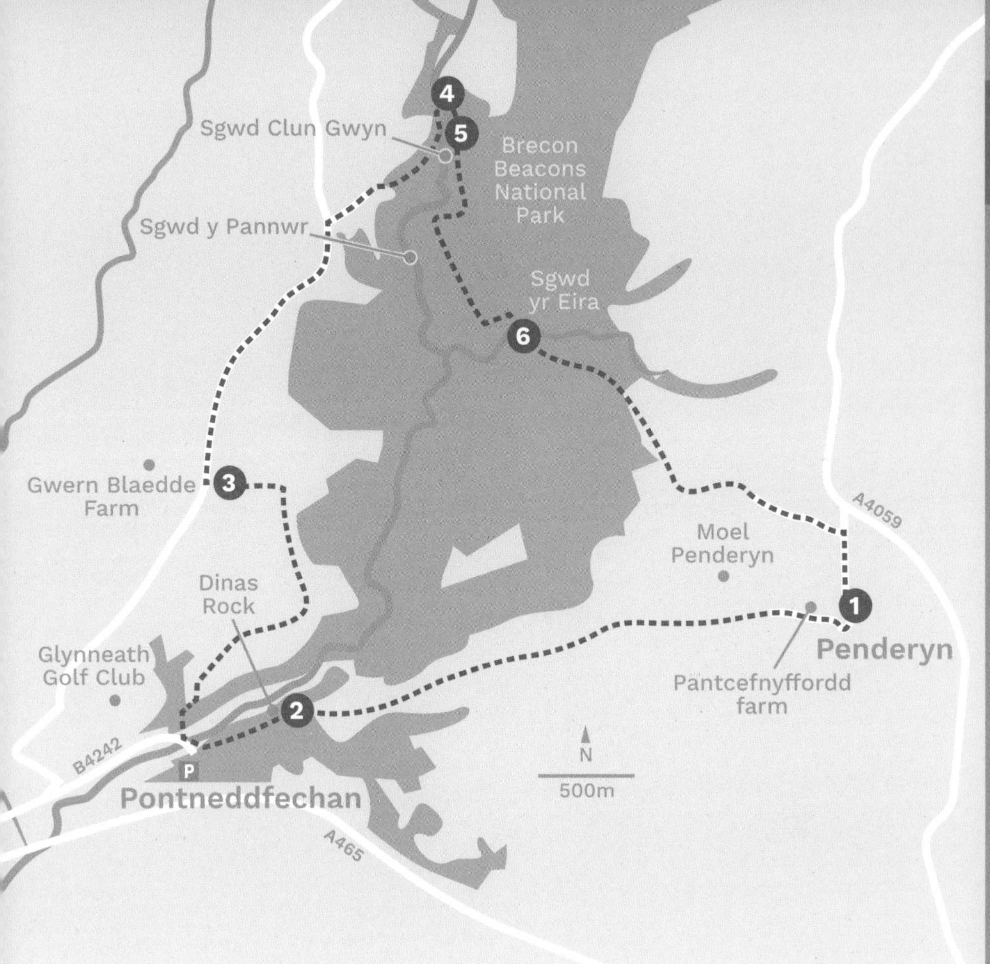

your left. Follow this to the farmhouse. Go through the metal gate just before the farmhouse, or over the stile on the right of the gate. Follow along the side of the small stream on your right until you have some trees in front of you and the farm buildings on your left. Cross diagonally left across this small field to the furthest barn (with corrugated sides and roof) and pass this on the right. Follow the farm track to the metal gate in front of you.

3 Go through the gate. Follow the farm track to the road, turn right and follow the road gently uphill. Ignore the entrance to Gwern Blaedde Farm and the turning on your left with a 'No Through Road' sign and carry on along the main road, going straight past the track, by a fingerpost sign, on your right. When you get to a road sign indicating a cattlegrid and animals, take the track on your right to a bunkhouse. Pass through a metal gate with a cattlegrid, and a kissing gate on the right. Head straight up the path. There is an information board on your right about Sgwd Clun Gwyn and, ahead, a signpost. You are entering the Brecon Beacons National Park. At the fork in the road take the right path through a gate to Sgwd Clun Gwyn (White Meadow Falls) crossing over a small bridge made of railway sleepers and bearing left to cross another small sleeper bridge. Ahead is a metal gate with a kissing gate on the right. Go through this and

follow the track. Keep to the main track as it descends through the trees – soon you will hear the water and, looking through the trees, you can see Sgwd Clun Gwyn, the first waterfall. There is a bench here, which makes an ideal resting place, and a small track down to the best position for photographing Sgwd Clun Gwyn. Then continue along the main path, following the river with the fence on your right.

4 Cross the footbridge then turn right and follow the rocky footpath up. When the footpath meets a Y-junction, take the left fork up away from the river (the right fork has been closed).

5 At the top, follow the footpath right to an observation point to see Sgwd Clun Gwyn from the other side. A four-way marker post marked '13' (white number on a dark green disc) shows the direction to Sgwd-yr-Eira (Fall of Snow) towards marker post 16 in front of you. This is a very well-signposted footpath from here on and you will find waymarkers painted red. Follow the waymarkers to number 25, where you have an option to descend to the Sgwd y Pannwr (Waterfall of the Fuller) and Sgwd Isaf Clun Gwyn (Lower White Meadow Falls). Continue on to Sgwd-yr-Eira following waymarkers from 25 upwards. From 25, your next waymarker is 33 as waymarkers 26–32

The spectacular Sgwd Clun Gwyn (White Meadow Falls) thunders into the river below. When the river is in full spate, the fall can extend all the way across the ledge.

are down to the two falls Sgwd y Pannwr and Sgwd Isaf Clun Gwyn. On reaching waymarker 35 you head away from the red arrows and start following the green arrows down the path to Sgwd yr Eira. Follow this path down steps to the waterfall and waymarker 38 at the bottom (observing the safety notices on the way down). At this point (if you haven't already), put on your waterproofs before going behind the waterfall. Exercising extreme caution on the uneven, and in some places narrow, wet rocks, go along the left side to the waterfall and follow the route behind it. It is always wet and slippery under here and great care is required. Drovers used to herd their sheep behind this waterfall, as it was the only route across the river. On out the other side, follow the steep ascent to the top. This path is also very uneven, wet and slippery, and can be unstable; it will merge with an ash path. At the top of the ash path is a Y-junction with a noticeboard. Here, take the left path and you will reach a big rock.

6 This is a great place to rest, or to remove waterproofs or change into dry clothing. Continue on past the rock following the ash path. After passing the small wood on your left you will come to a Y-junction in the path. Do not cross the stile but take the right fork and walk along, keeping the fence on your left. When you come to a steel gate on your left, with a stile just before it, ignore the track to the right. Continue through a metal gate, over two small stone bridges, until you reach a waymarker post on a fence corner pointing straight ahead. Continue on, following the track. You will shortly come to a stile on your left; ignore this and follow the waymarked path on the main track. At the T-junction, turn left onto another main track to walk along the northern side of Moel Penderyn. You will come to a metal gate across the main track with a kissing gate on the right – pass through the kissing gate and continue on the main track. Ignore the double gate on your left and you will find yet another metal gate in front of you with a wooden kissing gate on the right; go through. Now the road bears left – follow it down. At the crossroads, turn right and then go up a slight incline. You will see a children's road sign in front of you; continue along this road going up the hill as it becomes a little steeper, returning to the Red Lion car park.

rambler profile

Kate Ashbrook

Kate is an active Ramblers member, having first become involved as a committee member of the Devon Area in the late 1970s. She is also general secretary of the Open Spaces Society, patron of the Walkers Are Welcome Towns network and a former chair of the Ramblers and Campaign for National Parks.

1. Tell us about some Ramblers' campaigns that you have been involved in.

Back in the late 1980s, I was a leader of the campaign for greater freedom to roam, which resulted in the Countryside and Rights of Way Act 2000. This gives us the right to walk responsibly on land that has been mapped as access land (mountain, moor, heath and down, and registered common land) in England and Wales. It was a significant achievement for walkers. I also led the campaign to reopen the notorious Framfield footpath 9 (East Sussex) after it had been heavily obstructed by a landowner who despised walkers, ending with a successful action in the Court of Appeal.

It's been 45 years since I first joined the Ramblers and I have been an active member for most of that time. I have been a member of the board of trustees for 40 years, except for four years as president, and chair three times. I am currently a vice-president.

Locally, I have been the Area footpath

Kate cutting the barbed wire across a footpath in Pensax in Worcestershire, 1989, at a Ramblers' rally.

Kate marching through a marquee that was blocking the Thames-side footpath at Henley Regatta in 1990. Photo by Bucks Free Press.

secretary for the Buckinghamshire, Milton Keynes and West Middlesex Area for 36 years.

2. Why do you think access to green spaces is so vital?

Green spaces give us the chance to relax and unwind, in fresh air away from traffic and pollution, listening to birdsong and enjoying nature. They are vital to people's health and wellbeing, and it is deeply worrying that so many people do not have ready access to a good-quality green space.

3. How can we fight for a greener world and protect our green natural spaces?

We need to generate a new movement and lobby the decision-makers – the Westminster government, Scottish Parliament, Welsh Senedd and the local authorities. We need to persuade them that green spaces are an investment in our health and wellbeing and that the relatively small sums needed to create, improve and manage them are money well spent. We must involve all sections of the community in this campaign.

4. Is activism still at the heart of the Ramblers?

Yes definitely, our members on the ground are keen activists, as they fight damaging path changes and carry out practical work to improve paths, but they probably don't realize that they are campaigning all the time, working for beneficial change. We must rekindle our movement in these difficult times when access to the outdoors has never been more important or so valued by the population, and give clear messages of what we want to achieve and how everyone can play a part in achieving it.

Above: Kate in 2013, at the gate she organised in the fence on access land at Cobstone Hill.

Left: Kate opening the 'Hoogstraten' Framfield 9 footpath in East Sussex in February 2003.

Resources and Further Information

The Ramblers recommends using public transport where possible to reduce carbon emissions. All transport information provided was correct at time of publication. Please do check with the relevant providers for up-to-date travel information before travelling. More information and contact details for local Ramblers Areas can be found at ramblers.org.uk

Falls of Foyers, Loch Ness

This route originally appeared in *Walk* magazine Winter 2011
Route developer: Graeme Ambrose
Visitor information: Fort Augustus Tourist Information Centre www.visitscotland.com
Transport: D&E coaches www.decoaches.co.uk
Local Ramblers Area: Highland & Islands

Ravensheugh Sands and Seacliff, East Lothian

This route originally appeared in *Walk* magazine Winter 2015
Route developer: Keith Fergus
Visitor information: Visit East Lothian visiteastlothian.org/
Transport: Eve Coaches www.eveinfo.co.uk/bus-services/
Local Ramblers Area: Lothian & Borders

Skelwith and Colwith, Lake District

Route developers: Brian and Joy Greenwood
Visitor information: Lake District National Park www.lakedistrict.gov.uk/visiting
Transport: Stagecoach Cumbria and North Lancashire www.stagecoachbus.com/about/cumbria-and-north-lancashire
Local Ramblers Area: Lake District

Farndale, North Yorkshire

This walk originally appeared in *Walk* magazine Summer 2010
Route developer: Neil Coates
Visitor information: North York Moors National Park www.northyorkmoors.org.uk
Transport: Moorsbus www.moorsbus.org/timetablesfares.html
Local Ramblers Area: North Yorks & South Durham

Parwich and Tissington, Derbyshire

Route developer: Andy Page
Visitor information: Visit Peak District www.visitpeakdistrict.com
Transport: High Peak Buses www.highpeakbuses.com/bus-services/
Local Ramblers Area: Derbyshire

Portbury, North Somerset

Route developer: Geoff Mullett
Visitor information: Visit Somerset www.visitsomerset.co.uk
Transport: First Bus Bristol, Bath, and the West www.firstbus.co.uk/bristol-bath-and-west
Local Ramblers Area: Avon

Child Okeford, Dorset

Route developer: James Austin
Visitor Information: Child Okeford Village www.childokeford.org/walks-around-the-village/
Transport: First Buses Somerset www.firstbus.co.uk/somerset
Local Ramblers Area: Dorset

South Malvern

Route developer: Michael Everitt
Visitor information: Visit the Malverns www.visitthemalverns.org
Local Ramblers Areas: Gloucestershire, Worcestershire

Near Dolgellau, Snowdonia

Route developers: Jacky Cross and Margaret Lowe
Transport: Lloyd's Coaches lloydscoaches.com/bus-timetables/
Visitor information: Snowdonia National Park snowdonia.gov.wales
Local Ramblers Area: North Wales

Cadair Berwyn, North Wales

Route developer: Roger Butler
Visitor information: Visit Mid Wales www.visitmidwales.co.uk/things-to-do/north-powys-cadair-berwyn-p1730111
Transport: Tanat Valley Coaches www.tanat.co.uk/public-services
Local Ramblers Areas: North Wales, Powys

The Ring of Steall, the Highlands

This route originally appeared in *Walk* magazine Spring 2011
Route developer: Keith Fergus
Visitor information: Walk Highlands www.walkhighlands.co.uk
Transport: Stagecoach North Scotland www.stagecoachbus.com/about/north-scotland
Local Ramblers Area: Highland & Islands

Buttermere, Lake District

Route developer: James Austin
Visitor information: Lake District National Park www.lakedistrict.gov.uk/visiting
Transport: Stagecoach Cumbria and North Lancashire www.stagecoachbus.com/about/cumbria-and-north-lancashire
Local Ramblers Area: Lake District

High and Low Force, Upper Teesdale

Route developer: Roger Carpenter
Visitor information: Bowlees Visitor Centre www.thisisdurham.com/things-to-do/bowlees-visitor-centre-p24781
Transport: Hodgsons Buses www.hodgsonsbuses.com/service_routes.html
Local Ramblers Area: North Yorks & South Durham

Robin Hood's Bay, North Yorkshire

Route developer: Andy Page
Visitor information: Welcome to Yorkshire www.yorkshire.com/places/yorkshire-coast/robin-hoods-bay
Transport: Arriva Bus Yorkshire www.arrivabus.co.uk/yorkshire
Local Ramblers Area: North Yorks & South Durham

Malham Cove, North Yorkshire

This route originally appeared in *Walk Britain: Great Views* (2009)
Route developer: This route was originally created by Walk Britain, supported by Craven Ramblers
Visitor information: Yorkshire Dales National Park www.yorkshiredales.org.uk/places/malham_national_park_centre
Transport: Dalesbus www.dalesbus.org/malham.html
Local Ramblers Area: West Riding

Stow-on-the-Wold, Cotswolds

Route developer: Andy Page
Visitor information: Visit Stow on the Wold www.stowinfo.co.uk
Transport: Pulham and Sons Coaches www.pulhamscoaches.com/bus/
Local Ramblers Area: Gloucestershire

Margate to Broadstairs, Kent

Route developer: Philip Cheesewright
Visitor information: Visit Thanet www.visitthanet.co.uk/plan-your-visit/visitor-information-services
Transport: Southeastern Railway www.southeasternrailway.co.uk/destinations-and-offers/popular-kent-destinations/margate
Local Ramblers Area: Kent

Ditchling Beacon, South Downs

Route developer: Charlotte Markham
Visitor information: National Trust www.nationaltrust.org.uk/ditchling-beacon
Transport: Compass Travel www.compass-travel.co.uk/compass-timetables/
Local Ramblers Area: Sussex

The Tarka Trail, Devon

This route originally appeared in *Walk* magazine Winter 2018
Route developer: Mark Rowe
Visitor information: Tarka Trail official website tarkatrail.org.uk
Transport: Stagecoach South West www.stagecoachbus.com/about/south-west
Local Ramblers Area: Devon

Rhossili, Gower Peninsula

This route originally appeared in *Walk Britain: Great Views* (2009)
Route developer: This route was originally created by Walk Britain, supported by Swansea Ramblers
Visitor information: The National Trust www.nationaltrust.org.uk/trails/rhosili-down-hillend-and-beach-walk
Transport: Adventure Travel www.adventuretravel.cymru/bus-services/
Local Ramblers Area: Glamorgan

Pentland Hills, Edinburgh

Route developer: Keith Fergus
Visitor information: Pentland Hills Regional Park www.pentlandhills.org
Transport: Stagecoach West Scotland www.stagecoachbus.com/about/west-scotland
Local Ramblers Area: Lothian & Borders

Tilberthwaite, Lake District

Route developers: Brian and Joy Greenwood
Visitor information: Lake District National Park www.lakedistrict.gov.uk/visiting
Transport: Stagecoach Cumbria and North Lancashire www.stagecoachbus.com/about/cumbria-and-north-lancashire
Local Ramblers Area: Lake District

Strid Wood and Bolton Abbey, Yorkshire

Route developer: James Austin
Visitor information: Bolton Abbey boltonabbey.com
Transport: Dalesbus www.dalesbus.org
Local Ramblers Area: West Riding

York's Walls

Route developer: Andy Page
Visitor information: Visit York www.visityork.org
Transport: By rail, London North Eastern Railway www.lner.co.uk/the-east-coast-experience/our-stations/york-station/. By bus, First Bus York www.firstbus.co.uk/york
Local Ramblers Area: East Yorkshire and Derwent

Wendover, Buckinghamshire

This route originally appeared in *Walk* magazine Autumn 2011
Route developer: Mark Rowe
Visitor information: Visit Buckinghamshire www.visitbuckinghamshire.org/article/wendover
Transport: Chiltern Railways www.chilternrailways.co.uk/routes-and-destinations/wendover
Local Ramblers Area: Buckinghamshire, Milton Keynes and West Middlesex

Walthamstow Wetlands, London

Route developer: Vicky Duff
Visitor information: London Wildlife Trust www.wildlondon.org.uk/walthamstow-wetlands-nature-reserve
Transport: Transport for London tfl.gov.uk/
Local Ramblers Area: Inner London, Hertfordshire and North Middlesex, Essex

Odiham Castle, Hampshire

Route developer: Deborah Gregory
Visitor information: Visit Hampshire www.visit-hampshire.co.uk/things-to-do/odiham-castle-p285561
Transport: South Western Railway www.southwesternrailway.com/travelling-with-us/at-the-station/hook
Local Ramblers Area: Hampshire

Westonbirt and the Arboretum, Wiltshire

Route developer: Geoff Mullett
Visitor information: Forestry England www.forestryengland.uk/westonbirt-the-national-arboretum
Transport: Stagecoach West www.stagecoachbus.com/about/west/stroud
Local Ramblers Area: Gloucestershire, Wiltshire & Swindon

Tintern and Offa's Dyke, Wye Valley

Route developer: Geoff Mullett
Visitor information: Visit Monmouthshire www.visitmonmouthshire.com/things-to-do/walking/offas-dyke-path
Transport: Phil Anslow and Sons Coaches www.philanslowcoaches.co.uk/bus-services/
Local Ramblers Area: Gloucestershire

Strumble Head, Pembrokeshire

Route developer: Andy Page
Visitor information: Visit Pembrokeshire www.visitpembrokeshire.com/explore-pembrokeshire/towns-and-villages/strumble-head
Transport: Richard Bros www.richardsbros.co.uk/Timetables
Local Ramblers Area: Pembrokeshire

Birnham Oak, Perth and Kinross

Route developer: Judith Dobson
Visitor information: Visit Scotland www.visitscotland.com/info/see-do/the-birnam-oak-p2571371
Transport: For rail travel, Scotrail www.scotrail.co.uk/plan-your-journey/stations-and-facilities/dkd. For buses, Stagecoach East Scotland www.stagecoachbus.com/about/east-scotland
Local Ramblers Area: Forth Valley, Fife, & Tayside

Loch Trool, Galloway

Route developer: Judith Dobson
Visitor information: Forestry and Land Scotland forestryandland.gov.scot/visit/forest-parks/galloway-forest-park/glentrool-visitor-centre
Local Ramblers Area: South West Scotland

The Wirral, Merseyside

Route developer: Liverpool Ramblers Group
Visitor information: Visit Wirral www.visitwirral.com
Transport: For rail travel, Merseyrail www.merseyrail.org/plan-your-journey/stations/west-kirby.aspx. For buses, Merseytravel www.merseytravel.gov.uk/bus/
Local Ramblers Area: Merseyside and West Cheshire

Bradgate Country Park, Leicestershire

Route developer: John Alton
Visitor information: The Bradgate Park Trust www.bradgatepark.org
Transport: Roberts Travel Group www.robertstravelgroup.co.uk/bus-timetables
Local Ramblers Area: Leicestershire and Rutland

Cley-next-the-Sea, Norfolk

This route originally appeared in *Walk Britain: Great Views* (2009)
Route developer: This route was originally created by Walk Britain, supported by Sheringham and District Ramblers
Visitor information: Visit North Norfolk www.visitnorthnorfolk.com/explore/visit/cley-next-the-sea
Local Ramblers Area: Norfolk

Windsor to Savill Garden, Berkshire/Surrey

Route developer: Bob Pedley
Visitor information: Windsor Great Park www.windsorgreatpark.co.uk
Transport: First Bus Berkshire & the Thames Valley www.firstbus.co.uk/berkshire-thames-valley
Local Ramblers Area: Berkshire, Surrey

The Seven Sisters, East Sussex

This route originally appeared in *Walk Britain: Great Views* (2009)
Route developer: This route was originally created by Walk Britain, supported by Metropolitan Walkers
Visitor information: Seven Sisters, South Downs National Park www.sevensisters.org.uk
Transport: For buses, Stagecoach South East www.stagecoachbus.com/about/south-east/eastbourne or Cuckmere Buses www.cuckmerebuses.org.uk/. For rail travel, Southern Rail www.southernrailway.com/
Local Ramblers Area: Sussex

Richmond, London

Route developer: Brian Hunt
Visitor information: Visit Richmond www.visitrichmond.co.uk
Transport: Transport for London tfl.gov.uk/
Local Ramblers Area: Surrey, Inner London

Abbotsbury and Chesil Beach, Dorset

Route developer: Fiona Barltrop
Visitor information: Visit Dorset www.visit-dorset.com/
Transport: For information visit First Buses www.firstbus.co.uk/wessex-dorset-south-somerset/plan-journey/jurassic-coaster or the Jurassic Coast Trust www.jurassiccoast.org/explore/visitor-information/travel-information
Local Ramblers Area: Dorset

Penderyn, Mid Glamorgan

Route developer: Clive Pleasants
Visitor information: Brecon Beacons National Park www.breconbeacons.org
Local Ramblers Area: Glamorgan, Powys

Index

Picture Credits

Special thanks to Alina and Juliet Congreve for the use of their photography throughout this book.

Pages 2–3 Shutterstock/Undivided; 6 © John Jackson; 8 Istock by Getty Images/Gollykim; 10 Istock by Getty Images/Mikedabell; 11 Istock by Getty Images/SolStock; 13 Shutterstock/Matt Gibson; 15 Shutterstock/Pixel-Shot; 16 © Chris Parkes; 17 © Louise Trewern; 18 © Lahari Parchuri; 19–20 Shutterstock/Vivvi Smak; 20–21 © Juliet Congreve; 25 (top) Shutterstock/DavidFM; 25 (bottom) Shutterstock/Russell Ouellette IV; 27 Shutterstock/Ben Queenborough; 28–29 © John Nichols; 30 Shutterstock/Charles Masters; 33 Shutterstock/Len Green; 36 Shutterstock/Angus Reid; 37 Richard Smith/Alamy Stock Photo; 38 Shutterstock/David JC; 41 Shutterstock/Chrislofotos; 42 Shutterstock/Oscar Johns; 44 Diana J Webb/Alamy Stock Photo; 47 Shutterstock/Lilly Trott; 48–49 Shutterstock/Steve R Johnston; 53 Shutterstock/David Crosbie; 56–57 Shutterstock/SuxxesPhoto; 58–59 Shutterstock/SuxxesPhoto; 60–61 Shutterstock/JoeEJ; 62 Shutterstock/Erni; 64–65 Simon Stapley/Alamy Stock Photo; 67 Shutterstock/Aleksandrs Goldobenkovs; 68–69 © Roy Marshall; 70–71 Shutterstock/Helen Cradduck; 72 Shutterstock/Helen Cradduck; 74–75 Shutterstock/Pajor Pawel; 75 (top) Shutterstock/Dani Ber; 76–77 Shutterstock/MNStudio; 78–79 Shutterstock/Milosz Kubiak; 81 Shutterstock/Helwoodmedia; 82–83 Shutterstock/Tim Lamper; 87 Shutterstock/Neal Rylatt; 89 Shutterstock/Nicola Pulham; 90 Shutterstock/Pete Stuart; 93 Shutterstock/Melanie Hobson; 94–95 Shutterstock/JJFarq; 98–99 Shutterstock/Christine Bird; 100 Shutterstock/John Sainsbury; 103 Shutterstock/Darrell Evans; 104–105 Shutterstock/Peter Cripps; 107 Shutterstock/Marek Mierzejewski; 108–109 Shutterstock/Sarah2; 110 (left) Shutterstock/Menno Schaefer; 110 (right) Shutterstock/Maratr; 112–113 Shutterstock/Salarko; 116–117 © Juliet Congreve; 118–119 Shutterstock/Stephen Bridger; 120 AidanStock/Alamy Stock Photo; 122–123 Shutterstock/Helen Hotson; 124 Istock by Getty Images/Millie Chamberlain; 127 Shutterstock/Phil Silverman; 129 Shutterstock/Alex Manders; 131 Shutterstock/David Ionut; 133 Shutterstock/Northalletonman; 134–135 Shutterstock/David Hughes; 136 Shutterstock/Neil Bussey; 139 © Juliet Congreve; 140–141 Shutterstock/cktravels.com; 142 Shutterstock/cktravels.com; 145 (top) Shutterstock/Annabel Russell; 145 (bottom) Shutterstock/BasPhoto; 146 Istock by Getty Images/Vincent Ryan; 148–149 Shutterstock/cparrphotos; 152–153 Shutterstock/John Corry; 155 Shutterstock/Billy Stock; 157 Shutterstock/Deatonphotos; 158–159 Shutterstock/Peter Moulton; 160–161 Shutterstock/Max R Hawkins; 162 Shutterstock/FJAH; 164 (top) Gavin Haskell/Alamy Stock Photo; 164 (bottom) Shutterstock/Dan Tiego; 166–167 © Juliet Congreve; 169 Shutterstock/Scotland's scenery; 171 (top) Shutterstock/Skye Studio LK; 171 (bottom) Shutterstock/S Buwert; 172–173 Shutterstock/Dave A Bennett; 175 Shutterstock/Kevin Eaves; 177 Shutterstock/John David Photography; 179 Shutterstock/Philip Brookes; 181 Shutterstock/MikOhWhy; 182 Shutterstock/GhostCreativeUK; 185 Shutterstock/Phil Harland; 187 Shutterstock/Helen Hotson; 188–189 Shutterstock/Gordon Bell; 191 (left) © Juliet Congreve; 191 (right) Shutterstock/Giedriius; 192–193 Shutterstock/Adam James Booth; 194 Shutterstock/Chrislofotos; 197 Shutterstock/James Ratchford; 201 Shutterstock/Anthony Shaw Photography; 202 Shutterstock/I Wei Huang; 204 David Woof/Alamy Stock Photo; 206–207 Shutterstock/Joe Dunckley; 209 Shutterstock/Mark Godden; 211 Shutterstock/Sebastien Coell; 212 Shutterstock/Fanni_2021; 214 Shutterstock/Steven Musgrove; 216–217 © Kate Ashbrook